THE TRUE FLAG

THE TRUE FLAG

THEODORE ROOSEVELT,
MARK TWAIN, AND THE BIRTH
OF AMERICAN EMPIRE

STEPHEN KINZER

HENRY HOLT AND COMPANY   NEW YORK

Henry Holt and Company, LLC
Publishers since 1866
175 Fifth Avenue
New York, New York 10010
www.henryholt.com

Henry Holt® and 🅷® are registered trademarks of
Henry Holt and Company, LLC.

Library of Congress Cataloging-in-Publication Data

Names: Kinzer, Stephen, author.
Title: The true flag : Theodore Roosevelt, Mark Twain, and the birth of
    American empire / Stephen Kinzer.
Description: First edition. | New York : Henry Holt and Company, 2016. |
    Includes bibliographical references and index.
Identifiers: LCCN 2016019840| ISBN 9781627792165 (hardcover) | ISBN
    9781627792172 (electronic book)
Subjects: LCSH: United States—Foreign relations—1897–1901. | United
    States—Politics and government—1897–1901. | United States—Foreign
    relations—1901–1909. | United States—Politics and government—1901–1909.
    | Spanish-American War, 1898—Influence. | Imperialism—History—19th
    century. | Imperialism—History—20th century. | United
    States—Territorial expansion.
Classification: LCC E713.K58 2016 | DDC 327.73009/034—dc23
LC record available at https://lccn.loc.gov/2016019840

Our books may be purchased in bulk for promotional, educational, or business use. Please contact your
local bookseller or the Macmillan Corporate and Premium Sales Department at (800) 221-7945, extension 5442, or by e-mail at MacmillanSpecialMarkets@macmillan.com.

First Edition 2017

Designed by Kelly S. Too

Printed in the United States of America
1 3 5 7 9 10 8 6 4 2

For Marianne

CONTENTS

THE TRUE FLAG

Introduction

How should the United States act in the world? Americans cannot decide. For more than a century we have debated with ourselves. We can't even agree on the question.

Put one way: Should we defend our freedom, or turn inward and ignore growing threats?

Put differently: Should we charge violently into faraway lands, or allow others to work out their own destinies?

Our enthusiasm for foreign intervention seems to ebb and flow like the tides, or swing back and forth like a pendulum. At some moments we are aflame with righteous anger. Confident in our power, we launch wars and depose governments. Then, chastened, we retreat—until the cycle begins again.

America's interventionist urge, however, is not truly cyclical. When we love the idea of intervening abroad and then hate it, we are not changing our minds. Both instincts coexist within us. Americans are imperialists and also isolationists. We want to guide the world, but we also believe every nation should guide itself. At different times, according to circumstances, these contrary impulses emerge in different proportions. Our inability to choose between them shapes our conflicted approach to the world.

Eminent figures have led the United States into conflicts from Indochina to Central America to the Middle East. Others rose to challenge them. They were debating the central question of our foreign policy: Should the United States intervene to shape the fate of other nations? Much of what they said was profound. None of it was original.

For generations, every debate over foreign intervention has been repetition. All are pale shadows of the first one.

Even before that debate broke out, the power of the United States was felt beyond North America. In 1805 a fleet dispatched by President Thomas Jefferson defeated a Barbary Coast pasha who was extorting money from American vessels entering the Mediterranean. Half a century later, President Millard Fillmore sent a fleet of "black ships" to force Japan to open its ports to American traders. Those were isolated episodes, though, and not part of a larger plan to spread American power. After both of them, troops returned home.

Civil war enveloped the United States from 1861 to 1865. Over the decades that followed, Americans concentrated on binding their national wounds and settling the West. Only after the frontier was officially declared closed in 1890 did some begin to think of the advantages that might lie in lands beyond their own continent. That brought the United States to the edge of the world stage.

In 1898, Americans plunged into the farthest-reaching debate in our history. It was arguably even more momentous than the debate over slavery, because its outcome affected many countries, not just one. Never has the question of intervention—how the United States should face the world—been so trenchantly argued. In the history of American foreign policy, this is the mother of all debates.

As the twentieth century dawned, the United States faced a fateful choice. It had to decide whether to join the race for colonies, territories, and dependencies that gripped European powers. Americans understood what was at stake. The United States had been a colony. It was founded on the principle that every nation must be ruled by "the consent of the governed." Yet suddenly it found itself with the chance to rule faraway lands.

This prospect thrilled some Americans. It horrified others. Their debate gripped the United States. The country's best-known political and intellectual leaders took sides. Only once before—in the period when the United States was founded—have so many brilliant Americans so eloquently debated a question so fraught with meaning for all humanity.

The two sides in this debate represent matched halves of the divided American soul. Should the United States project power into faraway lands? Yes, to guarantee our prosperity, save innocent lives, liberate the oppressed, and confront danger before it reaches our shores! No, intervention brings suffering and creates enemies!

Americans still cannot decide what the Puritan leader John Winthrop meant when he told his followers in 1630, "We shall be as a city upon a hill, the eyes of all people are upon us." He wanted us to build a virtuous society that would be a model for others! Wrong, he wanted us to set out into a sinful world and redeem it! Forced to choose between these two irreconcilable alternatives, Americans choose both.

The debate that captivated Americans in 1898 decisively shaped world history. Its themes resurface every time we argue about whether to intervene in a foreign conflict. Yet it has faded from memory.

Why has the United States intervened so often in foreign lands? How did we reach this point? What drove us to it? Often we seek answers to these questions in the period following World War II. That is the wrong place to look. America's deep engagement with the world began earlier. The root of it—of everything the United States does and seeks in the world—lies in the debate that is the subject of this book.

All Americans, regardless of political perspective, can take inspiration from the titans who faced off in this debate. Their words are amazingly current. Every argument over America's role in the world grows from this one. It all starts here.

1

White and Peaceful Wings

Where better to launch a patriotic uprising than Faneuil Hall in Boston? Colonists had gathered amid its Doric columns to protest the Boston Massacre and plot the overthrow of British rule. Abolitionists had denounced slavery from its stage. It is a lodestone of American liberty, a cathedral for freedom fighters.

That is why a handful of eminent Bostonians chose Faneuil Hall as the place to begin a new rebellion on the sunny afternoon of June 15, 1898. Like all Americans, they had been dizzied by the astonishing events of recent weeks. Their country had suddenly burst beyond its natural borders. American troops had landed in Cuba. American warships had bombarded Puerto Rico. An American expeditionary force was steaming toward the distant Philippine Islands. Hawaii seemed about to fall to American power. President William McKinley had called for two hundred thousand volunteers to fight in foreign wars. Fervor for the new idea of overseas expansion gripped the United States.

This appalled the organizers of the Faneuil Hall meeting. They could not bear to see their country setting out to capture foreign nations. That afternoon, they rose in protest.

Several hundred people turned out. "On all sides could be seen the well-known faces of leaders of good causes among us," one newspaper reported. According to another, "Nearly all the settees on the floor were filled, while the benches in the gallery were well fringed with ladies."

At three o'clock, Gamaliel Bradford, a prominent civic leader and proud descendant of the Pilgrim governor William Bradford, called the meeting to order. His speech was both a warning and a cry of pain.

Over the past year, Americans had grown enraged by the harshness of Spanish colonial rule in Cuba. Most cheered when Congress declared war on Spain. They were thrilled when President McKinley sent troops to help Cuban revolutionaries fighting to expel the Spanish. Before long, though, some in Washington suggested that instead of allowing Cuba to become independent, as promised, the United States should take the island and rule it. Then they began talking of seizing Puerto Rico and even the Philippines. Imperial fever had broken out and was spreading. This stirred Bostonians to bitter protest.

"We are not here to oppose the war," Bradford told the Faneuil Hall crowd. "We are here to deal with a far graver issue, to insist that a war begun in the name of humanity shall not be turned into a war for empire, that an attempt to win for Cubans the right to govern themselves shall not be made an excuse for extending our sway of alien peoples without their consent. . . . We are to be a world power, but the question is whether we shall be a power for beneficence or malfeasance. Everything is against the policy of conquest."

The next speaker was another New England patriarch, Charles Ames, a theologian and Unitarian pastor who had traveled the world promoting humanitarian causes. He warned that the moment the United States seized a foreign land, it would "sacrifice the principles on which the Republic was founded."

> The policy of imperialism threatens to change the temper of our people, and to put us into a permanent attitude of arrogance, testiness, and defiance towards other nations. . . . Once we enter the field of international conflict as a great military and naval power, we shall be one more bully among bullies. We shall only add one more to the list of oppressors of mankind. . . . Poor Christian as I am, it grieves and shames me to see a generation instructed by the Prince of Peace proposing to set him on a dunce's stool and to crown him with a fool's cap.

At the very moment that these words were shaking Faneuil Hall, debate on the same question—overseas expansion—was reaching a climax in Congress. It is a marvelous coincidence: the first anti-imperialist rally in American history was held on the same day that Congress voted, also for the first time, on whether the United States should take an overseas colony. That day—June 15, 1898—marked the beginning of a great political and ideological conflict.

The Faneuil Hall meeting was set to end at five o'clock. In Washington, the House of Representatives scheduled its decisive vote for precisely the same hour.

Every member of Congress understood that history was about to be made. President McKinley had decided that the United States should push its power into the Pacific Ocean and that, as a first step, it must seize the Hawaiian Islands. Some Americans found the idea intoxicating. Others despaired for the future of their country. One of them was the Speaker of the House, Thomas Reed, a figure so powerful that he was known as Czar.

Reed, a blunt-spoken Maine lawyer who had sought the Republican presidential nomination just two years before—and lost in part because of his anti-imperialist views—was repelled by the swaggering nationalism that had taken hold of Congress. Annexing Hawaii seemed to him not simply unwise but absurd. He told a friend that the United States might as well "annex the moon." So deep was Reed's anger, or depression, that he could not bring himself to preside over a vote that might lead to annexation. On the morning of June 15 he sent word that he would not appear.

Empire was the traditional way for rising states to expand their power, and in 1898 the American military had the means to make its imperial bid. Yet the United States had been founded through rebellion against a distant sovereign. It was pledged above all to the ideal of self-government. For a country that was once a colony to begin taking colonies of its own would be something new in modern history.

The most potent arguments against imperial expansion were drawn from American scripture. According to the Declaration of Independence, liberty is an inalienable right. The Constitution's opening phrase is "We the People." George Washington sounded much like an anti-imperialist when he asked, "Why quit our own to stand upon foreign ground?" So did Thomas Jefferson when he insisted, "If there be one principle more deeply written than any other in the mind of every American, it is that we should have nothing to do with conquest." Abraham Lincoln proclaimed at Gettysburg that governments should be "of the people, by the people, for the people." Later he declared, "No man is good enough to govern another man without the other's consent."

To all of this, the imperialists had a simple answer: times have changed. Past generations, they argued, could not have foreseen the race for colonies that consumed the world at the end of the nineteenth century. Nor could they have known how important it would be for the United States to control foreign markets in order to ensure stability at home. In 1863, Lincoln himself had admitted that "dogmas of the quiet past are inadequate to the stormy present." The same principle, expansionists argued, applied in 1898.

One of Speaker Reed's deputies gaveled the House of Representatives to order at midday on June 15. The debate began with due gravity.

"Since that fateful shot was fired at Sumter," Representative Champ Clark of Missouri said as it began, "a greater question has not been debated in the American Congress."

The first speakers argued that bringing Hawaii into the United States would be a step in the march of human progress. "This annexation is not a conquest or a subjugation of others, but a continuation of our established policy of opening lands to the colonial energy of the great colonizing nation of the century," argued Richard Parker of New Jersey. To pass up such a chance, he concluded, would be "antediluvian and thorough stupidity."

Edwin Ridgeley of Kansas agreed. "Civilization has ever moved westward, and we have every reason to believe that it will ever so continue," he reasoned. "We need not, nor do I believe we will, enter into a conquest of force but, to the contrary, our higher civilization will be carried across the Pacific by the white and peaceful wings of our rapidly increasing commerce."

Several congressmen asserted that the United States had no choice but to expand overseas because its farms and factories were producing more than Americans could consume and urgently needed foreign markets. "The United States is a great manufacturing nation," William Alden Smith of Michigan reasoned. "Eventually we must find new markets for our energy and enterprise. Such desirable territory is fast passing under the control of other nations. Our history is filled with unaccepted opportunities. How much longer shall we hesitate?"

Congressmen not only declaimed on that fateful day, but also debated, sometimes with considerable wit. One of their arguments was over the role of American missionaries, who had arrived in Hawaii during the 1820s and set in motion the process that led to this debate. Albert Berry of Kentucky said Hawaiians had benefited immensely from their "influence and inspiration."

"When the Americans sent missionaries there for the purpose of civilizing the natives," he asserted, "they found them in an almost barbarous condition, and set to work to bring about a condition of civilization."

That was too much for one opponent of annexation, John F. Fitzgerald of Massachusetts—the same "Honey Fitz" who would go on to become mayor of Boston and, more famously, grandfather to John, Robert, and Edward Kennedy. A Boston ditty held that "Honey Fitz can talk you blind / On any subject you can find." This day, his subject was the role of missionaries.

"My colleague," Fitzgerald said, "emphasized the pleasure that he felt in voting for annexation because of the fact that the islands had been redeemed from savagery by the devotion of American missionaries. In thinking the matter over, I have come to the conclusion that the native Hawaiian's view of the Almighty and justice must be a little bit shaken when he sees these men, who pretend to be the exemplars of Christianity and honor, take possession of these islands by force, destroy the government that has existed for years, and set up a sovereignty for themselves."

The day's most vivid exchanges were about a delicate but serious matter: the extreme foreignness of native Hawaiians. Both sides used racial arguments. Annexationists said the islanders' evident savagery made it urgent for a civilizing force to take their country and uplift them. Opponents countered that it would be madness to bring such savages into union with the United States, where they could corrupt white people.

"Hawaiian religion is the embodiment of bestiality and malignity that frequently lapses into crimes of lust and revenge," reported one opponent of annexation, John Rhea of Kentucky. "The various legends of their gods abound in attributes of the most excessive animalism and cruelty. Lewdness, prostitution, and indecency are exalted into virtues. . . . There exists today upon those islands, Mr. Speaker, a population for the most part a mixture of Chinese with the islanders, thus making a homogenous whole of moral vipers and physical lepers."

That brought Albert Berry back to his feet. "I want to say to the gentleman," he retorted, "if he would look about the streets of the capital of Washington, he would see that there is more immorality south of Pennsylvania Avenue than there is in the whole of the Hawaiian Islands."

"If I knew that to be true, I would blush to herald it on the floor of this House," Rhea replied. "But I deny it, Mr. Speaker. I deny that here in the capital city of the greatest government in the world, American womanhood has fallen to such a standard. Oh, for shame that you should speak such words!"

"I did not know that the gentleman ever blushed," Berry shot back.

Expansionists in Congress and beyond were visionaries seized by a radically new idea of what America could and should be. They saw their critics as standing in the way of progress: small-minded, timid, paralyzed by fears, maddeningly unwilling to grasp the prize that history was offering. "A certain conservative class," Freeman Knowles of South Dakota lamented, "would stand in the way of the glorious future and ultimate destiny of this Republic."

The eloquence of annexationists was matched by that of their opponents. One after another, these doubters rose to warn against the imperial temptation. Some of their speeches suggest that they realized they were likely to lose that day's vote on taking Hawaii. They knew, however, that this was only the opening skirmish in what would be a long struggle. They were speaking to Americans far beyond Washington—and far beyond 1898.

Time and again these troubled congressmen returned to their central theme: the American idea prohibits colonizing, annexing foreign lands, taking protectorates, or projecting military power overseas. Setting out to shape the fate of foreign nations, they argued, would not only require great military establishments and inevitably attract enemies, but also betray the essence of America's commitment to human liberty. "We are treading on dangerous ground," warned Adolph Meyer of Louisiana.

Meyer had been born into a family of German immigrants and was one of the few Jews in Congress. He had fought in the Confederate army, commanded Louisiana's uniformed militia, and acquired a reputation as a forceful orator. On the afternoon of June 15, 1898, he lived up to it.

> With monarchical governments, or governments only nominally republican but really despotic or monarchical, this system of colonies, however burdensome, however tending to conflict, may be pursued without a shock to their systems of government. But with us the case is different. Our whole system is founded on the right of the people— all the people—to participate in the Government. . . . Take this first fatal step and you cannot recall it. Much error we have corrected. Much that may hereafter be you can correct. But when this step is taken, you are irrevocably pledged to a system of colonialism and empire. There are no footsteps backward.

This was a debate over the very nature of freedom. Many Americans wished to see its blessings spread around the world. In 1898 they began disagreeing passionately on how to spread those blessings.

Anti-imperialists saw themselves as defenders of freedom because they wanted foreign peoples to rule themselves, not be ruled by Americans. They saw the seizure of faraway lands as blasphemy against what Herman Melville called "the great God absolute! The center and circumference of all democracy! His omnipresence, our divine equality!"

Expansionists found this preposterous. They believed that concepts like freedom, equality, and self-government had meaning only for developed, responsible nations—that is, nations populated and governed by white people. Others, they asserted, were too primitive to rule themselves and must be ruled by outsiders. By this logic, dusky lands could only be truly free when outsiders governed them. If natives did not realize how much they needed foreign rule, and resisted it, that was further proof of their backwardness.

No one promoted this view more colorfully or to greater effect than Theodore Roosevelt, the assistant secretary of the navy. In a letter to his fellow imperialist Rudyard Kipling, Roosevelt scorned "the jack-fools who seriously think that any group of pirates and head-hunters needs nothing but independence in order that it be turned forthwith into a dark-hued New England town meeting." As the national debate intensified, he came to embody America's drive to project power overseas.

Mark Twain believed Roosevelt's project would destroy the United States.

Roosevelt and Twain moved in overlapping circles and knew each other, but geography separated them for years. Twain traveled and lived abroad for much of the 1890s. In Fiji, Australia, India, South Africa, and Mozambique, he had been appalled by the way white rulers treated natives. His frame of historical and cultural reference was far broader than Roosevelt's. He saw nobility in many peoples, and found much to admire abroad—quite unlike Roosevelt, who believed that "the man who loves other countries as much as he does his own is quite as noxious a member of society as a man who loves other women as much as he loves his wife." Instead of seeing the United States only from within, Twain compared it to other powers. He saw his own country rushing to repeat the follies he believed had corrupted Britain, France, Belgium, Germany, Spain, Portugal, Russia, and the Ottoman and Austro-Hungarian Empires. That way, he warned, lay war, oligarchy, militarism, and the suppression of freedom at home and abroad.

These adversaries—Roosevelt and Twain—were deliciously matched. Their views of life, freedom, duty, and the nature of human happiness could not have been further apart. World events divided them even before their direct confrontation began. When Germany seized the Chinese port of Kiaochow (later Tsingtao) in 1897, both men were outraged, but for different reasons. Twain opposed all foreign intervention in China; Roosevelt worried only that Germany was pulling ahead of the United States in the race for overseas concessions. Roosevelt considered colonialism a form of "Christian charity." Twain pictured Christendom as "a majestic matron in flowing robes drenched with blood."

Even though Twain's most famous novel, *Huckleberry Finn*, is full of coarse language and portrays a runaway rascal as a hero, Roosevelt acknowledged it as a classic. He did not care for much else that Twain wrote, however, and especially disliked *A Connecticut Yankee in King Arthur's Court*. Twain treated the Knights of the Round Table as objects of lusty satire. Roosevelt had revered them since childhood and was appalled.

Yet in intriguing ways, Roosevelt and Twain were remarkably similar. Both were fervent patriots who believed the United States had a sacred mission on earth—though they defined that mission quite differently. Both were writers and thinkers as well as activists. Most important, both were relentless self-promoters, born performers who carefully cultivated their public images. They loved to preach, reveled in the spotlight, and could not turn away from a crowd or a photographer. Acutely aware of each other's popularity, neither publicly denounced the other. Among friends, though, both were free with their feelings. Roosevelt said he would like to "skin Mark Twain alive." Twain considered Roosevelt "clearly insane" and "the most formidable disaster that has befallen the country since the Civil War."

Roosevelt was not the conceptualizer or organizer or leader of the imperialist movement. Twain filled none of those roles for the anti-imperialists. Nonetheless they would become the most prominent, most admired, and most reviled spokesmen for their opposing causes. In mid-1898, Roosevelt was waiting impatiently for a chance to leap into history. Twain was planning his return to the United States. The stage was set for their confrontation.

Anti-imperialists enjoyed their country's light footprint in the world. They hated war and believed liberty was America's greatest gift to humanity. Imperialists considered war a purifying, invigorating, unifying force. In their imagined future, humanity would be guided by a virtuous United States and disciplined by American military power.

National unity, race, the meaning of liberty, the place of the United States in the world and in history—all of these grand themes shaped the debate that gripped Americans in 1898. At stake was nothing less than what kind of nation the United States would be in the twentieth century and beyond.

Anti-imperialists who convened at Faneuil Hall on that June 15 were abuzz with two pieces of exciting news. Reports had arrived from the Philippines that three days earlier, at a ceremony outside Manila, the Filipino rebel leader Emilio Aguinaldo had unfurled a new flag, led a chorus in singing a newly composed national anthem, and proclaimed a new nation: the Philippine Republic. Filipinos had declared an end to three and a half centuries of Spanish colonial rule.

This electrified American anti-imperialists. They insisted that as a freedom-loving nation, the United States must immediately recognize Philippine independence. This development added urgency—and, in their eyes, immense moral weight—to the anti-imperial cause.

The day's morning newspapers also carried reports of another thrilling declaration. The prairie firebrand William Jennings Bryan had delivered a powerful speech in Omaha that seemed certain to bring the debate over imperialism to the center of American life. Until this moment, no major political leader had spoken out against the rush to empire. Bryan had been the Democratic nominee for president in 1896 and was thought likely to run again in 1900. He was one of the most popular figures in the United States and arguably the country's most spellbinding orator.

Anti-imperialists in Boston immediately recognized the value of Bryan's support. Many of them were prosperous businessmen, lawyers, professors, philosophers, and aesthetes. Bryan was the opposite: a barn-storming, rabble-rousing populist beloved by millions of farmers, immigrants, and poor people. His speech in Omaha echoed several that had been given in New England salons, but it was delivered to a huge crowd by one of the nation's leading politicians. That took the anti-imperial cause into the American heartland.

Bryan began not with an exposition of history but with an apocalyptic warning rooted in his Christian fundamentalism: "Jehovah deals with nations as He deals with men—and for both, decrees that the wages of sin is death!"

History will vindicate the position taken by the United States in the war with Spain. . . . If, however, a contest undertaken for the sake of humanity degenerates into a war of conquest, we shall find it difficult to meet the charge of having added hypocrisy to greed.

Is our national character so weak that we cannot withstand the temptation to appropriate the first piece of land that comes within our reach? To inflict upon the enemy all possible harm is legitimate warfare, but shall we contemplate a scheme for the colonization of the Orient merely because our ships won a remarkable victory in the harbor of Manila? Our guns destroyed a Spanish fleet, but can they destroy that self-evident truth, that governments derive their just powers, not from superior force, but from the consent of the governed?

As organizers of the Faneuil Hall meeting took their places on the stage shortly before three o'clock that afternoon, they had reason to believe they were riding the crest of history. They could not imagine that Americans would wish to capture the Philippines after Filipino patriots had proclaimed independence, or that they would sully their national honor by seizing Puerto Rico, subjugating Cuba, or annexing Hawaii. The sudden emergence of Bryan as an ally seemed proof that multitudes were on their side.

When the anti-imperialist meeting was gaveled to order on the afternoon of June 15, the House of Representatives in Washington had been debating the annexation of Hawaii for several hours. By four thirty, both sessions were drawing to a close. The climactic speech in Boston was delivered by one of the city's most eloquent lawyers, Moorfield Storey.

"How can we justify the annexation of Hawaii, whose people—outside the small fraction now kept in power by us—are notoriously opposed to it?" Storey demanded. "Let us once govern any considerable body of men without their consent, and it is but a question of time how soon this Republic shares the fate of Rome!"

After Storey finished, one of his comrades came to the podium and read a four-part resolution. This was a historic moment: the first time an anti-imperialist resolution was presented to a public meeting in the United States. It echoed through air that once carried the defiant words of Samuel Adams and John Hancock, and later those of William Lloyd Garrison and Frederick Douglass.

> Resolved, that a war begun as an unselfish endeavor to fulfill a duty to humanity by ending the unhappy situation in Cuba must not be perverted into a war of conquest.
>
> Resolved, that any annexation of territory as a result of this war would be a violation of the national faith pledged in the joint resolution of Congress which declared that the United States disclaimed "any disposition or intention to exercise sovereignty, jurisdiction, or control over Cuba except for the pacification thereof," a disclaimer which was intended to mean that this country had no selfish purpose in making war and which, in spirit, applies to every other possession of Spain.
>
> Resolved, that the mission of the United States is to help the world by an example of successful self-government, and that to abandon the principles and the policy under which we have prospered and embrace the doctrine and practices now called imperial is to enter the path which, with other great republics, has ended in the downfall of free institutions.
>
> Resolved, that our first duty is to cure the evils in our own country.

Following a suggestion from the audience, a fifth clause was added, directing organizers of the meeting to name a committee charged with contacting like-minded groups in other cities—echoing the "committees of correspondence" of the revolutionary period, which were also organized at Faneuil Hall. The resolution was adopted by acclamation. This was the first time Americans had joined to oppose the idea of overseas expansion. It marked a portentous beginning.

As Bostonians approved their anti-imperialist resolution at Faneuil Hall, congressmen were making their fateful choice in Washington. All understood that although the immediate issue was Hawaii, the real question was immensely greater. It was nothing less than the future of the Republic: whether or not the United States should become a global military power and shape the fate of distant lands.

Late in the afternoon, at the same moment Moorfield Storey was speaking in Boston, Representative William Hepburn of Mississippi rose in Congress to deliver a speech that crystalized the pro-annexation position. "We have not a foot of territory that we have not taken from others," he reminded his colleagues. This uncomfortable truth proved, he said, that expansion is the logical path to national greatness.

"Who dares to say that, even if we should enter into this new policy, the fate which befell the Roman Empire would be ours?" Hepburn asked. "Look at England. What would she be today if confined to her insular domain? What could she be? The mistress of the seas? Ah, no! One of the leading nations of the earth? Ah, no! Giving her laws, her literature, and her civilization to the rest of the world? Ah, no! She would have been powerless for this great end. Had there not been a Frederick the Great, who can say that the little Duchy of Brandenburg would have extended itself into the great German empire of today? This same 'greed,' this thirst for annexation, this desire for new territory, this passion for extending civilization, has blessed the earth."

That brought William Terry of Arkansas to his feet. "A war solemnly declared for the cause of humanity, justice, and the vindication of the national honor and the national flag is being perverted from the plain and proper purposes for which it was authorized by Congress and endorsed by the American people," Terry declared. "That flag, sir, in all its history, was never unjust in conquest and aggression. It has always been glorious and honored among all the nations of the earth, because wherever it floated, upon the land or upon the sea, it was recognized as the emblem and very symbol of freedom, humanity and justice. . . . Let us stand true to the lofty principles of those who gave it to our keeping."

At five o'clock, congressmen began casting their votes. The margin was overwhelming. By 209 to 91, the House of Representatives voted, for the first time in its history, to endorse the seizure of an overseas territory. After the Senate acted and President McKinley signed, Hawaii would become American.

That day—June 15, 1898—marked the beginning of a debate that would soon consume the country. The American anti-imperialist movement was born at Faneuil Hall in Boston on the same afternoon Congress set the United States on its imperial path. Battle lines were drawn for an epic clash.

2

There May Be an Explosion

Heads turned and conversation stopped when the youngest member of the New York State Assembly arrived to take his seat on April 18, 1882. He looked like the parody of a Victorian dandy: hair curled and parted in the middle, muttonchop sideburns, a thin mustache, and a monocle in one eye with a gold chain looped over his ear. His formal morning coat, which swept down almost to his shoes, opened to reveal skin-tight bell-bottom trousers. In one hand he carried a gold-tipped cane, in the other a silk top hat.

"Who's the dude?" one bemused assemblyman asked another.

"That's Theodore Roosevelt of New York," came the reply.

For a time Roosevelt remained an object of curiosity and ridicule in Albany. Colleagues called him Young Squirt, Weakling, Jane-Dandy, and Punkin-Lily. A newspaper wondered if he was one of those men "given to sucking the knob of an ivory cane."

Roosevelt soon modified his dress and manner, but he turned out to have an even more remarkable quality. He was constantly and irrepressibly in motion, a hyperactive, frenetic bundle of energy. In the Assembly he ricocheted from one cause to another. He demanded civil service reform, warred on the liquor industry, and fought increases in the minimum wage. A fellow assemblyman called him "a brilliant madman." He had not yet, however, discovered the vehicle he would ride to power.

It appeared before him a couple of years later, in the figure of Henry Cabot Lodge, a gaunt, imperious Bostonian he vaguely remembered from the Porcellian Club at Harvard. In 1884 the two young men— Roosevelt was twenty-five, Lodge thirty-four—were delegates to the Republican National Convention in Chicago. They took an instant liking to each other. Lodge sensed that Roosevelt would become a "national figure of real importance." Here was born the partnership that, a decade and a half later, would push America toward empire.

Roosevelt entered politics, as many do, to see how far he could rise. Lodge was just as ambitious, but unlike his younger friend he had a cause, a focused goal. He wanted the United States to dominate the world. How he would drive his country to this imperial height he did not yet know, but he was resolved to make it his life's work. Roosevelt, who had been captivated by "hero stories" since childhood and loved nothing more than the dream of war, was Lodge's instinctive ally. Both believed two things passionately: that the United States must become one of the world's great powers, and that it could do so only by taking foreign lands. For years they waited for their country to catch up with them.

Lodge and Roosevelt wanted to do more than simply change the way the United States approached the world. They wanted Americans to begin ruling people far beyond their own continent, without those people's consent. It would be an immense historical leap.

This most astonishing of all American years began like any other. There was no hint that after 1898 nothing would ever be the same. But history exploded, and suddenly the audacious dreams of Lodge, Roosevelt, and their friends came within reach.

These are the lands that Abraham Lincoln's secretary of state, William H. Seward, wished the United States to acquire: Hawaii, Mexico, Cuba, Puerto Rico, the Dominican Republic, Haiti, the Virgin Islands, Canada, Greenland, and Iceland. By the time Seward died in 1872, none had become American. In that same year, though, Henry Cabot Lodge graduated from Harvard. It was a neat handoff. Lodge revered Seward and set out to pursue his imperial dream.

Expansion has always been central to the American idea. Jefferson doubled the size of the United States by purchasing the Louisiana Territory from France in 1803. Over the following decades, the United States secured its sovereignty in North America by clearing native peoples from the West and seizing a large part of Mexico. In 1867, Seward himself arranged the American purchase of Alaska. To Lodge he bequeathed the next challenge: ushering the United States from continental empire to overseas empire.

Lodge was an exemplar of America's aristocracy. His family had accumulated great wealth on the seas—as privateers during the American Revolution, as dealers in opium, rum, and slaves, and finally as masters of trade across the Caribbean, Mediterranean, and Pacific. Several of his ancestors had been politicians. He became the most powerful and prominent figure this globally ambitious family produced.

Known throughout his life as Cabot, he was born in 1850 and grew up on Beacon Hill and at his family's manor in the seaside village of Nahant. His upbringing was one of extreme privilege. Before he was out of his teens he knew half a dozen European capitals, but he never saw, understood, or cared about the tumultuous lives of ordinary Americans. In Boston his favorite outing was to Commercial Wharf, where amid sailors and salt air he watched exotic goods being unloaded from his father's ships: the *Argonaut*, the *Cossack*, the *Don Quixote*, the *Magnet*, the *Kremlin*, the *Storm King*.

When Lodge ran for a seat in the Massachusetts House of Representatives in 1879, Democrats ridiculed him as a "silver-spooned young man," a "lah-de-dah boy," and "the gentleman rider of Nahant." Nonetheless he won the third of his district's three seats. Blond and blue-eyed, already sporting the pointed beard he would keep all his life, he began plotting his rise. In 1881 he lost a race for the State Senate. The next year he failed to win nomination for Congress, but he remained active in Republican politics and in 1884 was chosen as a delegate to the Republican National Convention in Chicago. That led him to the partnership with Roosevelt through which he changed the course of history.

Lodge was vain, austere, and aloof. He spoke in a high-pitched, raspy voice that some compared to chalk screeching on a blackboard. Not only did he lack the common touch, he had no interest in cultivating it. Many saw him as an arrogant snob. He saw himself that way. From the beginning of his political career he realized that his character and personality would prevent him from ever winning the presidency. Yet only a president could lead the United States decisively toward empire.

In 1884, Lodge opposed the nomination of the corrupt James G. Blaine for the presidency. So did Roosevelt. The two men corresponded, met for dinner at Delmonico's in New York City, and cemented their friendship at the Republican convention in Chicago. Both were Harvard graduates from wealthy families, limitlessly self-confident, who loved horseback riding, were drawn to the sea, considered war glorious, and felt enough energy within themselves to move the world. They failed to prevent Blaine's nomination, but set out to become co-founders of the modern American empire.

Roosevelt welcomed Lodge's friendship, which came at a crossroads in the younger man's life. Earlier that year, Roosevelt had been shattered by the death of his mother and wife on the same day—February 14, 1884—and reacted by plunging into frenetic action. He bought a cattle ranch in North Dakota, hunted game, slept in tents, and gathered material for self-promoting books with evocative titles such as *Hunting Trips of a Ranchman*. It was therapy by playacting, the rich boy living out his fantasy of rugged life. When Roosevelt killed his first buffalo, according to one account, he "abandoned himself to complete hysteria," dancing around the carcass while "whooping and shrieking." For the rest of his life he rhapsodized about "the keen delight of hunting in lonely lands."

Humbug, scorned Mark Twain. Nothing in Roosevelt's public persona irritated him more than the "outdoorsman" image.

"He has no sympathy with any brand of nature study other than his own," Twain wrote. "In a word, Mr. Roosevelt is not a naturalist, but a game killer. Of the real spirit of animal life, of their habits as discovered with quiet watching with no desire to kill, he knows nothing, and never will learn until he goes into the woods, leaving his pack of dogs, his rifle, his prejudice, and his present disposition behind him."

Upon returning from a trip west in 1886, Roosevelt decided to run for mayor of New York. It was an ill-conceived campaign. He finished a

poor third and retired to his Long Island estate at Oyster Bay to rumi-
nate. Over the next two years he kept a low profile. Many thought his
political career was over.

For the first but not the last time, Lodge intervened. Following the
election of Benjamin Harrison as president in 1888, Lodge, who had just
completed his first term as a congressman, relentlessly lobbied the new
president to give Roosevelt a job in Washington. Harrison was reluctant,
but in 1889 he finally agreed to name Roosevelt to the three-member
Civil Service Commission.

Roosevelt and Lodge, living close to each other in Washington,
became intimate friends as well as political partners. Together they wrote
a book for young readers called *Hero Tales from American History*, a collection of idealized stories about Daniel Boone, Andrew Jackson, and
other swashbucklers who exemplified "the stern and manly qualities
which are essential to the well-being of a masterful race." They spent
countless hours discussing ways to awaken Americans to what they
considered the call of destiny. Few others heard it.

"We fear no encroachments on our territory, nor are we tempted at
present to encroach on that of others," the Naval Policy Board reported
in 1890. "We have no colonies, nor any desire to acquire them."

This approach to the world bitterly frustrated Roosevelt. He considered fighting to be the only way for a man to prove himself. One of his
Harvard friends wrote that "he would like above all to go to war with
someone . . . he wants to be killing something all the time." Later
the philosopher and psychologist William James wrote that Roosevelt
"gushes over war as the ideal condition of human society, for the manly
strenuousness which it involves, and treats peace as a condition of
blubberlike and swollen ignobility, fit only for huckstering weaklings,
dwelling in grey twilight and heedless of the higher life."

With America happily at peace during the 1890s, Roosevelt racked his
brain to find a possible enemy. "I should welcome almost any war, for I
think this country needs one," he wrote in 1895. For a time he mused
about fighting the "aboriginal owners" of Australia or Siberia, which
seemed to him a glorious prospect because "the most ultimately righteous
of all wars is a war with savages." Since no such war could be arranged, he
began to imagine fighting a European power instead. Any would do.

"Frankly I don't know that I should be sorry to see a bit of a spar with Germany," he wrote to a friend. "The burning of New York and a few other seacoast cities would be a good object lesson in the need of an adequate system of coastal defenses."

In 1892, Lodge won the job he coveted above all others and would hold until his death thirty-two years later: United States senator from Massachusetts. Roosevelt was an energetic civil service commissioner, but after a time he became bored with the job. In 1895 he returned to New York City to become president of the police board. He proved to be a zealous anti-corruption crusader and implacable enemy of Sunday drinking. His saloon smashing made great copy. Lodge saw the way to their grand goal becoming clearer.

"I do not say you are to be president tomorrow," he wrote to Roosevelt. "I do not say it will be—I am sure that it may and can be."

Lodge and Roosevelt wanted their country to strengthen its navy, project power, and rule faraway lands, but neither man had a systematic plan to accomplish it. It took the naval strategist Alfred Thayer Mahan to give order to their wild surmise.

Mahan had served in the navy during the Civil War and went on to command ships, but he was a poor captain, steering several of his vessels into collisions. Sometimes depression overwhelmed him so fully that he could not leave his cabin. Shore duty suited him better. In 1885 he secured appointment as a lecturer at the fledgling Naval War College in Newport, Rhode Island, and the next year became its president. There he met Theodore Roosevelt, who came to the college to deliver a speech in which he used the word "war" sixty-seven times. Roosevelt encouraged Mahan to collect his notes into a book. It emerged as *The Influence of Sea Power Upon History, 1660–1783*, and it remains one of the most influential works of military history ever written in the United States. Mahan argued that control of the seas is always crucial to countries seeking to achieve or maintain far-reaching power. If the United States wished to join the scramble for the world's wealth, he concluded, it would have to build warships and dispatch them to take distant islands, ports, peninsulas, and "strong places where a navy can be protected and refurnished."

"I am frankly an imperialist, in the sense that I believe that no nation, certainly no great nation, should henceforth maintain the policy of isolation which fitted our early history," Mahan wrote. "Imperialism, the extension of national authority over alien communities, is a dominant note in the world politics of today."

Mahan's book gave Lodge and Roosevelt the guide they had lacked, complete with historical detail that seemed to prove their case—though it did not explain the rise of land-based empires such as Russia or Germany. Mahan became the toast of Washington. He wrote articles and testified at congressional hearings. Until his book appeared, most Americans had thought of expansion as a movement within their own continent, to be accomplished with wagon trains and cavalry patrols. He encouraged them to look further.

"Captain Mahan has written distinctively the best and most important, and also most interesting, book on naval history which has been produced on either side of the water in many a long year," Roosevelt wrote in the *Atlantic*. "Our greatest need is the need for a fighting fleet. . . . We need a large navy, composed not only of cruisers but containing also a full proportion of powerful battleships, able to meet those of any other nation."

Mahan did not see power projection as simply an abstract good or an exercise of national ego. He promoted it above all as an answer to the central dilemma of American life. By the end of the nineteenth century, American farmers and factory owners had so fully mastered techniques of mass production that they were producing more than they could sell. They urgently needed new markets.

In 1893 the United States plunged into the worst depression its people had ever known. The collapse of the Philadelphia and Reading Railroad Company shocked the over-leveraged economy and set off a panic. Hundreds of banks failed. Thousands of businesses collapsed. Millions lost jobs. Bitter strikes were brutally suppressed. Commodity prices plummeted, leaving many farm families destitute. Hordes of angry unemployed converged on Washington. Chaos threatened.

Business and political leaders saw only one way out of this crisis: overseas markets. These would be the safety valve by which explosive social pressures inside American society would be eased. During the mid-1890s, politicians, businessmen, and editorial writers focused continually on the theme of "glut" and the absolute necessity of finding new markets for American products. Mahan reminded them that overseas commerce would have to be protected, or imposed on unwilling nations, by naval power. He fused America's commercial and strategic interests into a global strategy that captured many imaginations.

"The great nations are rapidly absorbing for their future expansion and their present defense all the waste places of the earth," Lodge wrote. "As one of the great nations of the world, the United States must not fall out of the line of march."

Several times Lodge and Roosevelt saw encouraging glimmers of militarism in the United States. In 1891, Americans were roused to a fury by news that two American sailors had been stabbed to death in a fight outside the True Blue Saloon in Valparaiso, Chile. "We are actually at the mercy of a tenth-rate country!" Roosevelt fumed. Behind this manufactured crisis lay a desire to slap down the powerful Chilean navy and ensure access to nitrate deposits that were bringing profit to an American company, W. R. Grace. Finally, threatened with retaliation, Chile agreed to pay the United States a $75,000 indemnity.

In 1894 the United States sent five warships to intervene in a civil war in Brazil, breaking a blockade that prevented the unloading of American goods at Rio de Janeiro. A year later the United States declared its right to dictate the settlement of a boundary dispute between Venezuela and British Guiana. These episodes produced momentary bursts of martial pride. They were practice runs, psychic preparations for the explosion of American intervention that lay ahead.

As the presidential election of 1896 approached, the Republican candidate, Governor William McKinley of Ohio, was asked what the country needed in order to complete its recovery from depression. "We want a foreign market for our surplus products," he replied simply. That was what businessmen wanted to hear. McKinley became the first American presidential candidate to receive large campaign donations from wealthy capitalists. Many were arranged by his close friend and political manager Mark Hanna, who had made a fortune in oil, steel, coal, and railroads. Captains of industry had rarely contributed to political campaigns. Hanna persuaded them that this time they must—to block demonic power in the form of William Jennings Bryan.

Few presidential candidates in American history have stirred as much emotion as Bryan. To the established classes he was a paragon of

evil, promoter of radical policies certain to destroy the American economy. Masses of the poor and dispossessed idolized him. The 1896
presidential campaign framed class conflict more starkly than any in
American history. It was the first presidential election in which big
money played a decisive role. At its heart was the life-or-death debate
over "free silver."

Millions of Americans, especially farmers, were being crushed by
debt or had already lost their land. They blamed the gold standard for
keeping commodity prices low and mortgage interest rates crushingly
high. Cheaper currency and easier money, they believed, would ease their
burden. This they would achieve through what was called free silver,
legalizing the coinage of silver at the same rate as gold even though its
intrinsic value was far less. The result would be inflation, which they
presumed would raise prices for their crops and make it easier for them
to pay off their debts. To creditors and many others, this sounded like
a recipe for wiping out established fortunes—robbing the rich to aid
the poor.

Bryan promoted free silver with religious fervor. He arrived at the
1896 Democratic National Convention in Chicago as a little-known
former congressman from Nebraska, just thirty-six years old and a
most unlikely presidential candidate. In the space of less than an hour
on the afternoon of July 9, he changed the course of the convention, the
campaign, and American political history with one of the most famous
speeches of the age. It was a ringing call for the Democratic Party to
support "the struggling masses" against "idle holders of idle capital."

> There are those who believe that if you will only legislate to make
> the well-to-do prosperous, their prosperity will leak through on those
> below. The Democratic idea, however, has been that if you legislate to
> make the masses prosperous, their prosperity will find its way up
> through every class which rests upon them. You come to us and tell us
> that the great cities are in favor of the gold standard; we reply that the
> great cities rest upon our broad and fertile prairies. . . . We will answer
> their demand for a gold standard by saying to them: "You shall not press
> down upon the brow of labor this crown of thorns, you shall not crucify
> mankind upon a cross of gold!"

The arena exploded. Bryan was borne through the aisles like a conquering hero. "Bedlam broke loose, delirium reigned supreme," the *Washington Post* reported. Less than twenty-four hours later, delegates nominated Bryan as the Democratic candidate for president.

McKinley warned that free silver was too dangerous an experiment to try at a moment when the country was recovering from depression. Voters agreed. Propelled by large sums that Hanna raised from frightened robber barons, among them John D. Rockefeller, Cornelius Vanderbilt, and J. Pierpont Morgan, McKinley won the election with 271 electoral votes to 176 for Bryan.

In his inaugural address, McKinley said he "cherished the policy of non-interference with affairs of foreign governments" and then pointedly added, "We want no wars of conquest; we must avoid the temptation of territorial aggression." Nonetheless his victory at the polls produced a little-noticed result that decisively advanced the imperialist cause. Lodge had campaigned for the Republican ticket, and after the election he traveled to McKinley's home in Canton, Ohio, to ask "one personal favor" as a reward. He wanted McKinley to name Theodore Roosevelt assistant secretary of the navy.

McKinley gave no reply. He told a friend he was hesitant because he had heard that Roosevelt was "always getting into rows with everybody" and might be "too pugnacious" for such a sensitive post. Lodge did not give up. He lobbied for months, painstakingly arranging for one Washington insider after another to put in a good word with the president. Finally McKinley relented and made the appointment.

"Lodge did a brilliant selling job for Roosevelt," the diplomatic historian Warren Zimmerman has written. "He saw in Roosevelt the battering ram he needed to achieve a powerful navy and a muscular policy of expansion. . . . The warmth he could not show his friends or his wife he bestowed generously on Roosevelt. As Roosevelt clearly recognized, he owed his political success to Lodge more than anyone else."

That reference to Lodge's wife was not casual. Lodge and Roosevelt came from a class of Gilded Age men who idealized women, knew little about them, and viewed romantic passion as a sign of weakness. This left Nannie Lodge unfulfilled. She was the daughter of an admiral, highly intelligent and sophisticated, who read widely, played the piano, and could recite Shakespeare at length. "It was said of her that she knew the names and technical details of almost every ship in the Navy," according to one account, "and that she could discuss the controversies of staff and line vividly and accurately with any sea dog. . . . Lodge never prepared a speech or essay without submitting it to her for verification." Nonetheless the two had an uneasy relationship. Lodge said he admired Nannie for "that ignorance which is born of wide knowledge." It was not enough. While her husband was empire building, Nannie conducted an affair with one of his close friends, John Hay. Lodge was too busy to notice.

"It is unmitigated Boston that you see recorded," one of Lodge's friends wrote when he saw John Singer Sargent's portrait of the rising imperialist. "The eye of a robust, stiff-necked race of seventeenth and eighteenth century dissenters, with its plain living, high thinking, dauntless intolerance, bleak bad manners, suppression of feeling, tenacity in its stern beliefs, and its cantankerousness, stares down on you with cold disapprobation."

During 1897, Lodge and Roosevelt did all they could to promote the building of warships, expansion of naval bases, and better conditions for seamen. Nonetheless they felt like unrecognized prophets, lonely warmongers in a country happily at peace. At the end of the year Roosevelt wrote that he felt "a good deal disheartened at the queer lack of imperial instinct that our people show." If they did not change, he worried, "it will show that we either have lost, or else wholly lack, the masterful impulse which alone can make a race great."

On a January night in 1898, street fighting broke out in Havana between groups favoring and opposing Cuban independence. American newspapers, eager to print whatever would excite readers, reported falsely that Spaniards had assaulted American citizens. NEXT TO WAR WITH SPAIN! screamed one headline. The American minister in Madrid, Stewart Woodford, was appalled.

"Foreign correspondents at Havana, who are a disreputable set, are doing all they can to raise a war scare between America and Spain, spreading no end of lies and succeeding in exciting bad feeling," he wrote to President McKinley. "In order to obtain peace, the best would be to send away some of these correspondents."

In Washington, Roosevelt felt destiny calling. Combat—hearing bullets fly just as his boyhood heroes had—was his all-consuming dream. His father had paid a substitute to fight in his place during the Civil War, and Roosevelt believed he could redeem his family's honor only by going to war himself. As soon as he heard the news of rioting in Havana, he stormed into the office of his boss, Secretary of the Navy John Long, and announced that the moment war was declared, he would resign his post and enlist to fight.

"The impetuosity and fierceness with which he insists upon this are rather amusing," Long wrote in his diary. "I called him a crank, and ridiculed him to the best of my ability, but all in vain."

Soon afterward, following a long cabinet meeting at which no notes were taken, President McKinley ordered a lumbering armored cruiser docked at Key West, the USS *Maine*, to set sail for Havana. Officially this would be a friendly visit. It also served as a "gunboat calling card," a sign that Uncle Sam was watching. On January 25 the *Maine* dropped anchor beneath Morro Castle, a three-hundred-year-old symbol of Spanish power. Those who wished for war saw this as a hopeful sign because it increased the possibility of confrontation.

"There may be an explosion any day in Cuba which would settle a great many things," Lodge wrote to a friend.

A radically new force in American life ensured that millions of people would feel this explosion instantly: the mass press. Literacy rates had skyrocketed just as technology made the speedy production and distribution of newspapers possible. Journalism entered a new era. With it came a hard-charging breed of cutthroat media entrepreneurs. They fought furious battles for readers, filling their pages with lurid tales of sex, crime, and scandal. The most powerful of them, William Randolph Hearst, proprietor of the *New York Journal*, became the crucial third member of the troika that pushed the United States into war and toward global power. These three willful men—Lodge, Roosevelt, and Hearst— joined to reshape the world.

In the order of imperial battle that emerged at the beginning of 1898, Lodge was the consummate Washington insider and Roosevelt his ever-eager public face. The two of them alone, though, could not have roused America. They needed a mighty megaphone. Hearst provided it. He used his media empire to bombard Americans with a daily barrage of super-patriotic chauvinism that drove them wild.

Hearst had begun his newspaper career at the age of twenty-four by taking over the *San Francisco Examiner* from his father, who had acquired it as settlement of a gambling debt. In 1895 he moved his base to New York and bought a failing newspaper, the *Morning Journal*. He built it into a powerhouse in part by raiding the staff of its main competitor, Joseph Pulitzer's *New York World*. Then he reduced the newsstand price to a penny. Instead of a single edition he published three: morning, afternoon, and German language. To increase his reach he bought newspapers in other cities, ultimately winding up with more than two dozen.

Hearst's formula was simple: be the most sensational, thereby selling more papers and becoming steadily richer and more powerful. This worked phenomenally well. When Hearst bought the *Journal*, its daily circulation was less than eighty thousand. Within a year he had pushed it close to one million. He called this "an achievement not only unparalleled in the history of the world, but hitherto undreamed-of in the realm of modern journalism."

On most days the *Journal* published a garish mix of stories about murder, suicide, adultery, family tragedy, and political corruption. After a while Hearst, with an entrepreneur's sharp eye, concluded that these stories were starting to blur together. He looked for something new, a "running story" that would capture attention not just momentarily but for weeks or months—and drive people to buy a newspaper every day.

War is the best running story of all. It grips nations and creates a lust for news. Hearst saw that he could profit from this passion. He was, as the novelist and muckraking journalist Upton Sinclair wrote, "willing by deliberate and shameful lies, made out of whole cloth, to stir nations to enmity and drive them to murderous war."

The frenetic climate in America during the late 1890s allowed Lodge, Roosevelt, and Hearst to develop breathtaking dreams. During those years, Mark Twain was living in Europe, inhaling very different air. Lodge, Roosevelt, and Hearst considered colonialism a thrilling patriotic adventure. Twain saw it through the eyes of its victims.

After visiting Hawaii, Twain wrote that white traders and missionaries there were pursuing the "long, deliberate, infallible destruction" of the local population. He called British-ruled Rhodesia "a land of piracy and pillage" where natives suffered "insult, humiliation, and forced labor for a man whose entire race the victim hates." When agitation against Czar Nicholas II erupted in Russia, he became a founding member of the American Society of Friends of Russian Freedom. He defended the wrongfully accused Jewish officer Alfred Dreyfus against charges of treason in France. In early 1898 he published a moving dispatch in *Harper's* describing anti-Semitic violence in Vienna and Prague.

"In some cases the Germans being the rioters, in others the Czechs," he wrote, "and in all cases the Jew had to roast, no matter which side he was on."

Twain was far away when the United States set out on its imperial quest. He thought little about Cuba. Nonetheless he was sharpening his anti-colonialism and his instinctive sympathy for the oppressed. Expansionists would never have sympathized with native Hawaiians or Africans, much less revolutionaries in Russia. Twain did. Because he was abroad during the late 1890s, he was insulated from the tumult at home. That prepared him to be more virulent in his anti-imperialism than any other American.

William Randolph Hearst began his campaign for war in 1898 with wildly inflammatory coverage of the January upheaval in Havana, which the *Journal* portrayed as anti-American rioting although in fact it had little to do with the United States. He had his next chance a couple of weeks later. An agent working for Cuban revolutionaries stole a letter written by the Spanish minister in Washington, Enrique Dupuy de Lôme, that contained an unflattering reference to President McKinley. De Lôme described him— quite aptly—as "weak and a bidder for the admiration of the crowd, besides being a slippery politician who tries to leave a door open behind him while keeping on good terms with the jingoes of his party." The Cubans, guessing that this might interest Hearst, passed the letter to him.

WORST INSULT TO THE UNITED STATES IN ITS HISTORY, the *Journal* screamed in a front-page banner on February 9.

Over the next few days, the yellow press exploded in its first coordinated campaign of that decisive year. Newspapers turned de Lôme into a reviled symbol of Spanish impudence. The *Journal* said it was "impossible to exaggerate the seriousness of De Lôme's malevolent comment." Quickly the indiscreet diplomat resigned. Spain formally apologized.

JOURNAL'S LETTER FREES COUNTRY FROM DE LÔME was the *Journal* headline.

Flushed with this success, the *Journal* began demanding that McKinley immediately ask Congress for a declaration of war on Spain. It published a flood of heartrending dispatches about atrocities in Cuba, some fabricated by writers and illustrators who had never been there. In the space of a couple of weeks, millions of Americans were whipped into an anti-Spanish fury. All they needed was another provocation. It came quickly and with devastating force.

For three weeks after arriving at Havana, the *Maine* lay peacefully at anchor, a glistening white hulk with a deck the length of a football field. The warm evening of February 15 was as calm as others had been. When taps sounded shortly after nine o'clock, the captain, Charles Sigisbee, was in his cabin writing a letter to his wife.

> I laid down my pen and listened to the notes of the bugle, which were singularly beautiful in the oppressive stillness of the night. . . . I was enclosing my letter in its envelope when the explosion came. It was a bursting, rending, and crashing roar of immense volume, largely metallic in character. It was followed by heavy, ominous metallic sounds. There was a trembling and lurching motion of the vessel, a list to port. The electric lights went out. Then there was intense blackness and smoke. The situation could not be mistaken. The *Maine* was blown up and sinking.

This was the moment for which war hawks—jingoes, as they were called—had been waiting. It was tragic, but also an answer to their prayers. On February 17 the *Journal* published one of the most powerfully mendacious front pages in the history of American journalism. A drawing of the *Maine* at anchor, showing an enemy's bomb attached to her hull below the waterline, was surrounded by brilliantly composed headlines.

DESTRUCTION OF THE WAR SHIP MAINE WAS THE WORK OF AN ENEMY,
blared the top line. Below ran a flood of dazzling phrases.

Assistant Secretary Roosevelt Convinced the
Explosion of the War Ship Was Not an Accident

The Journal Offers $50,000 Reward
For the Conviction of the Criminals Who
Sent 258 Americans to Their Death

Naval Officers Unanimous That the
Ship Was Destroyed on Purpose

Hidden Mine or a Sunken Torpedo
Believed to Have Been the Weapon Used
Against the American Man-of-War

Officers and Men Tell Thrilling Stories of
Being Thrown Into the Air Amid a
Mass of Shattered Steel and Exploding Shells

Spanish Officials Protest Too Much

Our Cabinet Orders a Searching Inquiry

Journal Sends Divers to Havana to
Report on the Condition of the Wreck

Not everyone jumped to blame Spanish treachery. President
McKinley urged Americans to withhold judgment. Secretary of the
Navy Long wrote in his diary that the explosion was probably "the
result of an accident." The country's principal expert on maritime explo-
sives, Philip Alger, a professor at the Naval Academy, told the Washington
Evening Star that "no torpedo such as is known in modern warfare can of
itself cause an explosion as powerful as that which destroyed the *Maine*."
He theorized that the tragedy was caused by combustion of the ship's

ordnance set off by sparks from an adjacent coal bunker. Seventy-six years later an official inquiry determined that he was right. Americans were in a fury, though, and in no mood for such an explanation. They seized on the navy's false conclusion that the *Maine* "was destroyed by a submarine mine." Investigators said they were "unable to obtain evidence fixing the responsibility," but Spain was the obvious culprit.

"*Maine* is a great thing," Hearst cabled to one of his correspondents. "Arouse everybody."

Roosevelt reacted to news of the sinking with outrage but also immense excitement. "Being a jingo," he wrote to a friend, "I would give anything if President McKinley would order the fleet to Havana tomorrow. This Cuban business ought to stop. The *Maine* was sunk by an act of dirty treachery on the part of the Spaniards, I believe—though we shall never find out definitely, and officially it will go down as an accident."

Suddenly Cuba obsessed everyone. Crowds gathered in front of the White House. Spaniards were burned in effigy. Demands to fight echoed in editorials, speeches, and sermons. Newspapers published patriotic ditties. War songs became part of vaudeville shows.

> *Uncle Sam, tell us why are you waiting?*
> *Hear you not the call to arms?*
> *For our noble land has been degraded.*
> *Let us wake to war's alarms!*

Naval planners in Washington had concluded that in case of war, their first task would be to destroy the Spanish fleet to prevent a counterattack. They determined that most of the fleet was anchored at Manila Bay in the Philippine Islands, which had been a Spanish colony for centuries. The navy awaited an order from McKinley to attack. It did not come.

McKinley was the last president to have served in the Civil War. He fought at Antietam, where more than twenty thousand Americans fell in a single day. "I have been through one war, I have seen the dead piled up, and I do not want to see another," he told a friend. Several times he sought a negotiated peace in Cuba, but since he insisted that Spain renounce sovereignty over its "ever-faithful isle," he could not succeed. Secretary Long also tried and failed. Long wrote in his diary that he was unable to sleep and suffered from "much nervous trouble." President McKinley was no better, "oppressed and care-worn."

Long had learned of a "mechanical massage" machine that he hoped would ease his muscle spasms. He took February 25 off from work to test it. His deputy Roosevelt saw his chance and seized it as few American bureaucrats ever have.

As soon as Roosevelt realized he was alone in the office, he summoned his friend Lodge. Then, with Lodge at his side, he began dashing off telegrams to naval units at home and abroad. One ordered that warships be loaded with ammunition. Another authorized recruitment of new seamen. A third directed that naval cannon be prepared for action. The most important was to Admiral George Dewey, commander of the Asiatic Squadron.

"Order the squadron, except the [paddle-wheeler] *Monocracy*, to Hong Kong," he wrote. "Keep full of coal. In the event of a declaration of war with Spain, your duty will be to see that the Spanish squadron does not leave the Asiatic coast, and then offensive operations in the Philippine Islands."

Long rose early the next morning. Before dressing, he wrote in his diary that he had passed "a splendid night." His mood changed abruptly when he arrived at work.

"During my short absence, I find that Roosevelt, in his precipitate way, has come very near to causing more of an explosion than happened to the *Maine*," he wrote. "The very devil seemed to possess him."

Despite their displeasure, neither Long nor President McKinley countermanded Roosevelt's orders. That emboldened him. He pressed McKinley to ask Congress for a declaration of war. McKinley resisted, but agreed to submit a bill appropriating $50 million to fortify American ports and build new warships. That held off the jingoes for another week. It also provoked protests from congressmen alarmed at the rush to war.

"I have had letters from my people wanting us to take Cuba, to punish Spain," Representative David Henderson of Iowa, a leading Republican, told his colleagues. "I simply write back that no international law makes the United States the regulator of the wrongs of the earth. God has written no motto on the banner of our country that demands of us the regulating of the wrongs of other countries to their people. We all sympathize with the liberty-loving and fighting Cubans, but they are citizens of another government. So long as that question is before us, I follow the advice of Washington, recommending that we mind strictly our own business."

Views like these became harder to sustain as war fever intensified. They fell further out of favor after Senator Redfield Proctor, a respected Republican from Vermont, rose from his seat on the morning of March 17 to hurl a new thunderbolt. Proctor had just returned from an extended tour of Cuba. Until this moment he had refused to say anything about what he had found. His tone was calm. By one account he read his speech "with as little apparent feeling as if it constituted an agricultural report instead of a record of almost inconceivable horror."

Proctor said he had set out for Cuba with "a strong conviction that the picture had been overdrawn; that a few cases of starvation and suffering had inspired and stimulated the press correspondents, and that they had given free play to a strong, natural, and highly cultivated imagination." What he found, though, was a tragic panorama of Cubans "torn from their homes," many of them "so diseased that they cannot be saved," their children "walking about with arms and chests terribly emaciated." He called the situation in Cuba so awful that "it is not within the narrow limits of my vocabulary to portray it." If the United States intervened, he concluded, these horrors would end and "bounty will reach the sufferers."

Although Proctor did not say anything senators had not already heard, he was known to be close to President McKinley, and according to some reports had cleared his speech with McKinley in advance. That gave it special weight. Cynics growled that Proctor, who owned quarries in Vermont, was encouraging American intervention in Cuba to increase the market for gravestones. Nonetheless his speech touched many hearts. It gave expansionists their most emotionally powerful rallying cry.

Businessmen favored intervention in Cuba because they wanted markets and resources. Others saw it as a strategic imperative. Now the humanitarian argument was in place. McKinley recognized its appeal. In a message to Congress on April 11, he became the first American president to threaten war against another country because it was mistreating its own subjects.

"Forcible intervention of the United States as a neutral to stop the war [would be] in the cause of humanity, and to put an end to the barbarities, bloodshed, starvation, and horrible miseries now existing there, and which the parties to the conflict are either unable or unwilling to stop or mitigate," McKinley wrote. "It is no answer to say this is all in another country, belonging to another nation, and is therefore none of our business. It is specially our duty, for it is right at our door."

Americans hate the thought of suffering anywhere. Expansionists of 1898 played to this compassion. They realized, as have their successors, that the best way to bring Americans to support a foreign intervention is to frame it as a rescue of oppressed people. Lodge did that in a long Senate speech on April 13. He finished with a rousing call to national and racial greatness.

> We are not in this crisis by accident. We have not been brought here by chance or by clamorous politicians or by yellow journals. We are face to face with Spain today in the fulfillment of a great movement which has run through the centuries.
>
> In our veins runs the blood of Holland and the blood of England. If after all the centuries it comes to us, much as we pray to avert it, to meet Spain face to face in war, it is because we are there in obedience to a greater movement than any man can hope to control. We are there because we represent the spirit of liberty and the spirit of the new time, and Spain is over against us because she is medieval, cruel, dying . . .
>
> Surely there was never a more righteous cause than this for any nation to ask for justice. That gigantic murder, the last spasm of a corrupt and dying society, which carried down our ship and our men, cries aloud for justice.

This chauvinism repelled some powerful men in Washington. Among the most disgusted was the iron-willed "Czar" Reed, Speaker of the House. In the weeks after the *Maine* exploded, he blocked bills to finance a bigger navy. His regal scorn drove expansionist congressmen to paroxysms of anger. On the day Lodge spoke in the Senate, they jeered Reed and demanded to be heard. He ignored them. Tempers passed the breaking point.

"Liar!" one member shouted at Reed.

"Scoundrel!" shouted another.

Pandemonium broke out. Congressmen lunged at each other. Books were thrown, including a bound volume of the *Congressional Record*. A stray punch knocked a House page unconscious. Women in the gallery screamed. "Members rushed up and down the aisles like madmen," one newspaper reported, "exchanging hot words with clenched fists and set teeth; excitement was at a fever heat." Order was finally restored, partly by a sergeant-at-arms who charged into the scrum swinging a wooden mace. Tempers did not cool, however. The great debate was breaking out.

A couple of days later Lodge proposed an ultimatum: a Senate resolution declaring that if Spain did not withdraw from Cuba, the United States would declare war. Given the passions consuming Washington, this resolution was sure to pass. Anti-expansionist senators, however, found a way to turn it to their advantage. Lodge and his comrades always insisted that they wanted to fight in Cuba only to help Cubans win independence from Spain, not to annex or colonize the island. Senator Henry Teller of Colorado took them at their word. He introduced an amendment declaring the purity of American motives and asked that it be appended to Lodge's resolution.

"The people of the Island of Cuba are, and of right ought to be, free and independent," the Teller Amendment said. "The United States hereby disclaims any disposition or intention to exercise sovereignty, jurisdiction, or control over said Island except for the pacification thereof, and asserts its determination, when that is accomplished, to leave the government and control of the Island to its people."

Lodge was displeased but did not resist. In the predawn hours of April 19, the Senate and House agreed by voice vote to append the Teller Amendment to his war resolution. Then they passed the resolution, by a vote of 42 to 35 in the Senate and 311 to 6 in the House. McKinley signed it the next day.

Spain rejected the demand that it abandon Cuba. McKinley ordered a blockade of Havana. On April 24 and 25, Spain and the United States declared war on each other.

"Dissuade them!" Speaker Reed fumed after one of his supporters urged him to dissuade congressmen from their aggressive course. "He might as well ask me to stand out in the middle of a Kansas waste and dissuade a cyclone!"

In the months after the *Maine* exploded, Americans were gripped by patriotic frenzy. People thrilled to the prospect of war against evil. Some, however, felt a nagging fear.

American companies owned plantations, mines, and other rich properties in Cuba. Nearly all manufactured goods sold in Cuba were imported from the United States. Congress had promised that as soon as fighting ended, American troops would withdraw from Cuba and allow Cubans to shape their own destiny. The scale of these investments led skeptics to doubt. Would the coming war really be aimed only at helping Cubans win freedom, they wondered, or would expansionists try to turn Cuba into an American territory or protectorate as soon as the Spanish were gone? More frightening: If the United States took Cuba, would it then proceed to take other lands?

These were reasonable fears, but although Speaker Reed and others gave voice to them in Washington, the doubters still had no coherent national leadership. The first figure to step forward was Carl Schurz, one of the most brilliant immigrants to the United States during the nineteenth century. Schurz would go on to become a towering figure in the anti-imperialist movement, but he first made his case privately, in a letter to President McKinley.

"It would very grievously hurt this Republic in the opinion of mankind, which after all is of high importance to all of us, if the suspicion were to grow up that the ultimate annexation of Cuba was a secret motive of our action," Schurz wrote as the war drums began to beat. "Such an impression cannot be too carefully guarded against."

Over the course of nearly half a century in public life, Schurz had become a unique political and moral leader. As a teenager he fought in the 1848 revolution in his native Germany. Four years later he arrived in the United States, became a passionate abolitionist, and campaigned for Abraham Lincoln. He was rewarded with a post as minister to Spain. Less than a year later he resigned, returned to the United States, joined the Union Army, was commissioned as a brigadier general, and commanded troops at Chancellorsville and Gettysburg. Later he was elected to the U.S. Senate from Missouri. In 1877 President Rutherford B. Hayes named him secretary of the interior. He was the first immigrant from Germany to become a senator, and one of the first foreign-born cabinet secretaries. After leaving office, he spoke out regularly and wrote trenchant articles in national magazines. By one account he became "the self-constituted, but exceedingly useful, incarnation of our national conscience." Had it not been for his foreign birth, he might have run for president.

"During the stormy period between the outbreak of the Civil War and the close of the nineteenth century, most Americans grew familiar with the tall, erect, and vigorous figure of Carl Schurz, known as 'the Dutchman,'" one of his biographers has written. "Something about his irregular features lent itself readily to caricature, and his whiskers became as well known as Roosevelt's square teeth or Mark Twain's shaggy moustache."

One of Schurz's principles became his most famous maxim: "My country, right or wrong; if right, to be kept right; and if wrong, to be set right." In the matter of Cuba—and the larger temptation of global power—he believed the United States was going profoundly wrong. McKinley had promised him in a letter soon after taking office in 1897, "There will be no jingo nonsense under my administration." Soon afterward McKinley told Congress that annexing any foreign land against the will of its people "would be criminal aggression." By the spring of 1898 he seemed to have changed course. Schurz begged him to reconsider.

"The man who in times of popular excitement boldly and unflinchingly resists hot-tempered clamor for an unnecessary war, and thus exposes himself to the opprobrious imputation of a lack of patriotism or of courage, to the end of saving his country from a great calamity, is, as to 'loving and faithfully serving his country,' at least as good a patriot as the hero of the most daring feat of arms," Schurz wrote in *Harper's* soon after sending his letter to McKinley.

Such noble principles may fit a peaceful era, but Americans were aflame in the spring of 1898. Schurz's warning was terribly timed. The United States was about to erupt in jubilant self-congratulation.

Before dawn on May 1, less than a week after the declaration of war, Admiral Dewey led six warships into Manila Bay and arrayed them in battle formation. Across the harbor lay the slow-moving, poorly armored Spanish fleet. By 5:20 Dewey's maneuver was complete. He gave the captain of his flagship, USS *Olympia*, an order that has gone down in history: "You may fire when you are ready, Gridley." The barrage was devastating. When it was over, three Spanish ships were sunk and six others had been scuttled. Spain suffered 381 casualties, including 161 killed. The Americans lost no ships and had just six men wounded, plus one dead from heat stroke. All was finished by midday.

VICTORY! COMPLETE! GLORIOUS! was the banner headline in the next day's *Journal.* Hearst's editorial said this triumph proved "the right is with us, and God is with the right." An astonishing 1.6 million papers were sold. Americans were delirious. Dewey became a hero such as the United States had never known.

The victory at Manila Bay, however, was far from complete. Dewey had destroyed the Spanish fleet but could do no more. His ships did not carry nearly enough men to attempt an amphibious assault. Even if they had, no assault had been authorized. No one in Washington had thought about what should come next.

"If old Dewey had just sailed away when he smashed that Spanish fleet," McKinley later mused, "what a lot of trouble he would have saved us."

Even the nimble-minded Lodge could not immediately grasp the scope of the opportunity suddenly at hand. "The victory at Manila was at first so overwhelming I did not take in all its possibilities," he wrote afterward. Only after "a day's reflection," he recalled, did he reach his three conclusions: "We must on no account let the islands go; we must hold the other side of the Pacific; and the value to this country is almost beyond imagination." Later he began imagining what that "value" might be.

"With our protective tariff wall around the Philippine Islands," he wrote to a friend, "its ten million inhabitants, as they advance in civilization, would have to buy our goods, and we should have so much additional market for our home manufactures."

Lodge did not confess these ambitions in public. Instead he took advantage of his friendship with McKinley to press his case privately. The two men represented New England and Ohio, twin pillars of the Republican Party. They needed each other. During that spring, Lodge haunted the White House.

McKinley knew no more about the Philippines than any other American. When asked where they were, he placed them "somewhere away around the other side of the world." Later he confessed that when he received Dewey's cable announcing victory at Manila Bay, "I could not have told you where those darned islands were within a thousand miles." Nor had McKinley considered what the United States might do with the Philippines after Dewey's victory. He dispatched an expeditionary force under General Wesley Merritt, and before departing Merritt asked him in a telegram "whether it is your desire to subdue and hold all of the Spanish territory in the islands, or merely to seize and hold the capital." McKinley replied vaguely that Merritt's mission would be "completing the reduction of Spanish power" and "giving order and security to the islands." War was approaching in Cuba, and McKinley did not want to be distracted by the Philippines.

No one looked forward to this war more impatiently than Roosevelt. On May 6, as he had promised, he quit his job as assistant secretary of the navy and announced that he was ready to fight in Cuba. Secretary Long wrote in his diary that Roosevelt's "unbounded energy and force" had clouded his judgment.

"He has lost his head to this unutterable folly of deserting his post, where he is of most service, and running off to ride a horse and, probably, brush mosquitoes off his neck on the Florida sands," Long wrote. "His heart is right and he means well, but it is one of those cases of aberration—desertion—vainglory; of which he is utterly unaware. He thinks he is following his highest ideal, whereas, in fact, as without exception every one of his friends advises him, he is acting like a fool."

"And yet," Long added as an afterthought, "how absurd this will sound if, by some turn of fortune, he should accomplish some great thing."

Roosevelt believed he had the makings of an ideal soldier. Few agreed. He applied to join the staff of General Fitzhugh Lee, a former consul general in Havana, but Lee would not have him. Regiments were being organized by state, and Roosevelt asked the governors of New York and Massachusetts to commission him. Both refused. Finally his friend and fellow expansionist Colonel Leonard Wood persuaded the territorial governor of Arizona to commission Roosevelt as a lieutenant colonel. He was ordered to proceed to Fort Sam Houston in San Antonio, Texas, and raise a cavalry unit. Officially he was second in command, under Wood, but the public saw only him. According to one newspaper, "Colonel Wood is lost sight of entirely in the effulgence of Teethadore."

"I know now that I would have turned from my wife's deathbed to have answered the call," Roosevelt told a friend afterward. This war gave him, he said, "my chance to cut my little notch on the stick that stands as a measuring rod in every family."

Some of the men who turned up to fight alongside Roosevelt were cowboys used to hard work in punishing heat. To join them, Roosevelt recruited a pack of eastern swells "from Harvard, Yale, Princeton, and many other colleges; from clubs like the Somerset of Boston and the Knickerbocker of New York; and from among the men who belonged to neither club nor to college, but in whose veins the blood stirred with the same impulse which once sent the Vikings overseas." They found each other odd but invigorating company. One wrote that his comrades included "millionaires, paupers, shyster lawyers, cowboys, quack doctors, farmers, college professors, miners, adventurers, preachers, prospectors, socialists, journalists, insurance agents, Jews, politicians, Gentiles, Mexicans, professed Christians, Indians, West Point graduates, Arkansan wild men, baseball players, sheriffs, and horse thieves."

Reporters from the *Journal* and other newspapers swarmed over Roosevelt's training camp. All found his unit's official name—First United States Volunteer Cavalry—impossibly boring. They tried out various alternatives: first the Fifth Avenue Boys and the College and Club Men, then the Cowboy Regiment and the Rustler Regiment, then Teddy's Terrors, Teddy's Texas Tarantulas, Teddy's Gilded Gang, Teddy's Cowboy Contingent, and Teddy's Riotous Rounders. Finally a correspondent from the *Arizona Weekly Star* came up with "Rough Riders." It was with that name that they entered history.

"The eyes of the civilized world are upon you," Roosevelt told his men in one rousing camp speech, "and I want your watchword to be, 'Remember the *Maine!*'"

Resplendent in a white dress uniform, Admiral Dewey welcomed a uniquely important guest aboard the *Olympia* on the morning of May 18, 1898. This was one of the most fateful meetings in the history of American foreign policy. No one knows what transpired.

Dewey's guest was the Filipino rebel leader Emilio Aguinaldo, whose revolutionaries had been fighting Spanish rule for four years. Aguinaldo had been in exile in Hong Kong, and Dewey dispatched an American warship, the USS *McCullough*, to bring him home. The Filipino force under his command numbered several thousand. Dewey realized that it could be expanded almost without limit if the United States would provide enough weaponry. He had crushed Spanish sea power; he wanted Aguinaldo to do the same on land.

Their partnership bore quick results. Dewey sent Aguinaldo ashore with a hundred rifles and directed the United States consul in Hong Kong to buy him two thousand more. Nonetheless this must have been an odd meeting. Neither man spoke the other's language well, and no interpreter was present. That may have served American purposes. Aguinaldo came away believing he had a deal: Filipino rebels would fight and defeat the Spanish, after which the United States would recognize the Philippines as an independent country. Dewey later insisted that he had promised no such thing.

"It is the word of a Malay adventurer—a Malay 'patriot,' if you please—against the word of an American admiral and gentleman," reasoned the *Hartford Courant*. "We believe George Dewey."

During the last days of May and the first days of June, the United States began deploying soldiers to fight on two fronts nearly ten thousand miles apart. The vanguard of the Philippine Expeditionary Force landed at Cavite, near Manila, on May 25. Two days later the United States Navy began a blockade of Santiago in eastern Cuba. On June 10, U.S. Marines landed at Guantánamo Bay. Roosevelt's Rough Riders made their way by train from San Antonio to Tampa, Florida, and sailed for Cuba on June 13.

At this moment the Spanish-American War, as it later came to be known, took its strangest territorial twist. The war was originally about Cuba. Puerto Rico would become a target because it was near Cuba. The Philippines were vulnerable after Dewey destroyed the Spanish fleet there. Then, most unexpectedly, a fourth land emerged as a candidate for annexation: Hawaii.

Five years earlier, in 1893, the United States had supported an uprising in which white planters and their allies deposed the Hawaiian monarchy. They tried to bring Hawaii into the United States, but before Congress could accept, the anti-imperialist Grover Cleveland returned to the presidency and blocked their ambition. White-ruled Hawaii became a sovereign nation, and remained so for five years. Now, with Cleveland out of the White House and war threatening in the Philippines, senators who favored annexing Hawaii saw a second chance.

Annexation would serve various interests. President Sanford Dole of Hawaii wanted to open the American market to Hawaiian sugar and fruit. Lodge, Roosevelt, and Captain Mahan saw Hawaii as an ideal base from which to project military power across the Pacific. Merchants and manufacturers salivated at the prospect of a launching pad for trade with China; magazines and newspapers were full of calculations about the fabulous wealth that awaited them if they could persuade the Chinese to wear cotton clothes, use American kerosene, build with American nails, or begin eating bread and meat instead of rice and vegetables. For five years these arguments had failed to persuade Congress that the United States needed Hawaii. That changed in the tumult of 1898.

At the beginning of May, Lodge introduced a measure to annex Hawaii. He cleverly shaped it to improve its chances for passage. Rather than frame it as a treaty, which would require a two-thirds majority in the Senate, he submitted it as an amendment to the War Revenue bill. That would allow it to be adopted by a simple majority in the House and Senate. McKinley liked the idea.

Carl Schurz, who had campaigned for McKinley, was shocked to see him supporting the seizure of a distant archipelago. On May 9 he wrote again to McKinley. He insisted that despite Dewey's "brilliant victory" at Manila, Americans must "remain true to our promise that this is to be a war of deliverance."

But if, as newspapers foreshadow, the Administration takes advantage of the war to press the annexation of Hawaii now—that annexation having been violently discountenanced by the public opinion of the country before the war began—it is certain that the confidence of the world in the unselfishness of our policy will be destroyed. . . . From that time on it would be useless to protest that this is not a war of selfish ambition and conquest.

Schurz wrote to McKinley every couple of weeks, but Lodge was in the White House almost every day. With gentle persistence he pressed a simple case: now that the United States had become involved in the Philippines, taking Hawaii, which lies halfway across the Pacific, was a "military necessity." Slowly McKinley came to agree. He called for another seventy-five thousand volunteers and began sounding like a convert.

"We need Hawaii just as much and a good deal more than we did California," he told a visitor to the White House. "It is manifest destiny."

On May 31, the Senate met in closed session to debate the annexation of Hawaii. The transcript, which remained secret for more than seventy years, shows that Lodge remained in the background and allowed others to press his case. They made two arguments: Hawaii is our way into the vast China market, and Hawaii has become a "military necessity" because it is a way station to the Philippines.

Anti-imperialist senators scorned these arguments as trivial and distracting. To them the question was cosmic—greater than Hawaii, greater than trade, greater than geopolitics. It touched the very essence of the American idea. The United States was born as an exemplar of freedom, they argued, and could not rule over distant peoples without betraying its most sacred principle. After one pro-annexation speech, Senator Augustus Octavius Bacon of Georgia rose to crystallize the question.

"Seeing that the Executive only has such powers as are given in the Constitution," Bacon demanded, "I want to know under what clause of the Constitution the Senator finds the power to seize the territory of a neutral country with which we are not at war."

Senator John Tyler Morgan of Alabama, a co-sponsor of Lodge's annexation resolution, replied that it was foolish to dwell on constitutional niceties when vital interests were at stake. Taking Hawaii, he insisted, was "absolutely necessary for properly providing for the situation." As precedent he cited Andrew Jackson's invasion of Florida in 1818, which brought the United States rich new territory that it probably could not have obtained legally.

"There are men still alive in this world who have the old Jackson stock in them," Morgan said, "and plenty of it."

Senators agreed not to vote on annexation until they could debate it publicly. This closed session, though, showed that many of them were excited at the prospect of overseas expansion. So were most Americans.

"A sort of bellicose fever has seized the American nation," the French ambassador wrote in a dispatch. For the London *Times* it was "the delirium of war." An Italian correspondent called it "manic passion for what has never been done before." To the *Kölnische Zeitung* it was "lust for conquest." *Le Temps* of Paris concluded that the United States had become "the predestined instrument of that imperialism that is latent in every democracy."

America's rush to world power began with astonishing suddenness in the spring of 1898. Over the course of just a few months, the United States and its people changed profoundly. Opponents of expansion scrambled to organize and marshal their arguments. As summer approached, they finally began to find their voice.

One of the first protests came from a dozen prominent New Yorkers including the novelist William Dean Howells, the social reformer Josephine Shaw Lowell, and Bolton Hall, treasurer of the American Longshoremen's Union.

"We desire to call attention to the manifest folly of contributing even in the slightest degree to the warlike feeling so prevalent in the country," they wrote in a manifesto that was published in New York and beyond. "The cruelty exhibited in Cuba is no peculiarity of the Spanish race; within the last few weeks instances of cruelty to Negroes have occurred in this country which equal, if they do not surpass, anything which has occurred in Cuba. . . . Our crusade in this matter should begin at home. We see every day the vast injustices prevailing in our own land, the hopeless toil, the wretched poverty, the armies of unemployed, and until we remove these beams from our own eyes we should not presume to take the mote from our brother's."

Soon after that statement was published in New York newspapers, a clarion voice rang out. It was that of Charles Eliot Norton, a much-admired Harvard professor who had begun his career in the East India trade and then forsaken it to become a scholar and social reformer. On June 7, as Congress was about to begin debating the annexation of Hawaii and as American warships were steaming toward Cuba and the Philippines, Norton addressed the Men's Club of the Prospect Street Congregational Church in Cambridge. This was the first major speech in the history of American anti-imperialism.

> A generation has grown up that has known nothing of war. The bless-ings of peace have been poured out upon us. . . . And now of a sudden, without cool deliberation, without prudent preparation, the nation is hurried into war, and America, she who more than any other land was pledged to peace and good-will on earth, unsheathes her sword. . . .
>
> My friends, America has been compelled against the will of all her wisest and best to enter into a path of darkness and peril. Against their will she has been forced to turn back from the way of civilization to the way of barbarism, to renounce for the time her own ideals. With grief, with anxiety, must the lover of his country regard the present aspect and the future prospect of the nation's life.

That day's audience included many of New England's most influential political, social, and intellectual leaders. Norton's words were the call to arms for which they had been waiting. Immediately a group of them, their hearts afire, resolved to present their case to a larger audience. They decided to hold a public rally at Faneuil Hall. The next available date was June 15, a week away. From that rally they charged forth into battle.

3

The Great Day of My Life

Sleek warships announcing America's surging ambition reached two ports on June 20, 1898. An enormous fleet—forty-eight vessels— approached Santiago, Cuba, as the sun set. Aboard one troop carrier was the newly commissioned Lieutenant Colonel Theodore Roosevelt. He was off on the adventure of a lifetime, and aching with anticipation.

"It is a great historical expedition and I thrill to think I am part of it," Roosevelt wrote in a letter home. "If we are allowed to succeed (for certainly we will succeed, if allowed), we have scored the first great triumph in what will be a world movement."

This was the most popular war in American history. Thanks to the telegraph, it was also the first one Americans were able to follow as it was being fought, reading about battles while they were still under way. The yellow press crackled with frenzied energy. Boatloads of correspondents flooded into Cuba. They needed heroes. The blunt-talking, bucktoothed, hyperactive Roosevelt fit the role perfectly.

Even the iconoclastic Mark Twain briefly shared his country's excitement. Twain was living in Vienna, where he was a major celebrity, and did not know that an anti-imperialist movement was growing at home. He spent his days writing and his evenings with a luminous circle of acquaintances including Gustav Mahler, Johann Strauss, Arthur Schnitzler, Gustav

Klimt, and Sigmund Freud—who skipped a medical lecture one evening and, by his own account, "treated myself to listening to our old friend Mark Twain in person, which was a sheer delight." In the spring of 1898, Twain's brother-in-law visited, and he reported that nearly all Americans considered the war in Cuba fully righteous. Twain agreed. For once he violated his own maxim "The majority is always in the wrong." What could be nobler, after all, than to liberate an oppressed nation and bless it with freedom?

"I have never enjoyed a war—even in written history—as I am enjoying this one," Twain wrote to his friend Joseph Twichell in Hartford. "For this is the worthiest one that was ever fought, so far as my knowledge goes. It is a worthy thing to fight for one's freedom; it is another sight finer to fight for another man's. And I think this is the first time this has been done."

Twain could not imagine how fully he would soon reverse this opinion. As he quietly applauded the war from far away, America's ambition grew. Roosevelt, his future antagonist, became the country's most outspoken expansionist.

Coverage of the Rough Riders at their Texas camp had already made Roosevelt a national figure. He was about to leap further, toward celebrity and myth. The reputation he won in Cuba during the summer of 1898 immeasurably strengthened his ability to rally Americans around his imperial vision. He raced into action while Twain dallied in Viennese drawing rooms.

On the same day that Roosevelt and his Rough Riders caught sight of Cuba for the first time, a single American warship seized another territory nine thousand miles away.

Secretary of the Navy John Long had ordered several warships based at Pearl Harbor in Hawaii to sail for the Philippines in case action was required there. He sent one commander, Captain Henry Glass of the USS *Charleston*, a set of secret orders, to be opened only at sea. Once Hawaii faded behind him, Glass assembled all hands on deck, dramatically broke the seal on his orders, and read them aloud. The *Charleston* was to proceed to the Philippines as planned, but not directly.

"On your way, you are hereby directed to stop at the Spanish Island of Guam," Long wrote. "You will use such force as may be necessary to capture the port of Guam, making prisoners of the governor and other officials and any armed force that may be there. You will also destroy any fortifications on said island and any Spanish naval vessels that may be there, or in the immediate vicinity. These operations at the Island of Guam should be very brief, and should not occupy more than one or two days."

Guam, a volcanic islet in the western Pacific, had been a Spanish colony since 1668 and was home to about fifty thousand people. Its principal value to outsiders was, and is, its strategic location. It is a short sail to ports in China and Japan, and an ideal base from which to project commercial or military power in East Asia. Americans decided they should have it.

The *Charleston* arrived at Guam on June 20, its crew eager to engage Spanish warships. To everyone's disappointment, the only vessel in the harbor was a Japanese brigantine picking up coconuts. With no ships to sink, Captain Glass ordered his men to bombard the crumbling Spanish citadel, Fort Santa Cruz. In a four-minute volley, they fired thirteen shells. There was no response. Soon afterward, a skiff flying the Spanish flag approached the *Charleston*. Two Spanish officers came aboard and apologized for not having returned the American "salute" because they had no gunpowder left in their arsenal. It turned out that they had not been resupplied for months and did not know the United States and Spain were at war.

The next morning an American lieutenant went ashore. At 10:15 he handed the Spanish commandant a message demanding surrender of the island within thirty minutes. The commandant retired to his quarters. Twenty-nine minutes later he emerged with a reply. "Being without defenses of any kind and without any means for meeting the present situation," he had written, "I am under the sad necessity of being unable to resist such superior forces and regretfully accede to your demands."

Upon receiving this surrender, Captain Glass sailed ashore. He assembled the fifty-six Spanish soldiers and officers and told them they were his prisoners, to be turned over to the American authorities in Manila. Then he ordered the American flag raised over Fort Santa Cruz. At this signal, the *Charleston*'s shipboard band struck up "The Star-Spangled Banner." Naval gunners fired a twenty-one-gun salute. When they finished, Glass declared Guam to be American. That made him the first officer ever to seize an overseas territory for the United States.

From Washington, Henry Cabot Lodge watched this operation with delight. The idea of taking small islands as "coaling stations" owed much to Captain Mahan, but it was Lodge who had brought it into mainstream Washington. Most Americans were too caught up in the Cuban drama to notice what had happened in Guam. Lodge understood that it marked the turn of epochs.

"The flag which had risen first on the distant Atlantic coast floated out before the afternoon breeze of these remote islands, which were henceforth to know new masters," he wrote in *Harper's*. "The first possession in the Pacific which Magellan had given to the Spain that dominated and frightened Europe had passed away forever from the Spain which had ceased to rule, and become a part of the Western republic."

Lodge was forty-eight, eight and a half years older than Roosevelt, and although he was just as vigorous a warmonger, he was not the sort of man to charge enemy lines himself. He recognized that he could do more for the cause by staying home. The corridors of Washington power suited him better than the battlefield. There he would fight for the duration of this conflict.

The third member of the jingo triumvirate, William Randolph Hearst, felt no such restraint. After the declaration of war on Spain, he ran a triumphant front-page headline that would have been outrageous if it was not at least partly true: HOW DO YOU LIKE THE JOURNAL'S WAR? Then, thirty-five years old and with no military experience, he applied for a commission as an officer in the United States Navy.

Hearst's newspapers had relentlessly taunted President McKinley for his reluctance to join the imperial crusade. Just a few days before he applied for his commission, the *Journal* published an insolent letter from "Uncle Sam" to McKinley. "We have this war with Spain on our hands," it said. "William, don't lack the moral courage. . . . Go in for action. Demand action. . . . Country above all, William." Not surprisingly, the navy rejected Hearst. He appealed. At one point he even offered to pay for his own warship if he could command it. It was to no avail. He had been a principal promoter of this war, though, and was determined not to miss it.

As soon as Hearst realized that he would not be commissioned as a naval officer, he bought a steamship, the *Sylvia*, from the Baltimore Fruit Company and turned it into a floating news bureau, crammed with everything from photographic supplies to a printing press on which he hoped to produce the first newspaper in "free" Cuba. His shipmates included a small army of correspondents, combat artists, personal attendants, and friends. They dropped anchor off eastern Cuba on June 18 and were soon joined by the pioneering motion picture cameraman Billy Blitzer, who would later help make film history as cinematographer to D. W. Griffith. Hearst spent hours with Blitzer and a parade of other camp followers, hosting them on deck for champagne lunches in his blazer and commodore's cap.

Among Hearst's companions aboard the *Sylvia* were two teenaged sisters, Millicent and Anita Willson, who had been his ostentatiously public companions in New York for more than a year. They were chorus girls in the risqué Broadway musicals he favored, and he loved showing up with them, one on each arm, at nightclubs and theater openings. Polite society was scandalized, but Hearst loved playing the showman. War did not change his style.

A few days after arriving in Cuban waters, Hearst went ashore to meet the legendary General Calixto García, commander of the revolutionary army in eastern provinces. As a sign of gratitude for Hearst's role in promoting American intervention, García presented him with a Cuban flag pockmarked by bullet holes. Hearst wrote a report of their encounter. He quoted García as saying that "the *Journal* had been the most potent influence in bringing the United States to the help of Cuba, and that they would always remember the *Journal* as a friend when friends had been very few."

Roosevelt and his men landed near Santiago on the afternoon of June 22. They made camp and soon afterward were told that their mission would be to help clear a path into the city. That required flushing Spanish troops out of the surrounding hills.

The Rough Riders fought twice. Their first taste of combat came on June 24, when they marched into an ambush on their way inland, near a village called Las Guásimas. Colonel Wood, accustomed to command, calmly gave orders as bullets flew. "Roosevelt, on the contrary, jumped up and down, literally, I mean with emotions evidently divided between joy and a tendency to run," a *Journal* correspondent reported. Shooting continued for ninety minutes. Eight Rough Riders were killed, including Hamilton Fish, captain of the Columbia University crew team. In later years Roosevelt would insist that he had not actually been ambushed, but had led his men in a planned maneuver aimed at drawing fire from Spanish positions.

Soon after that skirmish, Colonel Wood was named to relieve a general who had collapsed from fever. That left Roosevelt, "to my intense delight," in command of the Rough Riders—with a field promotion to colonel.

"The attack on Santiago is to begin in a few hours," the correspondent Richard Harding Davis wrote before dawn broke on July 1. "In the bushes of the basin beneath us, twelve thousand men are sleeping, buried in a sea of mist, waiting for the day."

Over the course of that morning, several American units were ordered to move against Spanish defenders. Roosevelt waited with growing impatience as volleys of fire echoed around him. Finally, at around one o'clock, a rider turned up bearing the command for which he had been waiting: "Move forward and support the regulars in the assault on the hills in front."

"The instant I received the order, I sprang on my horse and then my 'crowded hour' began," Roosevelt wrote afterward. "I waved my hat and we went up the hill with a rush."

What came to be known as the Battle of San Juan Hill was actually fought on a rise called Kettle Hill. It was part of a day-long wave of attacks that cost the lives of 205 Americans and 215 Spaniards. The result was a clear victory for the Americans, who by nightfall were in control of the ridgeline. Roosevelt later called it "the great day of my life."

As fighting subsided, one of the most famous correspondents on the scene, the *Journal*'s James Creelman, was seized by a wish to claim the flag of a defeated Spanish platoon. "I wanted it for the *Journal*," he wrote later. "The *Journal* had provoked the war, and it was only fair that the *Journal* should have the first flag captured in the greatest land battle of the war." Creelman dashed from cover and scooped up the flag he sought, but seconds after picking it up he was hit in the shoulder by a Spanish bullet. He staggered toward a hillside and fell. A few minutes later, stunned and bleeding, he felt a hand on his forehead.

"Opening my eyes, I saw Mr. Hearst, the proprietor of the New York *Journal*, a straw hat with a bright ribbon on his head, a revolver at his belt, and a pencil and notebook in his hand," Creelman recalled in his memoir. "The man who had provoked the war had come to see the result with his own eyes and, finding one of his correspondents prostrate, was doing the work himself. Slowly he took down my story of the fight. 'I'm sorry you're hurt, but'—and his face was radiant with enthusiasm—'wasn't it a splendid fight? We must beat every paper in the world.'"

While wounded reporter and excited editor were having this odd exchange, Roosevelt, a blue polka-dot kerchief waving from his sombrero, was reveling in his victory at Kettle Hill. His four hundred Rough Riders had dislodged a hundred-man Spanish position. He found the fight exciting beyond measure. At its height he gleefully shouted, "Holy Godfrey, what fun!"

Only the climactic scene remained. To complete the archetypal rite—to prove his full manliness, especially to himself—Roosevelt needed to kill an enemy soldier. The only ones in sight were fleeing into the distance.

Providentially, as Roosevelt and an aide-de-camp were surveying the aftermath of battle, two Spanish soldiers jumped from a trench about ten yards away and began firing blindly at them. Roosevelt was carrying an exquisitely symbolic revolver, a Colt .38 that his brother-in-law, a navy officer, had salvaged from the *Maine*. He drew it as the two Spaniards turned to run.

"I closed in and fired twice, missing the first and killing the second," he wrote afterward. "He doubled up as neatly as a jackrabbit." Later Roosevelt took pains to emphasize that he had not shot the fleeing soldier in the back, but rather "in the left breast as he turned."

On that day, Roosevelt redeemed what he saw as his family's shame and tasted the battlefield glory of which he had dreamed since childhood. He also assumed the identity that would soon make him the most captivating public figure of his age: gallant commander on horseback, saber in hand, charging into enemy gunfire in the cause of freedom. For years Roosevelt had promoted the idea of American conquest. Now he embodied it.

Screaming headlines in the *Journal* and other newspapers portrayed the fighting in Cuba as an epic conflict. Hearst knew better, but in search of readers he whipped his correspondents to ever bolder flights of fancy. As their copy flowed through his floating newsroom, he was seized by the desire to play at least a bit part in the war himself. Early on the morning of July 4 the part came his way.

The *Sylvia* had sailed up to the abandoned and still smoldering wreck of a Spanish cruiser, and Hearst went aboard for a look. Then, scanning the beach with his binoculars, he spotted a tattered troop of Spanish sailors who had escaped the wreck. Clad in his white yachting suit and cap, he leaped into a launch, was rowed to shore, and, waving a pistol, told the Spaniards they were his prisoners. Twenty-nine of them obediently came aboard the *Sylvia*. There Hearst treated them to a full meal and led them in two rounds of cheers, one for the Fourth of July and another for "George Washington and Old Glory." After a few hours he directed the *Sylvia* to approach the nearest American warship, the USS *St. Louis*, and announced to its captain that he had prisoners to deliver. With typical flair, he insisted on a receipt. An irritated officer complied, scrawling, "Received of W. R. Hearst twenty-nine Spanish prisoners." Hearst had a facsimile of this note published on the *Journal*'s front page. He framed the original. It hung on his office wall for years.

Roosevelt understood the value of self-promotion at least as well as Hearst. He not only used the war to push himself into the public limelight, as Hearst did, but also found a way to project his image into elite circles. From the moment he left Washington to join his Rough Riders, he maintained almost daily correspondence with Henry Cabot Lodge, who vicariously shared the adventure. Lodge sent him breathless encouragement, often accompanied by newspaper clippings.

"You have won yourself a high place already as one of the popular heroes of the war," Lodge wrote after the Kettle Hill engagement. "You can't win more distinction than you have already won so far as mere personal heroism is concerned!"

Roosevelt's letters overflowed with praise of his own bravery and battle skills. They were clearly written to be read aloud at salons and dinner parties back home. Lodge happily obliged.

"On the day of the big fight, I had to ask my men to do a deed that European military writers consider utterly impossible of performance, that is, to attack over open ground unshaken infantry armed with the best modern repeating rifles behind a formidable system of entrenchments," Roosevelt wrote in one letter that Lodge shared with friends. "The only way to get them to do it in the way it had to be done was to lead them myself."

No one could have managed Roosevelt's rise as deftly as Lodge. Groomed from childhood to command, he deeply understood the uses of power. He judged men shrewdly, cultivated them delicately, and manipulated them subtly. His web of social and political connections in Washington was dense. When fighting began in Cuba, he extended it by cultivating a group of admiring newspapermen. Through them he played an unseen role in shaping American public opinion.

"Each afternoon a group of correspondents would congregate in his committee room and discuss with him the progress and the conduct of the struggle," one biographer has written. "Senator Lodge referred to this select group as his 'Board of Strategy.' But in the press gallery they were referred to by a phrase that was to become famous in another respect thirty-four years later: the 'brain trust.' Throughout the war they met almost every day, and when the group later broke up, Senator Lodge presented each of the 'brain trusters' with a gold stickpin bearing the golden eagle from the great American seal."

With help from Lodge, as well as from Hearst's *Journal* and the rest of the popular press, Roosevelt emerged from his two months in Cuba as a famous hero. That made him a hot political commodity.

"The image that endured in public imagination was the charge of Teddy Roosevelt and his Rough Riders up San Juan Hill," according to one history of the war. "In reality, although the event was a crucial element of the American victory, it formed only one part of a larger engagement. . . . Roosevelt was a consummate politician, and the correspondents he courted so carefully highlighted his obvious courage in such a way that he became the linchpin of the battle. This undoubtedly also helped his future electoral prospects."

Only one other war hero was more popular than Roosevelt. By sinking the Spanish fleet at Manila Bay, Admiral Dewey became the most celebrated military commander in American history. His image adorned neckties, shaving mugs, fountain pens, baby bibs, and all manner of memorabilia. Streets, plazas, cocktails, and newborn boys were named for him. Songs and odes were composed in his honor. For a time there was talk that he would capitalize on his fame by running for president. He never became truly interested, though, and diffidently deflected political offers.

This cleared a path for Roosevelt. Every previous American war had produced successful politicians. In 1898, Dewey declined the role. Roosevelt seized it.

"I hear talk all the time about your being run for Governor and Congressman," Lodge wrote to his dear friend and protégé. In a second letter: "At this moment you could have pretty much anything you wanted." Soon afterward: "Ordinary rules do not apply to you."

To make himself a more formidable candidate—and to satisfy his private longings—Roosevelt decided that his "crowded hour" in Cuba qualified him for the Congressional Medal of Honor. He began campaigning for it immediately after the engagement at Kettle Hill, sending a barrage of letters and appeals to everyone in Washington he thought might help.

"I do wish you would get that Medal of Honor for me, I think I earned it," he wrote to Lodge. "I don't ask this as a favor—I ask it as a right."

Generals scoffed at Roosevelt's presumption. He was a volunteer officer whose military career barely spanned a summer and who had seen just two half days of combat. Nonetheless he relentlessly pressed his case. He was singularly unsuccessful until, eighty years after his death, President Bill Clinton, citing his "extraordinary heroism and devotion to duty," awarded him the Medal of Honor posthumously.

The American campaign in Cuba was not much of a war, just a few weeks of scattered engagements between mismatched armies and navies. There was little true heroism. Deaths from disease outnumbered combat deaths by eight to one. Yet none of this mattered to Americans. They had developed a yearning for glory, and in Cuba they found it. The incoming secretary of state, John Hay, captured the nation's exultant mood in a letter to Roosevelt.

"It has been a splendid little war," Hay wrote, "begun with the highest motives, carried on with magnificent intelligence and spirit, favored by that Fortune which loves the brave."

Newspapers overflowed with delirious reports of battlefield victories in Cuba. Patriotic pride gripped the national soul. Americans had their first taste of overseas conquest, and they loved it. Lodge decided to take advantage of the mood. On July 6 he asked the Senate to approve the annexation of Hawaii.

The House of Representatives had already approved annexation. President McKinley favored it. A vote in the Senate was all that stood between the United States and a colony more than two thousand miles beyond California.

Senator William V. Allen of Nebraska began the debate by calling this "the greatest question that has ever been presented to the American people." He warned that taking Hawaii would be only "the first act in the drama of colonization," and that as the drama unfolded the United States would be tempted to seize "every little dimple in either the Atlantic or Pacific Ocean that may force its head above the surface of the water."

Another prairie populist, Richard Pettigrew of South Dakota, read from documents showing that the overthrow of Hawaii's monarchy five years earlier had been the work of white planters and their friends, supported by the United States, and that natives strongly opposed it

> The government which now exists in Hawaii, with which we are treating for a title to that country, is a government existing without the consent of the people of those islands. . . . Will senators vote to take this title tainted by fraud? Will senators vote to ratify this robber revolution brought about by us, and refuse to consult the people most interested? If they will, it is an astonishing thing. . . .
>
> We based our government on the doctrine promulgated in the Declaration of Independence that all men are created free and equal and are by nature entitled to certain inalienable rights, which are mentioned in the declaration. We did not say that all men in the United States were born free and equal, but we said that all men, wherever they are born, stand on terms of equality. . . .
>
> No nation can afford to be guilty of dishonor or perfidy. The man who gains a reputation in the neighborhood in which he lives for being uncertain in his promises is always a loser. Honesty is the best policy, not only in individual life but in national life. The nation that makes and declares one thing and then seeks to accomplish the reverse of it will stand condemned in the eyes of the nations of the world, as the individual would stand condemned in the eyes of the community.

Supporters of annexation took these assaults calmly because they were confident of victory. Lodge did not rise from his seat. Among the few annexationists who did was Eugene Hale of Maine, who had a special interest in Hawaii because many of the first missionaries there came from his home state.

"To all intents and purposes these islands for years have been an appendage of the United States," Hale said. "Their business is ours. Their property is largely owned and controlled by men who have gone there from the United States. . . . We have today a moral protectorate over the Hawaiian Islands, and it is the sense, I believe, of the American people that the union be made complete."

Shortly after four o'clock, Vice President Garret Hobart, who was presiding, recognized anti-annexation senators for the last time. Knowing they were likely to lose the coming vote, these senators introduced a series of amendments aimed at weakening the annexation resolution— or at least embarrassing its sponsors. One amendment stipulated that Hawaiian election law must permit all adult males to vote. Another required a plebiscite on the islands before annexation could take effect. A third banned contract labor, a mainstay of the sugar industry. The Senate rejected all of them.

That cleared the way for a final vote. It was almost as lopsided as the one in the House had been three weeks earlier: forty-two in favor of annexation to twenty-one opposed, with twenty-six not voting. Moments later the House passed the War Revenue bill, to which the annexation proposal was attached. McKinley signed it the next day. For the first time in its history, the United States absorbed an overseas nation.

"Hurrah for Hawaii!" Roosevelt wrote to Lodge from his camp in Cuba when he heard the news. Then he added: "Did I tell you that I killed a Spaniard with my own hand when I led the storm of the first redoubt? Probably I did."

Americans who hated the idea of overseas expansion were aghast at the vote to annex Hawaii, but in one way it helped their incipient movement. It brought them another potent leader and spokesman: Grover Cleveland, who had served eight years in the White House and finished his second term just sixteen months before.

As president, Cleveland had blocked the annexation of Hawaii and even tried to reinstate the deposed queen. On the day his successor signed the annexation resolution, he sent a disgusted letter to a friend that showed how far some Americans were from Roosevelt's "Hurrah for Hawaii" triumphalism.

"Hawaii is ours," Cleveland wrote. "As I look back upon the first steps in this miserable business and as I contemplate the means used to complete the outrage, I am ashamed of the whole affair."

During the summer of 1898, many New Englanders worked intently to build a national anti-imperialist movement. Two widely popular leaders immediately enlisted: the dynamic former senator Carl Schurz, a lifelong Republican, and William Jennings Bryan, unofficial leader of the Democratic Party. Grover Cleveland became the third. He was fresh from the presidency, immersed in practical politics, and determined to stop the expansionist juggernaut. As soon as what he called "the Hawaiian monstrosity" was consummated, he began speaking and writing against "schemes of imperialism" that were luring the United States into "dangerous perversions of our national mission."

"Our government was formed with the express purpose of creating in a new world a new nation," Cleveland said in one speech, "the foundation of which should be man's self-government, whose safety and prosperity should be secured in its absolute freedom from Old World complications and in its renunciation of all schemes of foreign conquest."

Hearst, who had supported the annexation of Hawaii, ridiculed Cleveland's anti-imperialism. He directed one of his cartoonists to draw an image of an expiring Cleveland trying unsuccessfully to rise from his deathbed. "Burdened with ponderous platitudinosities, Grover Cleveland has again burst the cerements of the tomb and croaked his sepulchral protest against American progress," said the accompanying commentary. "If Mr. Cleveland were alive, it would be in order to ask him how it happens that our Government has taken root in the vast domain over which it serves a free, happy, and prosperous people."

Cleveland's outspoken statements gave anti-imperialists new reason for hope. They had believed from the beginning that justice was on their side. For three months their message had been drowned out by public cheering for triumph at Manila Bay, battlefield victories in Cuba, and the annexation of Hawaii. Now they were attracting first-rank leaders.

The Cuban war ended quickly. On July 16, commanders on both sides agreed to terms of capitulation. Their accord was special in one way. Spain surrendered not to Cuban rebels but to the United States. The message was clear: Americans, not Cubans, would replace Spain as the island's new masters.

"The president I think feels very strongly about Cuba," Lodge wrote to Roosevelt with evident pleasure. "He means to take firm military possession and not withdraw the troops until the island is in perfect order and a stable government is established."

On August 12, in a second-floor office at the White House that became known as the Treaty Room, representatives of Spain and the United States signed a formal surrender, called a "protocol of peace." Three days later the Rough Riders returned home. An adoring crowd was waiting when their troop carrier docked at Montauk, Long Island.

"How are you, Colonel Roosevelt?" one spectator shouted.

"I am feeling disgracefully well!" the hero replied. "Oh, but we have had a bully fight! I feel as big and strong as a bull moose!"

Reporters clamored for more. Roosevelt obliged by showing them the pistol he had used to kill a Spanish soldier. "When I took it to Cuba I made a vow to kill at least one Spaniard with it, and I did," he said. Adulation enveloped him.

"Will you be our next governor?" called a voice from the crowd.

"None of that!" Roosevelt replied. "All I'll talk about is the regiment. It's the finest regiment that ever was, and I'm proud to command it."

Not satisfied with being cheered at Montauk, Roosevelt decided he should lead his Rough Riders in a parade down Fifth Avenue in Manhattan. The War Department, already irritated by his campaign for the Medal of Honor, refused to allow it. Nonetheless Roosevelt's fame did not escape the notice of political bosses.

Republicans in New York faced a difficult election. They held the governorship, but their incumbent had been shown to be corrupt and seemed unlikely to win re-election. Only with a new candidate could they hope for victory. Republican bosses mistrusted Roosevelt, who was an impetuous reformer and notoriously difficult to control. Without him, though, they faced defeat at the polls.

Roosevelt had a complementary problem. He was bursting with ambition but had no political organization, no machine to propel him into office. Soon he and New York's Republican barons came to understand how much they could help each other. Political wheels began to turn. The hero of San Juan Hill prepared to enter the next phase of his career.

This should have pleased Hearst. He had played a decisive role in creating the Roosevelt legend. The *Journal* ran many stories about the Rough Riders, some of them highly romanticized and several printed alongside iconic drawings by Frederic Remington and other gifted illustrators showing Roosevelt sometimes as a thoughtful statesman, other times as a death-defying combat commander. In the run-up to the war, Hearst devoted almost an entire front page to an interview with Roosevelt, who not only promised that there would be "no backing down" over Cuba, but added: "It is cheering to find a newspaper of the great influence and circulation of the *Journal* that tells the facts as they exist, and ignores the suggestions of various kinds that emanate from sources that cannot be described as patriotic or loyal to the flag."

Yet this was neither a true friendship nor a true alliance. Hearst had always regarded Roosevelt with a combination of envy and resentment. Roosevelt returned his disdain. Each was a man of limitless ego who believed the world revolved around him, or should. Neither had any trouble imagining himself president of the United States.

Hearst and Roosevelt had been brought together as putative allies at the head of America's war party. Even while pursuing the same goals in Cuba, though, they never actually worked together. In a sense they were natural rivals, separated not only by politics—Roosevelt was a die-hard Republican, Hearst a populist Democrat—but also by chasms of class, style, and habit. Roosevelt came from old money, while Hearst's father was a rough prospector and land grabber. When in New York City, Roosevelt dined at the Metropolitan Club, across from Central Park. Hearst, who flaunted his mistresses and was known for what one colleague called "ways of sultanic languor and sybaritic luxury," was not admitted there.

For a while Hearst reveled in his iconoclasm and the notoriety that came with it. As the Cuban war ended, though, he was overwhelmed by a sense that Roosevelt had bested him. "I feel like hell," he told his star correspondent James Creelman. Soon afterward he poured out his regrets in a letter to his mother, who had financed his Cuban adventure.

> I guess I'm a failure. I made the mistake of my life in not raising the cowboy regiment I had in mind before Roosevelt raised his. I really believe I brought on the war, but I failed to score in the war. I had my chance and failed to grab it, and I suppose I must sit on the fence now and watch the procession go by. It's my own fault. I was thirty-five years old and of sound mind—comparatively—and could do as I liked. I failed and I'm a failure, and I deserve to be for being as slow and stupid as I was. . . . I feel about eight years old—and very blue.

Hearst's emotions led him to the extreme of trying to secure the Democratic nomination for governor so he could run against Roosevelt. He had lived in New York for just three years and could not persuade Democratic leaders to support him. His frustration made him steadily more combative.

"That Theodore Roosevelt, who was less than five years older, was already so far ahead of him only whetted Hearst's ambition," one biographer has written. "It is impossible to measure the depths of his loathing for Roosevelt, who had preceded him at Harvard, been a member of many of the same clubs, including the prestigious Porcellian, been elected to Phi Beta Kappa, and graduated at age twenty-one. Roosevelt, he was convinced, was now and had always been a charlatan."

This marked the demise of the Lodge-Roosevelt-Hearst troika, which became the Lodge-Roosevelt axis. Yet in the space of less than a year, these three secular missionaries had changed the course of history. Their cabal pushed the United States to war in Cuba and toward overseas empire. Each played a role no one else could have. All were compulsive activists who wished the United States to seize what they saw as fate's proffered gift.

"The athlete does not win his race by sitting habitually in an armchair," Lodge reasoned. "The pioneer does not open up new regions to his fellow men by staying in warm shelter behind the city walls."

Not even visionaries as powerfully driven as Lodge, Roosevelt, and Hearst, however, could have led Americans to the fateful leap of 1898 against their collective will. They were in a boisterous mood. The grand global adventure of colonialism was in full swing and promised rich rewards. Many wanted the United States to join the fray. A more decisive president might have sought to master this tide. McKinley allowed it to carry him away.

"The march of events rules and overrules human action," he reasoned.

Once victory over the Spanish was secured in Cuba, victory in the Philippines was only a formality. On August 13, American and Spanish forces staged a mock battle near Manila. Spanish commanders agreed to the charade because they preferred surrendering to the United States Army than to Filipino rebels. There were casualties, but as one American correspondent reported, "the gloves were padded." Spain surrendered to the United States before sundown.

"The governor-general arranged with me," Admiral Dewey explained later, "that I was to go up and fire a few shots and then I was to make the signal, 'Do you surrender?' and he would hoist the white flag, and then the troops would march in."

Following the pattern set in Cuba, American commanders did not invite Aguinaldo to the surrender ceremony and refused to allow his fighters to parade through Manila afterward. It was a bitter blow for the rebel leader who, less than two months earlier, had assured his followers that the United States had no desire to rule the Philippines. By summer's end he and his comrades, like their counterparts in Cuba, were left to grasp the scope of their misjudgment.

With Cuba and the Philippines in their power, Americans cast their eyes on a subsidiary prize, Puerto Rico. American warships had bombarded the Spanish fortress at San Juan, but McKinley had not yet added this island to his list of targets. The expansionists had. "Do not make peace until we get Porto Rico," Roosevelt had written to Lodge from his Rough Rider camp in Texas. "Porto Rico is not forgotten and we mean to have it," Lodge replied. "Unless I am utterly and profoundly mistaken, the administration is now fully committed to the large policy that we both desire."

Historians have suggested various names for America's practice of using force to extend its power overseas. For many in the period around 1898, it had an obvious name: imperialism. Others have called it colonialism or neo-colonialism. Some find "expansionism" more precise. In more recent formulations it is "liberal internationalism," "democracy promotion," "the freedom agenda," or "humanitarian intervention." Lodge's phrase best captures its essence. It is in every sense "the large policy." Its central purpose is to enlarge American power, wealth, and influence. It is large in scale and ambition. Lodge coined the phrase in reference to Puerto Rico, but it conveyed his inclination, as the essayist Gore Vidal wrote, "toward the annexation of, if possible, the entire world."

American troops landed in the Puerto Rican town of Ponce on July 25. By a wonderful quirk of history, if such it was, Lodge's twenty-three-year-old son George was the naval cadet who received the town's surrender. Soldiers met little resistance as they marched across the island to San Juan. With the signing of the "protocol of peace" at the White House in mid-August, Puerto Rico came under American control.

This operation was an afterthought. Puerto Rico was a lovely little prize, arguably of some strategic value, but the main reason Roosevelt and Lodge wanted it was simply that it was there. The fact that Puerto Ricans had accepted a far-reaching autonomy agreement with Spain and had just installed an elected government meant nothing to them. What mattered most was that this was the last Spanish colony in the hemisphere. Expansionists in Washington reasoned that by the principle of war conquest, the United States had won the right to own it. They took it because they could.

In a ravenous fifty-five-day spasm during the summer of 1898, the United States asserted control over five far-flung lands with a total of 11 million inhabitants: Guam, Hawaii, Cuba, the Philippines, and Puerto Rico. Never in history has a nation leaped so suddenly to overseas empire.

At his seaside manse in Nahant, Lodge decorated one room with booty his son and other returning soldiers had "judiciously looted" from Caribbean battlefields. On his walls hung a Spanish saber, the porthole of a destroyed Spanish warship, a Spanish flag bearing the royal ensign, and a Puerto Rican machete. He deserved every bit of the pride he felt when sitting among these trophies.

Lodge conceptualized all that "the large policy" could encompass. He was the key member of the expansionist triumvirate that emerged during the spring and summer of 1898. Hearst was invaluable in stirring the masses but commanded no respect in Washington. Roosevelt, the troika's public face, was eager to be steered. "Lodge is the Mephistopheles whispering poison in his ear all the time," wrote the anti-imperialist editor Edward Atkinson. Another interpretation of their relationship—that Lodge was Roosevelt's manipulative Lady Macbeth—may have been inspired by a striking photo of Lodge in full drag playing Lady Macbeth in a Hasty Pudding production at Harvard a quarter century earlier. Whatever the metaphor, it was Lodge who nurtured the expansionist idea through years when it was unpopular, Lodge who knew how to pounce when the moment was right, and Lodge who played the decisive role in Roosevelt's rise.

"What a wonderful war it has been!" he exulted after the protocol of peace was signed. "Nothing but victory, and at such small cost."

For anti-imperialists, the summer of 1898 was a horror. Pious pledges that the United States was intervening abroad only to liberate oppressed peoples turned out to have been part of a giant deception, or self-deception. America's war began in June as a drive to liberate colonies. By August it had become a campaign to capture them.

"The government must not be held too rigidly to purposes and expectations declared before the commencement of the war and in utter ignorance of its possible results," reasoned the lawyer-diplomat Joseph Choate, who would soon become ambassador to Great Britain. "In war, events change the situation very rapidly."

Grabbing Hawaii had been the breaking point that brought Grover Cleveland out of retirement and into the nascent anti-imperial movement. An equally eminent figure broke his peace when it became clear that expansionists would also try to take the Philippines. Their vaulting ambition turned the richest man in America into an anti-imperialist crusader.

Few immigrants embodied the rags-to-riches dream more fully than Andrew Carnegie. His fortune, and the ruthlessness with which he used it, brought him immense power. It also allowed him time to develop political passions, including a strong interest in promoting dialogue among nations. In 1898 he was entering the phase of his career in which he would finance projects such as the Central American Court of Justice and the Carnegie Endowment for International Peace. Some of his friends were surprised when he announced his support for the American war in Cuba. He told them he did it because, like Mark Twain, he believed President McKinley's assurance that this war was being waged for purely humanitarian reasons and "was not undertaken for territorial aggrandizement."

"Cuba must be freed from Spanish oppression," Carnegie wrote to a concerned friend. "When the proper time comes, when I can urge liberal treatment of Spain and the surrender of the Philippines, believe me, you shall find me, as you did before, pleading the right."

That time came sooner than anyone had expected. The "protocol of peace" stipulated that American and Spanish negotiators would meet in Paris to sign a final treaty with terms of surrender. War victory gave the United States the power to take what it wished, including the Philippines. This prospect outraged Carnegie. He resolved to prevent the signing of any treaty that would bring the Philippines under American rule. If he failed, he would try to block the treaty's ratification in the Senate. He would speak publicly, finance anti-imperialist campaigns, and even try to buy the islands himself in order to set them free.

When that tumultuous summer began, calls for restraint were weak, heard only in Faneuil Hall and a few other bastions of dissent. They were all but drowned out during the frenzy that followed victory in Cuba. By autumn, however, anti-imperialist committees had sprung up across the country. Organizers in Boston worked to weave them into a national league. As they were about to unveil it, a surge of excitement coursed through their movement. Andrew Carnegie published an essay in the *North American Review* announcing his unconditional commitment to their cause. He entitled it "Distant Possessions—The Parting of the Ways."

Is it possible that the Republic is to be placed in the position of the suppressor of the Philippine struggle for independence? Surely that is impossible. With what face shall we hang in the schoolhouses of the

Philippines our own Declaration of Independence, and yet deny independence to them? What response will the heart of the Philippine Islander make as he reads Lincoln's Emancipation Proclamation? Are we to practice independence and preach subordination, to teach rebellion in our books yet stamp it out with our swords, to sow the seed of revolt and expect the harvest of loyalty? . . .

Tires the Republic so soon of its mission, that it must, perforce, discard it to undertake the impossible task of establishing Triumphant Despotism, the rule of the foreigner over the people? And must the millions of the Philippines who have been asserting their God-given right to govern themselves be the first victims of Americans, whose proudest boast is that they conquered independence for themselves?

Carnegie's tirade changed all equations. Carl Schurz might be dismissed as a dreamy idealist, William Jennings Bryan as an ambitious candidate, Grover Cleveland as an embittered has-been. Carnegie, however, was a colossal figure legendary for his ability to achieve the impossible. Now he resolved to turn the United States off the path of empire.

Businessmen as a class were at first reluctant to join the rush to war, but by midsummer many had been won over. They came to see the prospect of new markets and resources as outweighing the dangers of temporary upheaval. Carnegie, by many standards the most successful of them all, demanded that they think again.

Soon after Carnegie published his declaration, the American Civic Federation, made up of opinion leaders from across the country, convened a conference in Saratoga, New York, to debate it. Carl Schurz presented the anti-imperial case. To no one's surprise, he was profound and eloquent.

The war with Spain was virtually initiated by a resolution adopted by Congress, April 19th, which declared that the people of Cuba should be free and independent. . . . It may be somewhat old-fashioned, but I still believe that a nation, no less than an individual man, is in honor bound to keep its word; that it can neither preserve its self-respect nor safe standards of morality among its own people, nor the esteem and confidence of mankind, unless it does. . . .

Let the thought of annexing those islands and their population to the United States either as States or as subject provinces be abandoned.... In this way we shall do our full duty to them without disregard of the superior duty which we owe to our own Republic. We shall have delivered them from Spanish misrule and given them a chance to govern themselves. The governments they then receive will indeed not be ideal governments. They will be Spanish-American governments, somewhat tempered and mitigated, perhaps, by the influence which American enterprise may carry there. But those governments will, at any rate, be their own, and if they become disorderly and corrupt, they will at least not infect with that disorder and corruption this Republic of ours.

Schurz was always impressive, but as soon as applause for this speech died down, other delegates clamored to dispute him. By one account it was a "tense moment" when the first of them, the essayist William Dudley Foulke, rose in challenge, "leveling his finger at Mr. Schurz, his voice shaking with dramatic fervor."

"Mr. Schurz, you are too late!" Foulke cried. "What you have just said would have been pertinent six months ago. Since then, however, we have taken Hawaii and Puerto Rico, our battleships have destroyed the Spanish fleet off Cavite and the peace conference has been called in Paris to determine whether we should return the Philippines to Spain, leave them alone without any government having destroyed the one they had, turn them over to some other power, or undertake their government ourselves. Mr. Schurz, again I say, you are too late! We have already expanded. The question now is not whether we expand, but what are we to do with the problems now confronting us, for the solution of which we have become responsible and which we cannot shirk if we are to hold up our heads in the society of nations."

The Saratoga conference convened for its final session on August 21. Before departing, delegates were asked to choose between pro- and anti-imperial resolutions. By clear majorities, they chose resolutions declaring that "the rescued and liberated people of the surrendered islands are in a sense temporarily wards of the conquering nation" and that "until such time as they may be able to govern themselves, they should continue under the protection of the United States."

This reflected America's momentary consensus. Congress and President McKinley had embraced "the large policy." The press promoted it. Much of the nation cheered it.

Yet a powerful protest movement was taking shape. By the time the tempestuous summer of 1898 drew to a close, four of America's most influential men had emerged to lead the anti-imperial crusade. Carl Schurz was a revered moral clarion. William Jennings Bryan led the country's political opposition and commanded fervent loyalty across the American heartland. Grover Cleveland had just completed eight years in the White House. Andrew Carnegie was a mythic plutocrat and master of a vast fortune. They made a formidable group.

For better or worse, the United States had come to hold decisive power over an array of foreign lands. Now the question was how it would dispose of them. For the first but not the last time, the world waited for Americans to decide.

Moments like these, when nations must make fateful choices, often produce larger-than-life figures. So it was in 1898, when the United States plunged into its most fateful debate since the Civil War. What giants arose to face each other! Lodge, Roosevelt, and Hearst led the imperial charge. Arrayed against them were Schurz, Bryan, Cleveland, and Carnegie. More gladiators were soon to enlist on both sides.

This debate would have been profound in any case. The emergence of such splendidly matched combatants guaranteed that it would also be a riveting spectacle.

4

Islands or Canned Goods

In the Republican politics of New York during the 1890s, arteries of power converged at the Fifth Avenue Hotel, a luxurious Italianate palazzo across from Madison Square Park. From one of its downstairs salons, lined with mahogany panels and wine-dark curtains, U.S. senator Thomas Platt brokered deals and dispensed justice like a medieval baron. Real decisions were made here, not at the State Capitol in Albany.

Platt, whose smooth style had earned him the nickname Easy Boss, lived at the hotel. He held his most delicate meetings in a private suite upstairs. One such meeting, on September 17, 1898, was to strike an uneasy deal with Colonel Theodore Roosevelt, the state's newest political star.

In public, Roosevelt was still denying that he wanted to run for governor. Privately, however, he had let Platt know that he was interested in the Republican nomination, and he had approved the manufacture of ten thousand buttons bearing the slogan "Our Teddy for Our Governor." Local satraps had told Platt that voters in Buffalo and surrounding Erie County, key electoral battlegrounds, were mad for the hero of San Juan Hill. Still the Easy Boss hesitated.

"If he becomes governor of New York, sooner or later, with his personality, he will have to be president of the United States," Platt told one of his men. "I am afraid to start that thing going."

Platt was pondering his options when one of his trusted deputies, the railroad lawyer and future senator Chauncey Depew, visited him in mid-September. He presented Depew with his dilemma. The incumbent governor, Frank Black, was loyal to the machine but had lost support after being charged with stealing money allocated for maintaining the Erie Canal. Roosevelt was the Republican of the hour, but headstrong and independent-minded. Whom should he nominate?

"Mr. Platt, I always look at a public question from the view of the platform," Depew replied. "Now if you nominate Governor Black and I am addressing a large audience—and I certainly will—the heckler in the audience will arise and interrupt me, saying, 'Chauncey, we agree with what you say about the Grand Old Party and all that, but how about the Canal steal?' I have to explain that the amount stolen was only a million—and that would be fatal. If Colonel Roosevelt is nominated, I can say to the heckler with indignation and great enthusiasm: 'I am mighty glad you asked that question. We have nominated for governor a man who has demonstrated in public office and on the battlefield that his is a fighter for the right, and always victorious. If he is selected, you know and we all know from his demonstrated characteristics, courage and ability, that every thief will be caught and punished, and every dollar that can be found will be returned to the public treasury.' Then I will follow the colonel, leading his Rough Riders up San Juan Hill, and ask the band to play *The Star-Spangled Banner*."

That convinced Platt. "Roosevelt will be nominated," he decreed.

Platt summoned Roosevelt to the Fifth Avenue Hotel on September 17 to tell him of his anointment. Intermediaries had already shaped their deal. Platt would make Roosevelt the Republican candidate for governor. Roosevelt promised in writing that, if elected, he "would adopt no line of policy and agree to no important matter or nomination without previous consultation."

This deal angered many Republicans. Reformers, who had considered Roosevelt an ally, denounced him as a "dough-face" and a "half-good man" for trafficking with the "standard-bearer of corruption." Regulars warned Platt that he would not be able to control his new protégé. Supporters of the tainted incumbent tried to block Roosevelt on the grounds that he was not a New York resident. Platt crushed them all. When he shook hands with Roosevelt at the end of their hotel meeting, he was officially welcoming the Rough Rider into the upper echelon of American politics.

"There is no humiliation to which Mr. Roosevelt will not submit that he may get the nomination for Governor," Hearst's *New York Journal* fumed. "The Theodore Roosevelt that was, was a humbug. The Theodore Roosevelt that is, is a prideless office-seeker."

After leaving Platt's suite, Roosevelt descended to the sumptuous lobby and walked along carpeted hallways past salons where the New York elite gathered for drinks and gossip. No one can know whether a copy of the new issue of *Century* was lying on a table in one of those salons. Quite possibly, though, some conversation was being devoted to the slashing attack on imperialism by Carl Schurz that was the issue's centerpiece. The article did not mention Roosevelt by name, but it signaled Schurz's emergence as the colonel's deepest ideological enemy.

We are told that as we have grown very rich and very powerful, the principles of policy embodied in Washington's Farewell Address have become obsolete—that we have "new responsibilities," "new duties," and a peculiar "mission." When we ask what these new responsibilities and duties require this Republic to do, the answer is that it should meddle more than heretofore with the concerns of the outside world for the purpose of "furthering the progress of civilization"; that it must adopt an "imperial policy" and make a beginning by keeping as American possessions the island colonies conquered from Spain. . . .

What, then, will follow if the United States commits this breach of faith? What could our answer be if the world should say of the American people that they are wolves in sheep's clothing, rapacious land-grabbers posing as unselfish champions of freedom and humanity, false pretenders who have proved the truth of all that has been said by their detractors as to their hypocrisy and greed, and whose word can never again be trusted? . . .

Will not those appear right who say that democratic government is not only no guaranty of peace, but that it is capable of the worst kind of war, the war of conquest, and of resorting to that kind of war, too, as a hypocrite and a false pretender? Such a loss of character, in itself a

most deplorable moral calamity, would be followed by political consequences of a very serious nature.

Roosevelt could not immediately reply to this attack because during
the last days of September he was busy preparing for the Republican
nominating convention. Schurz took advantage. His *Century* article—the
first to question imperial ambition since America's victories in Cuba
and the Philippines—was a sensation. Buoyed by the response, he wrote
again to President McKinley. This time he not only warned against taking foreign colonies, but offered an alternative.

"Would it not be perfectly feasible to settle the future status of
the Philippines by a conference with the Powers most interested in that
region, and at the same time to obtain all the commercial and strategi-
cal advantages we require?" Schurz asked. "And would it not be equally
feasible, with equal advantage to ourselves, to help Porto Rico to an
independent government as we are helping Cuba, and then endeavor to
bring about a 'Confederation of the Antilles,' embracing Cuba, Porto
Rico, Santo Domingo and Hayti—which would give those islands a
respectable international standing, while it would, of course, recognize
our leadership?"

McKinley did not reply. In public he committed himself neither to
keeping America's new possessions nor to setting them free. Nonetheless his political instincts were telling him, as he wrote to one of his
friends, that the United States "cannot let go."

Augustus van Wyck, a colorless judge and Democratic Party stalwart
from Brooklyn, ran against Theodore Roosevelt for governor in 1898, but
he was not Roosevelt's real opponent. Nor did the main issue have
anything to do with New York. Roosevelt's true adversary was Carl
Schurz—and the central campaign issue was "the large policy."

Roosevelt, who always relished a battle, plunged avidly into this one.
As soon as he officially secured the Republican nomination for governor,
he began writing a far-reaching speech that would stand as testament to
his deepest beliefs. He delivered it on October 5, intending it as both an
answer to Schurz and a rousing call to American greatness.

"Jammed from top to bottom with a shouting, cheering throng, Carnegie Hall was the scene tonight of the great mass meeting that opened the campaign of Col. Roosevelt for governor of New York," one newspaper reported. "The hall quickly filled, and so great was the jam outside that Col. Roosevelt and the other speakers had to have the aid of the police in forcing their way into the hall. Four overflow meetings were held. . . . Col. Roosevelt was received with a tremendous outburst of cheering. His speech was devoted almost wholly to national affairs. He asserted that the time had come when the nation must assume a new position among the nations of the world."

One historian has called this speech a "soaring, chauvinist oration." According to another, "It sounded more like the oratory of a Commander-in-Chief than plain gubernatorial rhetoric." This was Roosevelt's first coherent distillation of the potent beliefs that had shaped him and the modern United States, a clarion call for Americans to break out of their "fossilized isolation" and fulfill their "mighty mission."

There comes a time in the life of a nation, as in the life of an individual, when it must face great responsibilities, whether it will or not. We have now reached that time. We cannot avoid facing the fact that we occupy a new place among the people of the world, and we have entered upon a new career. . . .

The guns of our warships in the tropic seas of the West and the remote East have awakened us to the knowledge of new duties. Our flag is a proud flag, and it stands for liberty and civilization. Where it has once floated, there must and shall be no return to tyranny or savagery. We are face to face with our destiny and we must meet it with a high and resolute courage. For us is the life of action, of strenuous performance of duty. Let us live in the harness, striving mightily. Let us run the risk of wearing out rather than rusting out. . . . The only defense that is worth anything is the offensive. A peaceable man must not brawl, but when forced to fight, if he is worth his salt, he will defend himself by hitting and not parrying.

Roosevelt closed this speech with its logical conclusion: voting for any Democrat would mean "a repudiation of that war from which we have just emerged triumphant." This was the basis of his campaign. He refused to feign more than passing interest in excise taxes, licensing fees, supervision of local election boards, and other issues facing the state of New York. His only promise was that he would help lead the United States to global power.

"Expansion and our imperial destiny are about the only subjects that really wake him up; he turns a sleepy eye upon all state issues," the *New York Times* wrote. "Here is a man who aspires to the governorship of New York. Many men believe that he aspires to be president of the United States. It is a high, a permissible and an honorable ambition. But when he talks in this earnest way about heavier battalions and more battleships, when men remember his inborn pugnacity and his reputation as a terrible fighting man, and hear him talk in this strain about 'hitting not parrying,' will not the sober, conservative voters of New York hesitate a good deal before they cast a vote that may start this Hotspur on his way to a greater office?"

Never before had anyone campaigned for governor of an American state on a platform urging overseas expansion. Yet Roosevelt's obsession was with an ideal far grander than that diffuse thing called "foreign policy." He believed that humanity was entering a new age, that his own country was destined to dominate it, and that he knew best how to guide the country. What more profound theme could there be for a political campaign?

Early on the morning of October 17, Roosevelt set out on a whirlwind campaign tour by chartered railcar. He made seventeen stops along the Hudson River that first day, spent two more days barnstorming through towns in the Adirondacks and along the St. Lawrence River, ended with seven speeches in New York City, and then set out again on a whistle-stop tour during which he gave a hundred and two speeches in the space of a week. Each rally began with a troop of Rough Riders trotting out in battle fatigues, accompanied by bugle calls. One would theatrically recount the dangers they had faced in Cuba until "out of the woods came a hero." Then the candidate would appear, wearing his sombrero and flanked by a uniformed color guard. His stock speech, which was essentially a series of slogans about the glories of war and empire, never lasted more than ten minutes. Crowds went wild, even when, in the town of Port Jervis, the warm-up speech went a bit wrong.

"When it came to the great day, he led us up San Juan Hill like sheep to the slaughter!" cried that night's designated speaker, a former sergeant named Buck Taylor. "And so will he lead you!"

Roosevelt later acknowledged that this remark "hardly seemed a tribute to my military skill." Nonetheless the crowd took it well. The candidate had discovered that, as one observer wrote, "any remark to do with the Rough Riders stimulated applause from old and young, male and female." In Roosevelt, a suddenly energized America saw itself.

Schurz was a generation older than Roosevelt, but their careers in New York politics overlapped. They knew each other well, shared interests in history and environmental preservation, respected each other's intellect, and corresponded for years. On the great question of 1898, they were brilliantly matched antagonists.

Immediately after Roosevelt delivered his fiery Carnegie Hall speech, Schurz wrote that his "wild imperialistic ideas" were "an encouragement to the craziest sort of jingoism." He set out to compose a reply, and was working on it when he received a most unexpected letter: Roosevelt wanted his endorsement. Under the circumstances, this overture was odd indeed.

"We have long been friends, and I ardently hoped to be able to support you for the Governorship," Schurz wrote in reply. "I continued to hope until I read the report of your Carnegie Hall speech, [which] it makes it impossible to support you. . . . I cannot tell you, remembering our long and sincere friendship, how painful it is for me to be obliged to say this."

Schurz announced his decision in an open letter published in the *New York Post*. This was not only his angriest attack yet on the imperial idea. It was also the first time he focused directly on Roosevelt as its main promoter, and singled him out as the enemy.

He virtually asks us to endorse, by electing him, his kind of militant imperialism, which has no bounds. . . .

Election to the governorship of New York, as it repeatedly has been, may again become, in Colonel Roosevelt's case, the stepping-stone to a nomination for the Presidency. Indeed, it is in everybody's mouth that if Colonel Roosevelt succeeds, it will be so. . . .

I would not put him in a position, nor to him the way to a position, in which he would exercise any influence upon the foreign policy of the Republic; for I candidly believe that, owing to his exceptionally belli-cose temperament and to the sincerity of his fantastic notions as to the bodily exercise the American people need to keep them from Chinese degeneracy, and as to the necessity always to "live in the harness and strive mightily," he is very dangerously deficient in that patient pru-dence which is necessary for the peaceable conduct of international relations. . . . A vote for him is to mean an approval and encouragement of the manifest-destiny swindle. I call it so because it is a flagrant breach of faith in turning a solemnly proclaimed war of humanity into a vul-gar land-grabbing operation, glossed over by high-sounding cant about destiny and duty and what not.

Roosevelt was disgusted. "If we ever come to nothing as a nation," he wrote to Lodge, "it will be because the teaching of Carl Schurz and the futile continentallsis of the international arbitration type bears its legitimate fruit in producing a flabby, timid type of character, which eats away the great fighting features of our race." Still, Roosevelt's speech at Carnegie Hall and Schurz's harsh rebuttal gave both men what they wanted. Americans were caught up in a profound debate, but there was no presidential election in 1898. The question had to be put to a vote some-where. Roosevelt and Schurz determined that it would be in New York.

Newspapers occasionally published articles comparing Roosevelt to his Democratic opponent, but his battle with Schurz was infinitely more interesting. They were debating a question that would shape world his-tory. A couple of weeks before Election Day, the *New York Times* reflected on its meaning.

"The chief of the reasons why Mr. Schurz reluctantly withholds his vote from Mr. Roosevelt is the manner in which that gentleman has advocated, in his own speeches, an extreme policy of expansion," the *Times* wrote.

For our own part—though we fear Mr. Roosevelt will hardly thank us for the opinion—we are inclined to think that he has erred more in the statement of his ideas than in the ideas themselves, and that in the face of actual responsibility he would probably act with more sobriety than he talks. But it remains true that he has talked very wildly; that his talk in this direction was uncalled for, and that in some salient regards it has been extremely offensive. He has distinctly appealed to rational men to vote for him as Governor on the ground that to vote against him would tend to provoke "a hitch" in the peace negotiations in Paris, and would be a vote to abandon all that we achieved in the war with Spain. Such an appeal is more than offensive; it is insulting. Mr. Schurz has made an obvious and effective response to it, and for this and the influence it may have Mr. Roosevelt has only himself to thank.

Although Schurz was Roosevelt's chief antagonist during this campaign, his most vituperative enemy turned out to be William Randolph Hearst. The frenetic publisher seethed at the Rough Rider's rise into politics. As soon as it became clear that Roosevelt was running for governor, Hearst began using the *Journal* to attack him relentlessly.

"Unable to assail Roosevelt from the campaign trail, Hearst went after him in his newspapers," one biographer has written. "The Hearst papers organized a brilliantly coordinated campaign of ridicule, seamlessly linking news reports, editorials, and editorial cartoons to reduce Roosevelt to size. While Homer Davenport and the *Journal*'s corps of cartoonists portrayed Colonel Teddy as an overgrown playacting child, with prominent front teeth, rimless spectacles, and a Rough Riders uniform, Hearst's editorial assassins . . . excoriated him for accepting the nomination of the boss-dominated state Republican party."

Debate over the imperial idea was intense in New York. It echoed across much of the nation. Voters everywhere faced the same question: Should the United States leap across the seas and begin taking overseas territories? The 1898 election was not precisely a referendum on this question, but zealots on both sides tried to make it one.

Among the most successful was a theatrically gifted Indiana lawyer named Albert Beveridge, whose emergence that autumn reflected the political power of the imperial idea. Beveridge was born to penniless English immigrants and, at an early age, after hearing several stirring public speakers, decided that he would use oratory to make his way in life. He entered law school, studied rhetoric, and won oratorical contests. After graduating, he found that his classically framed and passionately delivered speeches could hold crowds for hours. Expansionism became his favorite theme. In 1898 he decided to use it as a platform on which to run for the United States Senate. He was thirty-five years old and had never sought public office. His sole campaign pledge was that, if elected, he would "map out and advocate the imperial policy of the Republic."

Beveridge launched his campaign in his hometown, Indianapolis, with a brilliantly evocative speech called "March of the Flag." Two hundred of his jubilant supporters, many carrying torches, picked him up at his home, escorted him into a ceremonial carriage, and then, accompanied by a brass band, marched to the cavernous Marion Club. The atmosphere was so thrilling, according to one account, that anti-imperialists in the crowd "went away sadly lamenting that in the excitement they, too, had cheered."

The debate over imperial expansion that consumed Americans in 1898 produced dozens of powerful speeches. Many address deep questions of morality, religion, justice, duty, and national identity. "March of the Flag" is among the most stirring. In its appeal to manifest destiny, providential mission, and racial pride, it anticipates what Americans would be told repeatedly over the next century and beyond.

> The question is larger than a party question. It is an American question. It is a world question. Shall the American people continue their resistless march toward the commercial supremacy of the world? Shall free institutions broaden their blessed reign as the children of liberty wax in strength, until the empire of our principles is established over the hearts of all mankind? Have we no mission to perform, no duty to discharge to our fellow man? Has God endowed us with gifts beyond our deserts and marked us as the people of His peculiar favor, merely to rot in our own selfishness? . . .
>
> The opposition tells us that we ought not to govern a people without their consent. I answer: The rule of liberty—that all just government derives its authority from the consent of the governed—applies only to those who are capable of self-government. We govern the Indians without their consent. We govern our territories without their consent. We govern our children without their consent. . . .
>
> Is this an hour to waste upon triflers with nature's laws? Is this a season to give our destiny over to wordmongers and prosperity-wreckers?

No! It is an hour to remember our duty to our homes. It is a moment to realize the opportunities fate has opened to us. . . . We cannot fly from our world duties. It is ours to execute the purpose of a fate that has driven us to be greater than our small intentions. We cannot retreat from any soil where Providence has unfurled our banner. It is ours to save that soil for liberty and civilization!

Soon after Beveridge opened his campaign with these words, a quite opposite appeal came from a gray-haired sage who had entered the Senate when Beveridge was still a teenager. George Frisbie Hoar was the "other" senator from Massachusetts, part of a remarkably mismatched pair. Both he and Henry Cabot Lodge were Republicans, but on the issue of overseas expansion they were the bitterest of foes. What one wished for, the other abhorred. Hoar made that clear when, addressing a campaign rally in his hometown of Worcester, he warned that an accident of fate in the Philippines must not tempt the United States to "a vulgar greed of power or of gain."

I believe that the highest service the American people can render to mankind and to liberty is to preserve unstained and unchanged the Republic. The danger is that we are to be transformed from a Republic founded on the Declaration of Independence, guided by the counsels of Washington, the hope of the poor, the refuge of the oppressed, into a vulgar, commonplace empire founded upon physical force, controlling subject races and vassal states, in which one class must forever rule and the other classes must forever obey. . . . It is said that the Philippine Islands are already ours by right of conquest. . . . I deny this alleged right of conquest. Human beings—men, women and children, peoples—are not to be won as spoils of war or prizes in battle. . . . We will emancipate this maiden. We will make her, if it be necessary, a wedding present and help to give her a dowry. But we will not make her our slave, and certainly we do not propose to marry her.

"Wobbly Willie" was one of President McKinley's many nicknames. Famous for his lack of convictions, he had risen in politics not by leading but by divining the public mood and following it. One of his contemporaries, Representative Joseph Cannon, a future Speaker of the House, liked to joke that McKinley kept his ear so close to the ground that it was full of grasshoppers. In 1898 this consummate equivocator was called to make one of the most fateful decisions in American history: whether to lead the United States toward offshore empire. His instinct told him to see what voters wanted. In mid-October he set out on a tour of six midwestern states.

McKinley gave fifty-seven speeches during his two-week tour. In each one, he tested the rhetoric of expansion. He found much enthusiasm. Audiences cheered his assertions that the United States had fought Spain "in a holy cause" and that Americans were now called to rule "those who, by the fortunes of war, are brought within the radius of our influence." The crowd in Hastings, Iowa, roared when he declared, "We want new markets, and as trade follows the flag, it looks very much as if we are going to have new markets." In Omaha he asked, "Shall we deny to ourselves what the rest of the world so freely and so justly accords us?" and the crowd shouted back, "No!"

According to the official transcript of McKinley's speeches, there was "prolonged applause" in St. Louis when he asserted that "God bestows supreme opportunity on no nation which is not ready to respond to the call of supreme duty," and "great applause" in Terre Haute when he said, "The people of the United States want the victories of the army and navy to be recognized in the treaty of peace." By the time he reached Chicago, he was charged with nationalist adrenaline.

City fathers in Chicago had organized a weeklong "peace jubilee" to celebrate America's victory over Spain. On opening night a reported twelve thousand people packed the ornate Chicago Auditorium—more than twice its official capacity. They cheered wildly for McKinley. The toastmaster, Franklin MacVeagh, a banker and future secretary of the treasury, set the triumphal tone.

"Democracy has seriously begun to rule humanity, and the illuminating truth is that democracy's ideals are not the ideals of isolation," MacVeagh declared. "Its concern is mankind. We are the greatest exponents of democracy, and we are appointed to live up to its ideals."

Then, most unexpectedly, the mood turned somber. The evening's final speaker was Booker T. Washington, the most famous African American of his time. After duly praising war heroes, he urged the celebrants to reflect on the meaning of their triumph.

"This country has been most fortunate in her victories," Washington said.

> She has met the proud Spaniard, and he lies prostrate at her feet. But there remains one other victory for Americans to win—a victory as far-reaching and important as any that has occurred to our navy and army. We have succeeded in every conflict except in the effort to conquer ourselves in the blotting out of racial prejudices. We can celebrate the era of peace in no more effectual way than by a firm resolve on the part of the Northern men and Southern men, black men and white men, that the trenches which we together dug around Santiago shall be the eternal burial place of all that which separates us in our business and civil relations. Let us be as generous in peace as we have been brave in battle. Until we conquer ourselves, I make no empty statement when I say we shall have, especially in the southern part of our country, a cancer gnawing at the heart of this Republic that shall one day prove as dangerous as an attack from an army from without or within.

This was the first time an African American had publicly reminded a president that the uplifting rhetoric used to justify imperialism contrasted with the reality of race discrimination at home. "When Mr. Washington had given expression to these words the most interesting feature of the evening occurred," one newspaper reported. "The audience rose and cheered to the echo, while President McKinley, standing his box, acknowledged by repeated bows the compliments of the colored orator."

Across Chicago over the next few days, the burning issue of American expansion was debated at schools, colleges, clubs, churches, and public halls. General Nelson Miles, the army commander, and General William Shafter, who had commanded the American expeditionary force in Cuba, gave rousing speeches extolling the glories of conquest. Equally eloquent words came from the other side.

One of the week's best-attended sessions was chaired by Henry Wade Rogers, the president of Northwestern University, who was in the process of losing his job because his opposition to imperialism upset the school's trustees. He spoke briefly and then introduced the country's most admired labor leader, Samuel Gompers. For several months Gompers had been suggesting that he would lead the labor movement toward anti-imperialism. Many tried to restrain him. Gompers led labor's mainstream, embodied in the American Federation of Labor, which stood against the more radical Industrial Workers of the World. He was respected across class lines. In Chicago he declared himself an unreserved anti-imperialist. Booker T. Washington had just urged African Americans to look skeptically on the imperial project. Gompers sent the same message to labor.

"It is worse than folly, aye, it is a crime, to lull ourselves into the fancy that we shall escape the duties which we owe to our people by becoming a nation of conquerors," Gompers told the crowd.

> If we attempt to force upon the natives of the Philippines our rule, and compel them to conform to our more or less rigid mold of government, how many lives shall we take? Of course, they will seem cheap, because they are poor laborers. They will be members of the majority in the Philippines, but they will be ruled and killed at the convenience of the very small minority there, backed up by our land and sea forces. The dominant class in the islands will ease its conscience because the victims will be poor, ignorant, and weak.

On McKinley's last day at the jubilee, he accepted an honorary doctorate from the University of Chicago and then shook 3,327 hands at the First Regiment Armory. That evening, he delivered the speech many Americans were awaiting. Its announced theme—"Duty Determines Destiny"—was calculated to stir the patriotic soul.

"President McKinley last night gave some hint of what his policy is upon territorial expansion," one newspaper reported. "No public utterance of the President previous to that at Wednesday night's banquet was fraught with so much meaning to the country. None gave so clear a vision of the views of the executive on the question of expansion, which has become paramount in the discussions of the nation." McKinley's words were indeed unequivocal.

We cannot avoid the serious questions which have been brought home to us by the achievements of our arms on land and sea. Accepting war for humanity's sake, we must accept all obligations imposed upon us. . . .

We must give to the world the full demonstration of the sincerity of our purpose. Duty determines destiny! My countrymen, the currents of destiny flow through the hearts of the people. Who will check them, who will divert them, who will stop them? And the movements of men, planned and designed by the Master of Men, will never be interrupted by the American people.

This speech was the clearest signal yet that McKinley intended to keep at least part of the Philippines under American rule. Many newspapers reprinted it in full. The most famous bartender in America, Mr. Dooley, also had an opinion.

A creation of the Chicago humorist Finley Peter Dunne, Mr. Dooley was the central figure in a stream of newspaper columns that were syndicated across the country beginning in 1898. His homespun wisdom, delivered with an Irish brogue, delighted millions of readers. He was even quoted at McKinley's cabinet meetings. One historian has concluded that Mr. Dooley "probably did as much to deflate the American militarists and imperialists as did the treatises of the Boston Brahmins."

"Mack r-rose up in a perfect hurricane iv applause," Mr. Dooley said in his report of the Chicago speech. "'Now,' he says, 'th' question is what we shall do with th' fruits iv victhry?' he says. 'We ar-re bound,' he says, 'to—to re-elize our destiny, whatever it may be,' he says. 'We can not tur-rn back,' he says, 'th' hands iv the clock that, even as I speak,' he says, 'is r-rushin through th' hear-rts iv men . . . I will tur-rn th' job over to destiny.'"

"What do you think ought to be done with th' fruits iv victory?" asked Hennessy, his favorite customer.

"Well," replied Mr. Dooley, "if 'twas up to me, I'd eat what was r-ripe an' give what wasn't r-ripe to me inimy. An' I guess that's what Mack means."

The warm reaction to McKinley's patriotic speeches in Chicago and across the American heartland persuaded him that the masses supported overseas expansion. His trip left him more inclined than ever to lead the United States toward empire. "None of us have been able to move him since he returned from the West," Secretary of the Interior Cornelius Bliss wrote to Andrew Carnegie. "Had an interview with him, but he was obdurate. Withdrawal would create a revolution at home, he said."

Various forces united to push McKinley toward his decision to seize the Philippines. Navy commanders recognized Manila Bay as a magnificent platform from which to project American strategic power into East Asia. Business leaders saw millions of new customers for American goods, the prospect of rich resources, and a springboard to the potentially immense China market. Missionaries and religious groups swooned at the prospect of saving millions of lost souls for Christ. McKinley himself recognized above all the political value of annexation—and the furor he feared would engulf him if he turned away from empire at this crucial moment.

Soon after McKinley returned to Washington from Chicago, probably on the night of October 24, he had the most influential divine visitation in recorded presidential history. By his own account, he was pondering the Philippines question while walking along the corridors of the darkened White House. Gripped by a sudden urge, "I went down on my knees and prayed Almighty God for light and guidance." When he opened his eyes, he knew what he must do.

"I don't know how it was," he said afterward, "but it came."

When McKinley emerged from his trance, he found himself believing that the United States could not grant independence to the Philippines because its people were "unfit for self-government," and that "there was nothing left for us to do but to take them all, and to educate the Filipinos, and uplift and civilize and Christianize them and by God's grace do the very best we could by them, as our fellow men for whom Christ also died."

McKinley was deeply religious, and his account of this vision was no doubt sincere. Nonetheless he must have recognized the happy coincidence: what God wanted him to do would also be popular with voters.

This time, God sounded remarkably like Theodore Roosevelt and Henry Cabot Lodge.

On November 8, election results confirmed McKinley's reading of the American mood. Republicans held their majority in both houses of Congress. Lodge, the most powerful expansionist in Washington, was guaranteed re-election by a landslide in Massachusetts that filled the state legislature, which in that era elected U.S. senators, with Republicans. Most important, Roosevelt won the governorship of New York. His margin was narrow—eighteen thousand votes out of 1.3 million cast—but it raised him to a new political level. "There is no denying that Theodore Roosevelt has grown mightily in the public estimation," the *Troy Times* observed. Over the course of just a few months, the cowboy from Oyster Bay had acquired a heroic reputation and used it to propel himself into high office.

"I have played it with bull luck this summer," Roosevelt wrote to a friend after the election. "First, to get into the war; then to get out of it; then to get elected. I have worked hard all my life, and have never been particularly lucky, but this summer I *was* lucky, and I am enjoying it to the full."

Five days after the election, McKinley made a decision he had not wanted to make before. He directed Secretary of State John Hay to send decisive instructions to American negotiators in Paris. Hay sent the cable as McKinley ordered.

"Willing or not, we have the responsibility of duty which we cannot escape," he wrote. "You are therefore instructed to insist upon the cession of the whole of the Philippines and, if necessary, pay to Spain $10,000,000 to $20,000,000."

Expansionists won at the polls in 1898, but their opponents were hardly ready to concede. On the contrary, they were charged with energy and believed their fight had just begun. Many Americans were just beginning to realize that their country was about to start ruling millions of people in far-flung lands. Once they understood the dangers of the leap they were being asked to take, anti-imperialists believed, they would step back.

Working from offices in Boston, impassioned activists had spent the summer and fall writing letters to potential sympathizers across the country. Among the most vigorous was eighty-year-old George Boutwell, who had helped organize the Faneuil Hall meeting in June. Boutwell was a co-founder of the Republican Party; America's first commissioner of internal revenue, named by Abraham Lincoln; secretary of the treasury under Ulysses S. Grant; and a congressman, U.S. senator, and governor of Massachusetts. He had helped lead the abolitionist movement, campaigned against the Ku Klux Klan, and played important roles in securing passage of the Fourteenth and Fifteenth Amendments to the Constitution, which were aimed at securing civil and voting rights for African Americans. In his mind, every abolitionist was a natural anti-imperialist, since anyone who opposed keeping human beings as slaves must also oppose ruling other nations against their will.

A few days before the election, Boutwell took time from his correspondence to address a ladies' club in Cambridge. In his speech he posed a question many Americans were asking: What would be the alternative to expansion and conquest? Unexpected events had given the United States power to determine the fate of overseas nations. How should it dispose of those nations, if not by taking them? Boutwell had a concise reply:

(1) Give to Hawaii a territorial government and upon a liberal basis;
(2) Insist on an independent government for Cuba and give no encouragement for the project of annexation; (3) Abandon Porto Rico and the Spanish islands of the Pacific Ocean without controversy, debate, or negotiations with anyone.

The simplicity of Boutwell's proposal, along with his many letters to civic and political leaders across the country, brought thousands of supporters to the anti-imperialist cause. From nearly every state, people reported that they had established local groups and were eager to become part of a national movement. Months of intense work came to fruition on November 18, when an eager crowd packed into a law office on Milk Street in Boston to witness the founding of the Anti-Imperialist League.

At that inaugural meeting, Boutwell was chosen by acclamation as the league's first president. Eighteen others became vice presidents, among them Grover Cleveland, Carl Schurz, Samuel Gompers, and Andrew Carnegie—who underlined his commitment with a check for $10,000. Then it was announced that the league would move its office from Boston to Washington, where it would be better able "to bring together the united efforts of men of repute throughout the country without regard to party." One of its first jobs would be to collect signatures on a petition expressing "protest against any extension of the sovereignty of the United States over the Philippines in any event, or any foreign territory, without the free consent of the people thereof." This was also the theme of an "address to the public" that the league issued to mark its birth.

> The Constitution gives to the United States no more than to the individual the right to hold slaves or vassals, and recognizes no distinction between classes of citizens—one with full rights as free men, and another as subjects governed by military force.
>
> We are in full sympathy with the heroic struggles for liberty of the people in the Spanish Islands, and therefore we protest against depriving them of their rights by an exchange of masters. Only by recognizing their rights as free men are all their interests protected. Expansion by natural growth in thinly-settled contiguous territory, acquired by purchase for the expressed purpose of ultimate statehood, cannot be confounded with, or made analogous to, foreign territory conquered by war and wrested by force from a weak enemy. A beaten foe has no right to transfer a people whose consent has not been asked, and a free Republic has no right to hold in subjection a people so transferred. . . .
>
> Shall we now prove false to our declaration and seize by force islands thousands of miles away whose peoples have not desired our presence and whose will we have not asked? Whatever islands we take must be annexed or held in vassalage to the Republic. Either course is dangerous to the physical and moral safety of the nation.

For months, opposition to the expansionist project had been sporadic and scattered. The founding of the Anti-Imperialist League at the end of

1898 marked the beginning of a sustained counterattack. It was impressively led, widely supported, and focused on a specific short-term goal: to prevent the United States from annexing the Philippines.

No officer of the Anti-Imperialist League was more outspoken than Carnegie. "Should we undertake to hold the Philippines, we immediately place the whole Republic within the zone of wars and rumors of wars," he warned in a public statement two days after the league was founded. Over the next year he sent streams of letters to newspapers, members of Congress, fellow tycoons, and even President McKinley.

"The true friend not only warns a friend of what he sees to be dangers that surround him, but he ventures to counsel him as to what he should do in the crisis," Carnegie wrote in one letter to McKinley. "Were I President of the United States, I should announce in my message to Congress that I demanded the Philippines from Spain that I might give to them the Independence which every people can claim as a God-given right, [and] that I had no idea of holding them in subjection."

Soon after sending that letter, Carnegie's tone hardened. The speeches McKinley made during his Midwest tour disgusted him because they mixed sweet-sounding calls for peace with declarations that the United States would now begin using military force to spread its power around the world. In a bitter letter to Secretary of State Hay, he called McKinley "Mr. Face-both-ways."

> When a jellyfish wishes to conceal its whereabouts, it does so with ebullitions of blubber. This is what people say the President did on his western tour. . . . I do not think he is well, and yet I see that if one American soldier's blood is spilt shooting down insurgents, either in Cuba or the Philippines, he is like another Mac, he shall sleep no more. . . .
>
> It is a great strain which the President is putting on the loyalty of his friends and supporters. Many are bearing it. It has proven too great for me.

Other anti-imperialists were just as passionate. Erving Winslow, secretary of the Anti-Imperialist League, visited McKinley at the White House and warned him, "If you should call upon the United States to make war on the Filipinos' government, it would be the severest strain ever yet put upon the loyalty of the people." A former Republican president, Benjamin Harrison, who while in office had favored annexing Hawaii, declared that he opposed further expansion and warned against trying "to deliver the oppressed the world around." No week passed without anti-imperialist meetings or protests.

"There is a wild and frantic attack now going on in the press against the whole Philippine transaction," Secretary Hay wrote to his friend Whitelaw Reid, who was then in Paris as part of the American negotiating team. "Andrew Carnegie really seems to be off his head. He writes me frantic letters, signing them 'Your Bitterest Opponent.' He threatens the President, not only with the vengeance of the voters but with practical punishment at the hands of the mob. He says henceforth the entire labor vote of America will be cast against us, and that he will see that it is done. He says the Administration will fall into irretrievable ruin the moment it shoots down one insurgent Filipino."

As Americans celebrated that year's Thanksgiving, they had much for which to be grateful. Many exulted in the amazing leap their country had made in a few short months. It was the subject of President McKinley's holiday proclamation.

"Few years in our history have afforded such cause for thanksgiving as this," he wrote. "The skies have been for a time darkened by the cloud of war, but as we were compelled to take up the sword in the cause of humanity, we are permitted to rejoice that the conflict has been of brief duration and the losses we have had to mourn, though grievous and important, have been so few, considering the great results accomplished, as to inspire us with gratitude and praise to the Lord of Hosts."

McKinley was eager to seal his triumph by securing the treaty of annexation. Spain had no choice but to accept. On December 10, Secretary of State Hay received a curt cable from the American negotiators in Paris.

"Treaty signed at 8:50 this evening," it said.

The Treaty of Paris was all that any expansionist could have wished. Spain, facing discontent at home and fearing a renewal of war, accepted all American demands. For a payment of $20 million, it gave up sovereignty over Cuba and ceded Puerto Rico, Guam, and the Philippines to the United States. These islands, pillars of a collapsing empire, would become the foundation of a rising new one.

"The President is naturally compelled to add that until complete tranquility prevails in the islands, and a system of government is inaugurated, the military occupation will be continued," the *London Chronicle* observed. "We shall not be thought discourteous or cynical if we remark that this is precisely the language that successive British Governments have maintained about Egypt, with a result known to the world, and an omen which is certainly not inapplicable."

Many shared the fear that the United States would impose a reviled colonial regime in the Philippines, just as the British had in Egypt. Critics furiously condemned the Treaty of Paris. Mark Twain was among the most deeply shaken.

Twain was in Vienna when the treaty was signed. Reading news of it—learning that the United States intended to annex the Philippines—instantly wiped away whatever hope or sympathy he still harbored for the American expansionist project. That pushed him inexorably toward the American anti-imperialist movement, shaping the next and least-known phase of his career.

Soon after the Treaty of Paris was published, Twain sent a troubled letter to Joseph Twichell, the same friend to whom he had written six months earlier calling the war in Cuba "the worthiest one that was ever fought." The treaty had changed everything. Until Twain read it, he had believed the United States was setting out into the world to liberate brutalized peoples. Now he began suspecting the opposite.

"Apparently we are not proposing to set the Filipinos free and give their islands to them, and apparently we are not proposing to hang the priests and confiscate their property," Twain wrote. "If these things are so, the war out there has no interest for me."

This letter provoked a quick response from Twichell, a thoughtful pastor who had been an ardent abolitionist and was Twain's closest counselor. Upon receiving Twain's letter declaring opposition to the Treaty of Paris, he wrote back with the obvious question: "Why don't you say something about it?"

Twain had recently completed a European speaking tour. He was finishing his novella *The Man That Corrupted Hadleyburg*, a wry tale of small-town hypocrisy. His daughter was ill. He was struggling with creditors. The time was not yet ripe for him to enter the fray. Nonetheless his change of heart was fateful. It reflected what many Americans were feeling.

"We are going to have trouble over the Treaty," Lodge predicted in a letter to Roosevelt. "How serious I do not know, but I confess I cannot think calmly of the rejection of that Treaty by a little more than one-third of the Senate. It would be a repudiation of the President and humiliation of the whole country in the eyes of the world, and would show we are unfit to enter into great questions of foreign policy."

"It seems impossible," Roosevelt replied, "that men of ordinary patriotism can contemplate such an outrage on the country."

No one, least of all Lodge himself, could imagine that a generation later he would help kill another highly ambitious treaty, the one creating the League of Nations. In 1898 he insisted that voting against a treaty negotiated by the White House constituted near-treason. He would need that argument and many others, along with less savory political weapons, to win his case in the Senate.

Trouble began quickly. Senator George Vest of Missouri submitted a resolution declaring that "under the constitution of the United States, no power is given to the federal government to acquire territory to be held and governed permanently as colonies." Senator George Frisbie Hoar warned in a newspaper interview, "If we take the Philippines under the treaty of peace, the downfall of the American Republic will date from the administration of William McKinley." Carl Schurz called for a national plebiscite in which all Americans, not just the Senate, would decide whether to take the Philippines. The American Federation of Labor, at the urging of its leader, Samuel Gompers, issued a proclamation "to give vent to the alarm we feel from the dangers threatening us and our entire people, to enter our solemn and emphatic protest against what we already feel: that, with the success of imperialism, the decadence of our republic will have already set in." William Jennings Bryan gave a speech declaring that "the imperialistic idea is directly antagonistic to the idea and ideals which have been cherished by the American people since the signing of the Declaration of Independence," and then gave another insisting that the American flag was meant to fly "not over a conglomeration of colonies and commonwealths, but over the land of the free and the home of the brave."

> The flag is a national emblem and is obedient to the national will. . . . When the American people want it raised, they raise it, and when they want it hauled down, they haul it down. . . . Shall we keep the Philippines and amend our flag? . . . Shall we add a new star—the blood star, Mars—to indicate that we have entered upon a career of conquest? . . . Or shall we adorn our flag with a milky way composed of a multitude of minor stars representing remote and insignificant dependencies? No, a thousand times better to haul down the Stars and Stripes and substitute the flag of in independent republic than to surrender the doctrines that gave glory to Old Glory.

The opposition had found its voice. "What a singular collection the so-called anti-Imperialists are getting together!" Lodge marveled in a letter to Roosevelt.

By the end of 1898 this "collection" was a truly stellar group: the brilliantly articulate former senator and interior secretary Carl Schurz; the legendary tycoon Andrew Carnegie; the country's most prominent labor leader, Samuel Gompers, and its most prominent civil rights advocate, Booker T. Washington; the leader of the Democratic Party, William Jennings Bryan; a co-founder of the Republican Party, George Boutwell; the previous two presidents, Grover Cleveland and Benjamin Harrison; and a dozen more of America's brightest lights. Arguably the most influential was the fictional bartender Mr. Dooley. As the debate over annexation intensified, Mr. Dooley's favorite customer and foil, Mr. Hennessy, dropped into the bar with advice for McKinley.

> "I know what I'd do if I was Mack," said Mr. Hennessy. "I'd hist a flag over th' Ph'lippeens, an' I'd take in th' whole lot iv thim."
>
> "An' yet," said Mr. Dooley, "tis not more thin two months since ye larned whether they were islands or canned goods. . . . If yer son Packy was to ask ye where th' Ph'lippeens is, cud ye give im anny good idea whether they was in Rooshia or jus' west iv th' thracks?"

"Mebbe I cudden't," said Mr. Hennessy, haughtily, "but I'm f'r takin' thim in, annyhow."

"So might I be," said Mr. Dooley, "if I cud on'y get me mind on it. Wan iv the worst things about this here war is th' way it's makin' puzzles f'r our poor, tired heads. . . . Ivry night, whin I'm countin' up the cash, I'm askin' mesilf will I annex Cubia or lave it to the Cubians? Will I take Porther Ricky or put it by? An' what shud I do with the Ph'lippeens? Oh, what shud I do with thim? I can't annex thim because I don't know where they ar-re. I can't let go iv thim because some wan else'll take thim if I do. They are eight thousan' iv thim islands, with a popylation iv wan hundherd millyon naked savages; an' me bedroom's crowded now with me an' th' bed. . . .

"It's a poverty-sthricken counthry, full iv goold an' precious stones, where th' people can pick dinner off th' threes an' ar-re starvin' because they have no step-ladders. Th' inhabitants is mostly naygurs an' Chinny-men, peaceful, industhrus, an' law-abidin', but savage an' bloodthirsty in their methods. They wear no clothes except what they have on, an' each woman has five husbands an' each man has five wives. . . . We import juke, hemp, cigar wrappers, sugar, an' fairy tales fr'm th' Ph'lippeens, an' export six-inch shells an' th' like. Iv late th' Ph'lippeens has awaked to th' fact that they're behind th' times, an' has received much American amminition in their midst."

That "amminition" was being sent to the Philippines, along with thousands of soldiers, to carry out what McKinley hoped would be a peaceful takeover. He had spent his life making political deals, and apparently believed he could reconcile Filipinos to American rule just as he had often patched up political squabbles in Ohio. Utterly ignorant of the land he wished to seize, he had no concept of Aguinaldo's insurgent movement, which had thirty thousand men under arms, and never expected that it would fight for independence against a new master just as it had fought against an old one. He presumed the Filipinos would welcome American rule.

In mid-December, newspapers reported that Carnegie had met McKinley and offered to pay the United States Treasury $20 million to buy the Philippine Islands so he could grant them independence. A newsman asked him if the report was true.

"Quite true," Carnegie replied. "I would gladly pay twenty millions today to restore our Republic to its first principles."

So determined was Carnegie to defeat the Treaty of Paris that he decided to make the most astonishing overture of his storied life. He offered to strike a partnership with the man he had once called "the most dangerous demagogue in the history of the Republic."

Carnegie and William Jennings Bryan differed as profoundly as any two public figures in turn-of-the-century America. One was spectacularly wealthy and dedicated to the conservatism that preserves great fortunes. The other was a self-educated midwesterner, homespun champion of the common man, and lifelong enemy of plutocracy. In practical politics, their differences boiled down to one enormous disagreement. Carnegie believed above all in monetary stability, guaranteed principally by the gold standard. Bryan's central theme was "free silver," which Carnegie, all other tycoons, and most Republicans were certain would lead to their ruin and the nation's economic collapse.

This presented Carnegie with a profound dilemma. The man whose economic ideas he detested shared his militant anti-imperialism. Slowly he developed the idea that if he could somehow persuade Bryan to abandon or soften his "free silver" rhetoric, the two could work together.

News of such a partnership would shock both men's friends, so it would have to be arranged in secret.

Bryan arrived in New York on December 17 and made a stirring speech warning that the United States must never annex the Philippines. Carnegie responded within hours, in a telegram to Bryan. "Your clear and most timely expression of risks this morning impels me to write to say that in this hour of grave danger to Republican institutions, all partisanship fades away," he wrote. "Labor is already against imperialism and I look to the farmer to be heard from. Holding out to you the hand of fellowship in the new issue before us & wishing you god-speed, Andrew Carnegie."

A few hours later, Bryan cabled back and asked Carnegie to visit him at the Bartholdi Hotel. That hotel, however, was not only Bryan's local base but also headquarters of the Free Silver Party, a loose band of his supporters. Carnegie thought it unwise to appear there. The two men agreed to meet at his Upper East Side mansion instead.

Neither man recorded details of their conversation. Undoubtedly they agreed that imperialism was an unalloyed evil. What they said about domestic issues is less clear. Carnegie came away believing that Bryan might be willing to back away from his "free silver" platform, making an alliance possible. By the time they parted, as one historian has observed, "the covers had been pulled back on the bed, even though this strangely matched pair were not quite ready to announce that they were climbing in together."

This late-night meeting held immense promise. If the richest man in America could unite with the champion of debt-ridden farmers and downtrodden immigrants, they might together slay the imperialist beast. Bryan had direct influence over at least half a dozen senators and could be decisive in killing the Treaty of Paris. Then, if he agreed to tone down his economic populism, Carnegie would give him decisive support that might propel him to the presidency. This would be the most astonishing alliance in American political history.

5

If They Resist,
What Shall We Do?

Ice covered many sidewalks and the temperature never rose to zero, but revelers who came to see Theodore Roosevelt sworn in as governor of New York threw the hottest party Albany had ever seen. Delirious crowds jammed the streets. Men dressed as Rough Riders waved make-believe sabers and blew bugles. Barrooms echoed with the chant, "What's the matter with Ted-dy? He's! All! Right!"

Roosevelt's celebrity is not enough to explain the passion that animated this crowd. People came to Albany for more than the inauguration of a governor. They sensed a new age dawning.

Three hundred fifty miles to the south, the United States Senate was about to begin the farthest-reaching debate in its history. During the first weeks of 1899 it would make a choice to shape the world. Roosevelt's inauguration, on January 2, was the curtain-raiser to this drama.

Spectators roared as Roosevelt, wearing a top hat and escorted by troops from the New York National Guard, paraded toward the newly completed State Capitol. He was the first governor to be inaugurated there. Soon he would be charging up the seventy-seven steps two or three at a time, but on this day he walked slowly and touched each one.

Nobody in the Assembly Chamber expected Roosevelt to give a substantive address. He obliged by speaking for less than five minutes. His few promises—honest government, thrift, low taxes—were those every public official makes. Then, just before taking the oath of office, he veered from the script. He offered a new pledge, most extraordinary for a governor: during his term in Albany, he would help make the United States "one of those world powers to whose hands, in the course of the ages, is entrusted a large part in the shaping of mankind."

The dawn of 1899 found Roosevelt and other expansionists flush with enthusiasm. As they had hoped, the Treaty of Paris gave the United States control over vast new territories. Then, just days before New Year's Day, President McKinley—moved by some combination of divine guidance, political calculation, and Henry Cabot Lodge's skillful lobbying—imposed military rule over the Philippines and directed Filipinos to accept "benevolent assimilation."

Since the United States had not officially assumed sovereignty over the islands—that could come only after the Senate ratified the treaty—this proclamation had no legal standing. From the moment McKinley issued it, however, it guided American policy in the Philippines.

> We come not as invaders or conquerors, but as friends, to protect the natives in their homes, in their employments, and in their personal and religious rights. . . . The mission of the United States is one of benevolent assimilation, substituting the mild sway of justice and right for arbitrary rule. In the fulfillment of this high mission, supporting the temperate administration of affairs for the greatest good of the governed, there must be sedulously maintained the strong arm of authority, to repress disturbance and to overcome all obstacles to the bestowal of the blessings of good and stable government upon the people of the Philippine Islands under the free flag of the United States.

This proclamation made no mention of self-rule. It offered not even a hint that the United States might one day grant independence to the Philippines. McKinley made it clearer than ever that America was determined to govern the islands indefinitely.

Members of the Anti-Imperialist League exploded in anger. They held public meetings in thirty states and gathered fifty thousand signatures on a petition demanding that the United States recognize the

Philippine Republic as an independent nation. A California newspaper called them "the kicking Bostonese."

The task of replying to McKinley's shattering proclamation fell, not surprisingly, to Carl Schurz, whose critiques of imperialism were always as meticulously argued as they were impassioned. Schurz had been invited to give the convocation address at the University of Chicago on January 4, and he decided to use the occasion to deliver a grand dismemberment of "the large policy." He composed a speech that ran to more than eleven thousand words, which he himself, in a letter to a friend, conceded was "very long." This was necessary, he wrote, because he intended the speech as a guide "for speakers or writers on our side of the question who will find in it answers, or at least suggestions for answers, to every argument brought forward on the other side."

Schurz sent Carnegie an advance copy of this speech, and Carnegie was so impressed that he directed Schurz to have it printed as a pamphlet and send him the bill. "You have brains and I have dollars," he wrote. "I can devote some of my dollars to spreading your brains."

Convocations at major universities were often national events in those days. Many eyes were on Schurz as he stepped to the University of Chicago podium to deliver the address he entitled simply "American Imperialism."

Arguments for taking the Philippines included, as Schurz listed them in this speech, (1) we need them as a market for our excess goods; (2) another country will take them if we don't; (3) holding them will open a rich China trade; (4) Filipinos cannot govern themselves and must be civilized; (5) our navy needs bases in the Pacific; (6) the flag cannot be "hauled down"; and (7) overseas expansion is America's destiny. Schurz refuted each one. Then he called on senators to resist "the intoxication of conquest."

Schurz knew that Senate debate on the Treaty of Paris was likely to begin soon. He could not have guessed that on the very day he spoke at the University of Chicago, President McKinley would send the treaty to the Senate. Along with McKinley's "benevolent assimilation" message, it was read to senators in closed session at midday on January 4. At that same moment, Schurz was telling his audience in Chicago that the Senate was about to debate "a subject fraught with more momentous consequence than any ever submitted to the judgment of the American people since the foundation of our constitutional government."

> The people of those islands will either peaceably submit to our rule or they will not. If they do not, and we must conquer them by force of arms, we shall at once have war on our hands. . . . Now, if they resist, what shall we do? Kill them? Let soldiers marching under the Stars and Stripes shoot them down? Shoot them down because they stand up for their independence? . . .
>
> Let us relax no effort in this, the greatest crisis the Republic has ever seen. . . . Let us raise high the flag of our country—not as an emblem of reckless adventure and greedy conquest, of betrayed professions and broken pledges, of criminal aggressions and arbitrary rule over subject populations—but the old, the true flag, the flag of George Washington and Abraham Lincoln, the flag of the government of, for, and by the people; the flag of national faith held sacred and of national honor unsullied; the flag of human rights and of good example to all nations; the flag of true civilization, peace, and good will to all men.

On January 4, 1899, the most intense phase of the struggle over American empire began. Three things happened on that day. In Washington, McKinley submitted the Treaty of Paris for Senate ratification, setting off a thirty-four-day debate. In Chicago, Schurz delivered his comprehensive attack on the imperial idea. And in Manila, General Elwell Otis, newly named American commander in the Philippines, stunned Filipinos by publishing McKinley's decree ordering them to show "honest submission" to the United States and accept "benevolent assimilation" rather than independence.

"My nation cannot remain indifferent in view of such a violation and aggressive seizure of its territory by a nation which has arrogated to itself the title, 'champion of oppressed nations,'" Emilio Aguinaldo wrote. "My government is disposed to open hostilities if the American troops attempt to take forcible possession. . . . Upon their heads be all the blood which may be shed."

Aguinaldo's protest rang through Washington as debate over the Treaty of Paris began. Anti-imperialists saw it as presenting, with poignant clarity, the case of a people who wanted the same independence Americans had sought in 1776. It imbued their cause with patriotic urgency.

For the treaty to be ratified, sixty of the ninety senators would have to vote in favor. Nearly all of the fifty-two Republicans had pledged to do so—with the notable exception of George Frisbie Hoar, who helped lead the opposition. President McKinley tried to ease Hoar out of Washington by offering to name him ambassador to Great Britain, but he would not be moved. Instead he devoted himself to the task of assembling the thirty-one votes necessary to block ratification. At 12:15 on Monday, January 9, he rose in the Senate to deliver the most important speech of his long career.

"There is always a certain inherent drama in the sight of a man torn between the loyalties of party and principle, and both the Senate floor and gallery were filled as Hoar rose to address his colleagues and the nation," Hoar's biographer has written.

> For those who liked their heroes handsome and youthful, there must have been a certain sense of disappointment. Hoar had fortunately given up the scraggly side-whiskers that some years earlier had given him a resemblance to Horace Greeley, but at seventy-two he was, with his round face, white hair, and appreciable stomach, an unlikely figure for a crusader as he stood facing Vice President Hobart, unconsciously juggling a key ring in his right hand. Hoar's usual custom was to carefully prepare his speeches but to bring to the Senate only a handful of notes containing key topic sentences and quotations. On this day he read from a typewritten manuscript. He made a conscious effort to read slowly and curb his high-pitched voice, but to his attentive audience on the floor and gallery, the anxiety and passion of the speaker were unmistakable.

Hoar's speech was long, dense, allusive, and heavily ornamented, a gem of neoclassical oratory. He discoursed at length on the fate of ancient empires; quoted Jesus Christ, Martin Luther, Louis Napoleon, William Makepeace Thackeray, and John Quincy Adams; expressed painful regret that he felt called to oppose "men with whom I have so long and so constantly agreed"; and meticulously analyzed the Constitution, in which he found no authority for the annexation of overseas territories. The United States, he insisted, must not "rush madly upon this new career," lest it become "a cheap-jack country raking after the cart for the leavings of European tyranny."

> It is the greatest question ever discussed in this Chamber from the beginning of the Government. The question is this: Have we the right, as doubtless we have the physical power, to enter upon the government of ten or twelve million subject people without Constitutional restraint? . . .
>
> Persons who favor the ratification of this treaty without conditions and without amendment differ among themselves, [but] the state of mind and the utterance of the lips are always in accord. If you ask them what they want, you are answered with a shout: "Three cheers for the flag! Who will dare to haul it down? Hold on to everything you can get. The United States is strong enough to do what it likes. The Declaration of Independence and the counsel of Washington and the Constitution of the United States have grown rusty and musty. They are for little countries and not great ones. There is no moral law for strong nations. America has outgrown Americanism." . . .
>
> The poor Malay, the poor African, the downtrodden workman of Europe will exclaim, as he reads this new doctrine: "Good God! Is there not one place left on earth where, in right of my manhood, I can stand up and be a man?"

This speech shook the country. Congratulatory letters and telegrams poured into Hoar's office. Overnight he became the talk of the nation.

HOAR ATTACKS IMPERIALISM AND TREATY, the *New York World* screamed. "Our Constitution Gives No Power to Hold Vassal States and Govern Them / No Nation Was Ever Created Good Enough to Own Another / Flag Raised in the East Means It Must Be Lowered from Independence Hall / No American Workman, No American Home Will Be Better for the Philippines."

Before Hoar had even finished speaking, a supporter of the treaty, Orville Platt of Connecticut, rose to challenge him. Hoar yielded the floor. Platt told him that his argument contradicted all of American history.

"The literal application of the Senator's doctrine would have turned back the *Mayflower* from our coast and would have prevented our expansion westward to the Pacific Ocean," Platt said. "I believe the hand of Providence brought about the conditions which we must either accept or be recreant to duty. I believe that those conditions were a part of the great development of the great force of Christian civilization on earth. . . . The English-speaking people, the agents of this civilization, the agency through which humanity is to be uplifted . . . is charged with this great mission. Providence has put it upon us. We propose to execute it."

"You have no right at the cannon's mouth to impose on an unwilling people your Declaration of Independence and your Constitution and your notions of freedom and notions of what is good!" Hoar cried in reply. Then, his indignation rising, he warned that if the Treaty of Paris was ratified, John Trumbull's iconic painting of the signing of the Declaration of Independence, which hangs in the Capitol as an emblem of American liberty, would have to be turned to face the wall. It might then be replaced, Hoar suggested, by a scene from the Philippines showing "some great battle where the guns of our army and navy are turned on the men struggling for their liberty."

This powerful performance inspired opponents of the treaty. Sensing momentum on their side, they pressed their advantage. The day after Hoar's speech, Senator Augustus Octavio Bacon of Georgia proposed that the treaty be amended with a clause declaring that it was "not the purpose of the Government of the United States to secure and maintain dominion" over the Philippines and promising that Americans would withdraw as soon as an "independent government" was established there.

> For over 100 years every lover of liberty has pointed to this sentence of the Declaration of Independence, "that all governments derive their just powers from the consent of the governed," as a reason for their fight for liberty. This sentence has been a pillar of fire by night and has stirred the hearts of the oppressed all over the world. . . . The Filipino is begging to treat with us as to his own land. He acknowledges our gallant service. There is no honest commercial treaty that an honest nation could ask that they are not ready to consent to. They want liberty as we did. . . .

Why not make them our friends forever instead of our enemies? Why withhold the jewel of independence? Why not finish this war as we began it, for humanity's sake?

This assault wounded the treaty's supporters. They decided it was time for a tactical retreat. On January 11, Senator Joseph Foraker offered it.

Foraker had risen through Ohio politics alongside William McKinley and was one of the president's closest confidants. Anyone hearing Foraker speak could easily believe that he was giving voice to McKinley's thoughts. When he stood to oppose Bacon's resolution, he made a concession that, according to one report, "created a sensation in the chamber." He said that although the United States had every right "to acquire territory by conquest," in the case of the Philippines it would not exercise that right.

"I do not understand that anyone desires anything but the ultimate independence of the people of the Philippines, neither the President nor anyone in this chamber," Foraker said.

Senators were astonished. This seemed to be an announcement that if the treaty was ratified and the Philippine Islands became American, McKinley would soon free them. Hoar jumped to his feet.

"What of the statement about hauling down the American flag?" he asked.

"No one desires to retain the Philippines permanently," Foraker repeated. "The President is as much a lover of liberty, truth, and justice as is the Senator from Massachusetts, and his love of liberty goes out to the people of the Philippines as unerringly as to his own."

"Then we are to understand, the statement that the American flag is not to be hauled down does not mean that we are to hold perpetual domain?" Hoar demanded. "If the people of the Philippines believe their happiness can be best secured by self-government, they are to be given an opportunity to govern themselves?"

"With the determination of the ultimate policy respecting the Philippines, their feelings will have much to do," Foraker replied. "No one, so far as I am able to learn, is prepared by force and violence to take and hold them. I am willing to trust the Administration. I have no sympathy with those who talk of making war on Aguinaldo."

"Thank God for that!" Hoar cried in triumph.

This first week of debate energized opponents of the treaty. They had made their case eloquently and effectively—so effectively that the treaty's supporters had felt forced to offer a major concession. Momentum was on their side. Then, suddenly, they were thrown off balance. From Washington cloakrooms came shocking news: one of their champions was switching sides.

For a combination of political and patriotic reasons, William Jennings Bryan volunteered for military service in Cuba when war broke out in the spring of 1898. He became colonel of the Third Nebraska Volunteer Infantry, which was deployed no farther than Florida and suffered its only casualties from typhoid and malaria. During his months in uniform he scrupulously curbed his tongue, but as soon as he was mustered out in mid-December he plunged back into the political fray. "The Philippines are too far away and their people too different from ours to be annexed to the United States, even if they desired it," he told one interviewer.

Bryan's first and most radical gambit was to meet secretly with Andrew Carnegie in New York. The partnership they discussed held immense promise for the anti-imperial cause and, more immediately, for the campaign to block Senate ratification of the Treaty of Paris. Rumors of their meeting spread. Pressed by reporters, Bryan gave a weak denial: "I did not go to New York on purpose to see Mr. Carnegie." Later he confessed, "I did see him for a few moments." That set off a wave of speculation.

"When silver and iron fuse and join forces versus imperialism, it's about time to reckon that something unusual is getting ready to drop," the *Boston Globe* observed.

Bryan, however, was not ready to weaken his "free silver" stand in ways that would allow Carnegie to support him for the presidency. "Just now I am talking against imperialism, not because I have changed my mind on the other questions but because this attack of the imperialists has to be met now or never," he wrote to Carnegie soon after they met. "You need not delude yourself with the idea that silver is dead." This difference of opinion, however, shadowed only the possibility of a long-term political alliance between the two men. They still stood shoulder to shoulder against the treaty.

A couple of days after his clandestine meeting with Carnegie in New York, Bryan set out on a barnstorming tour of the Midwest. At every stop he denounced imperialism. His rhetoric soared. Crowds cheered.

"The Bible teaches us that it is more blessed to give than to receive, while the colonial policy is based upon the doctrine that it is more blessed to take than to leave!" Bryan declared in Cincinnati on January 6. The next day, in Chicago, he asked whether Americans were ready "to change the title of our executive and call him President of the United States and Emperor of the Philippines."

> When the desire to steal becomes uncontrollable in an individual, he is declared a kleptomaniac and is sent to an asylum; when the desire to grab land becomes uncontrollable in a nation we are told that "the currents of destiny are flowing through the hearts of men" and that the American people are entering upon "a manifest mission." Shame upon a logic which locks up the petty offender and enthrones grand larceny!

After delivering that barrage, Bryan traveled to Washington. He planned a discreet series of meetings with senators who were his allies and looked to him for guidance. That seemed reasonable. Within hours after Bryan began his meetings, however, astonishing news leaked out: he was advising his followers to vote *for* the treaty. His comrades were by turns stunned, outraged, and alarmed.

"I was so incensed," Senator Pettigrew reported after meeting Bryan, "that I finally told him he had no business in Washington on such an errand."

Bryan, perhaps agreeing, quickly left town. He barely managed to avoid the near-apoplectic Carnegie, who rushed to Washington upon hearing the news, still unable to believe that the "great commoner" was defecting.

In a series of frantic telegrams, Carnegie implored Bryan to return and make clear that he opposed the treaty—or at least signal his allies in the Senate to that effect. "Friends here who know tell me the Treaty can be defeated with 2 or 3 votes to spare," Carnegie wrote on January 10. "Your advocacy of ratification has disorganized matters. . . . I wish you were here to be satisfied that you have the power to defeat the Treaty, thus giving the country time to reflect. . . . Our friends say situation looks better, but the two leaders separately said to me today, 'We were all right until Bryan came and somewhat disorganized us—wish he could be here to see the situation.' . . . I hope you can see your way to wire your friends."

The next day Carnegie wrote again: "Our friends assure me votes enough were secured to defeat the treaty, but your advice shakes several. The two chief leaders against the treaty tell me if you will acquiesce in your friends going with them as fixed, matter settled, reply free."

Bryan was unmoved. "Your plan is dangerous," he wrote back. "My plan is safe."

This shattered all calculations. "It is impossible now to make a confident prediction on the outcome," Hoar wrote to Carnegie on January 12, "Until Mr. Bryan spoke, I thought we were pretty sure to defeat the treaty. . . . But Bryan has undoubtedly demoralized some of our northwestern Democrats and one or two of the Populists. I still hope to defeat the treaty, though I confess to great anxiety and almost despondency."

Anger over Bryan's apparent conversion deepened as he continued to denounce expansionism. "Who can estimate, in money and men, the cost of subduing and keeping in subjection eight millions of people, six thousand miles away, scattered over twelve hundred islands and living under a tropical sun?" he asked in an essay published in the *New York Journal* on January 15. Two days later in Denver, he delivered a stirring declamation called "Naboth's Vineyard" that was steeped in religious and moral prophecy.

"Wars of conquest have their origin in covetousness, and the history of the human race has been written in characters of blood because rulers have looked with longing eyes upon the lands of others," he said. "The fruits of imperialism, be they bitter or sweet, must be left to the subjects of monarchy. This is the one tree of which the citizens of a republic may not partake. It is the voice of the serpent, not the voice of God, that bids us eat."

How could such a passionate anti-imperialist support a treaty that

embodied the very thing he detested? Bryan had a tortuous explanation. The best way to liberate Filipinos, he now argued, was to annex
their islands by ratifying the treaty, help them establish self-government,
and then give them independence.

Although Bryan may truly have believed this, his decision was political as well. The next year's presidential election was much on his mind.
He had reason to fear that if Democratic senators succeeded in killing
the Treaty of Paris, voters would hold him responsible. That stiffened
his will.

Bryan's support for ratification upset all calculations and made the
vote even more difficult to call. "No one would venture an independent
prediction," one newspaper reported in mid-January. Another quoted
an unnamed senator as counting fifty-five for ratification, twenty-five
opposed, and ten undecided.

"The fight that is being made on the Treaty is disheartening," Lodge
wrote to Roosevelt. "It is not very easy to bear."

Watching from Albany, Roosevelt was more sanguine. In his reply to
Lodge, he agreed that opponents of the treaty "have the best chance in
the world to beat us" but predicted that "at the last moment, when the
Administration pulls the string, enough of our people will fall down to
let the treaty be ratified."

Much of the Senate debate was conducted behind closed doors.
Thanks to cooperative senators who shared their texts and notes with
reporters, however, it was closely covered in the press. Newspapers published long excerpts from many speeches, along with colloquies in which
senators sparred over the Philippines, colonization, destiny, and the mission of the United States. Their arguments riveted the nation's attention.

Many Americans were having second thoughts about the expansionist project. Postwar triumphalism was still strong but inevitably had
begun to weaken. Arguments against the treaty grew louder. One of the
most widely discussed and reprinted was that of William Graham
Sumner, a renowned Yale professor now considered one of the founders
of sociology. He was also, not incidentally, the inventor of the term "ethno-
centrism." On January 16 he delivered a brilliantly prescient speech to
the Phi Beta Kappa Society at Yale provocatively titled "The Conquest of
the United States by Spain."

We have beaten Spain in a military conflict, but we are submitting to be conquered by her on the field of ideas and policies. Expansionism and imperialism are nothing but the old philosophies of national prosperity which have brought Spain to where she now is. . . .

We assume that what we like and practice, and what we think better, must come as a welcome blessing to Spanish-Americans and Filipinos. This is grossly and obviously untrue. They hate our ways. They are hostile to our ideas. Our religion, language, institutions, and manners offend them. They like their own ways, and if we appear amongst them as rulers, there will be social discord. . . .

The great foe of democracy now and in the near future is plutocracy. Every year that passes brings out this antagonism more distinctly. It is to be the social war of the twentieth century. In that war, militarism, expansion, and imperialism will all favor plutocracy. . . . Therefore expansion and imperialism are a grand onslaught on democracy.

Three senators assumed the job of rounding up votes necessary to ratify the Treaty of Paris. Lodge directed the campaign. When he needed to make shady deals, he worked through Nelson Aldrich of Rhode Island. The third of the treaty's managers, Mark Hanna of Ohio, was the fundraiser and political kingmaker who had helped propel McKinley to the White House.

These masters of legislative maneuver began by counterattacking in the Senate. They were reeling from assaults by Carl Schurz, George Frisbie Hoar, and William Graham Sumner. One of them had to reply. No one doubted who it would be. On January 24, Lodge rose to address a hushed chamber.

"If I did not have faith in the American people and their government, I would do my best to prevent the ratification of the treaty," he said simply. "But as I have a profound faith in both, I want to take those islands from Spain in the only way it can be done—by the ratification of the treaty—and then leave it to the President, wise, humane, and patriotic; to the American Congress; and to the American people, who have never failed in any great duty or feared to face any responsibility, to deal with them in that spirit of justice, humanity and liberty which has made us all that we are today or can ever hope to be."

Newspapers reported this speech as a resounding answer to the one Hoar had delivered two weeks before. "The two speeches go before the country as the voice of Massachusetts," one Washington correspondent wrote. "Her senior senator spoke for the conservative sentiment of the state, the traditional love of the Constitution and the Declaration of Independence, with their emphasis on equal rights and self-government; while her junior senator spoke today the policy expressed in the treaty, seemingly made necessary by the events of the war, and in doing so denied that his opponents possessed any monopoly of devotion to the Declaration of Independence."

These two speeches reflected deeply opposing views that have reverberated through American history. Hoar insisted that the United States remain faithful to its founding belief in self-government for all peoples. Lodge replied that it must adjust to the realities of the dawning new century, which he believed could become a golden age of American pre-eminence. They agreed that their country had immense gifts to offer the rest of the world, but disagreed profoundly on how those gifts should be bestowed. Hoar wished Americans to inspire humanity with the example of justice and noble morals; Lodge was ready to use force to impose America's rule over recalcitrant foreigners. It was the old debate over what John Winthrop meant by his "city on a hill" speech, framed for a new age.

As debate in the Senate reached this climax, reports of a remarkable event in the Philippines gave the anti-imperialists fresh momentum. A group of educated Filipinos, nominated by members of the newly elected Congress, announced that they had finished writing a constitution for their five-month-old republic. It was an enlightened document, drawn from the constitutions of Belgium, France, Mexico, and Brazil. Its central provision was a declaration that sovereignty always remains with voters, who may lend power to elected officials but may also take it back. No fewer than twenty-seven of its articles were guarantees of political and civil rights, including "the freedom and equality of all beliefs, as well as the separation of Church and State." As it ratified this constitution, Congress also named Emilio Aguinaldo "President of the Supreme Government."

The Philippine Republic now had a president, a congress, a flag, a national anthem, and a constitution. Anti-imperialists saw this as a breakthrough. Any honest American, they insisted, must now respect the Filipinos' wish to be free.

Supporters of the treaty replied that they, too, wished Filipinos to be free, but argued that annexing their country was the best way to free them. Lodge said that annexation would "give to those people more freedom, peace, and self-government than they could possibly get in any other way." Another supporter of the treaty, Senator Knute Nelson of Minnesota, went so far as to say that granting independence to the Philippines would be "the highest cruelty" to Filipinos.

"Providence has given the United States the duty of extending Christian civilization," Nelson said in his speech favoring ratification. "We come as ministering angels, not despots."

As the debate dragged on, President McKinley began showing signs of irritation. He wanted his treaty ratified quickly and without amendment. Using favored news correspondents—he did not like to be quoted directly—he began sharpening his tone.

"The President is puzzled at the attitude of the Senate in refusing to recognize the embarrassment which must result either from the rejection of the treaty or from an indefinite prolongation of its consideration," one newspaper reported from Washington. "He reasons that if there is a majority of that body favorable to giving the Philippines independence, the natural and orderly course would be to get possession of the islands by the ratification of the treaty, and then enact the necessary legislation to provide for their future. For himself, there is no reason to suppose that he has changed his view as to the unwillingness of our people to let the American flag be lowered on any ground where it has once been raised."

Speculating about the treaty's chances became an obsession in Washington. Millions of Americans followed the shifting Senate tally. "Final polling today shows 54 men solidly for the treaty and 36 against," one newspaper reported on January 25. That same day, Lodge sent an optimistic report to Roosevelt: "On the surface they have more than a third, but they have some very weak supporters, and it is quite in the cards that we shall ratify all right."

"To refuse to ratify the treaty would be a crime not only against

America, but against civilization," Roosevelt wrote back. "It is difficult for me to speak with moderation of such men as Hoar. They are little better than traitors."

The "traitors" were also optimistic. "I told the President two weeks ago we should beat the treaty & he was sure I was 'away off,'" Carnegie wrote to Bryan. "He knows now."

Determined not to lose control of the Senate debate, Lodge began speaking more often. He invoked the course of history and the duties of greatness. If the treaty was rejected, he warned, Americans would be "branded as a people incapable of taking rank as one of the greatest world powers."

"The President," Lodge reasoned, "cannot be sent back across the Atlantic, in the person of his commissioners, hat in hand, to say to Spain with bated breath: 'I am here in obedience to the mandate of a minority of one third of the Senate to tell you that we have been too victorious, and that you have yielded too much, and that I am very sorry I took the Philippines from you.' I do not think that any American president would do that, or that any American would wish him to."

Lodge's speeches were always well framed, but because he was such a sharp partisan, his words changed few if any votes. He needed speeches from senators who had not yet made strong statements, and whose emergence from neutrality might sway others. After consulting with Roosevelt, he came up with an ideal candidate: Thomas Platt, the Republican "Easy Boss" of New York. Roosevelt asked Platt if he would speak in the Senate on behalf of the treaty. Platt agreed. "He really is against the Philippines, but he stands by the President," Roosevelt confided to Lodge.

On January 27, Platt spoke to an attentive Senate. He found it difficult to understand, he said, why the idea of annexing the Philippines produced such "acute distress" in so many American hearts, since "we have been for a whole century annexing territory, annexing with a club or with a caress, just as the necessities demanded."

"There are reasons why the natives of those islands should misunderstand the presence at Manila of an American army, but there is no reason why an American senator should misunderstand it, and no justification of his course in misrepresenting it," Platt concluded.

He knows that there is no American in all this broad land who wishes any other fate to any single native of the Philippines than his free enjoyment of a prosperous life. He knows that close in the wake of American rule, there would come to the natives a liberty that they have never known, and a far greater liberty than they could ever have under the arrogant rule of a native dictator. . . . The native may not know these things yet, but every American senator knows them, and puts himself and his country in a false position when, by attributing the spirit of conquest and aggression to those whose policy has rescued the Philippines from Spain and would now rescue them from native tyrants, he encourages them to doubt the generous spirit of our people.

January ended with a flurry of petitions landing on senators' desks. The National Association of Manufacturers asked "most earnestly" that the treaty be ratified. Carl Schurz, Andrew Carnegie, George Boutwell, Grover Cleveland, Samuel Gompers, and a handful of others urged the opposite: the treaty "ought not to be ratified until provision is inserted, as part of its text, to the effect that the United States shall not annex the Philippine Islands or Porto Rico." A vote was scheduled for February 6.

"The week of tedious maneuverings for position in advance of the vote on Monday is drawing to a close with considerable evidence of ill feeling on the part of individual senators," the *Boston Transcript* reported. "The day of amicable discussion has passed. Threats and counter-threats among the actors behind the scenes are now of frequent occurrence."

Much opposition to the treaty, in Washington and beyond, grew from the Anti-Imperialist League. Its leaders fed information to friendly senators and heavily lobbied the handful who remained undecided. Members wrote letters, signed petitions, and held public meetings. The league also published a stream of pamphlets, called Liberty Tracts, aimed at bringing its arguments to a larger audience. Often their titles were questions. "Is it right for this country to kill the natives of a foreign land because they wish to govern themselves?" one asked. Another: "Which shall it be: Nation or Empire? Shall we still continue loyal to the American ideal: a Nation of free individuals . . . or shall we renounce our principles of equality and liberty and engage in conquest for commercial advantage, in colonial government of aliens and dependents, and in military dominion over subject races?"

The battle over imperialism erupted at a moment when writing political poetry was a national fad. Newspapers regularly published topical poems submitted by readers. During 1898 much of this doggerel mourned martyrs of the *Maine*, celebrated Admiral Dewey, and welcomed the age of empire. In early 1899, as the Senate debated, anti-imperialist poems began to appear. They were not the result of a coordinated campaign by the league, but many of the authors were members or sympathizers. One of them, Vincent F. Howard, wrote a poem called "Imperialism" about "the robbers of the earth."

> *Lo, ye are weak and ignorant,*
> *While we are strong and great;*
> *And so, in Christian Charity,*
> *We've come to rule your State.*
> *We've come to civilize ye, and*
> *We've come to teach ye pray.*
> *Bow down, bow down, ye savages,*
> *Or else we needs must slay!*

6

Stinkpot

As the Senate approached its momentous vote on taking the Philippines, tension crackled across uneasy cease-fire lines in Manila. American troops and Filipino nationalists had been allies against Spain. They were behaving more like enemies every day.

"Where these sassy niggers used to greet us daily with a pleasant smile and a Benhos Dias, Amigo, they now pass by with menacing looks, deigning not to notice us at all," one soldier reported in a letter home. Another wrote: "I believe it is only a matter of time when there will be a clash, for the two armies' outposts are within a mile or two of each other, and a single shot from either side could precipitate a general engagement."

As the Senate vote was approaching, Henry Teller of Colorado made what one newspaper called "a striking point of considerable present pertinency. He spoke of the troubles at Manila and declared that as soon as one American soldier fell in an attack from the natives of the Philippines, sentiment would vanish and the American people would stand behind their army as they had always done."

Teller's musing turned out to be as prophetic as Lodge's suggestion, shortly before the *Maine* exploded at Havana, that "there may be an explosion any day in Cuba which would settle a great many things."

On February 2, 1899, American commanders in the Philippines gave their men orders to patrol aggressively, even at the risk of provoking a clash. That afternoon, an American company charged into a rebel camp and demanded that the rebels abandon it. After a tense standoff, they agreed. One of Hoar's informants cabled him from Hong Kong that this was "a political move [to] influence the Senate vote . . . [an] insignificant skirmish due [to] intentional provocation."

From his headquarters in Manila, General Otis, the military governor, cabled his superiors to expect a clash "in a very short time." The War Department issued a public warning that Filipino fighters were "about to force an issue" and that, if they did, "the result cannot be foreseen" because General Otis was committed to "most vigorously defending himself and the instruments confided to his charge." A historic page was about to turn.

Fate's instrument turned out to be Private William Grayson, a twenty-two-year-old innkeeper who had enlisted in the First Nebraska Volunteer Infantry two days before it moved out of Lincoln. On the evening of February 4, he and a comrade named Miller advanced into what one account called "unoccupied territory the insurgents regarded as their own." Grayson later recounted what happened next.

> Something rose up slowly in front of us. It was a Filipino. I yelled "Halt!" . . . Then he immediately shouted "Halto!" to me. Well, I thought the best thing to do was to shoot him. He dropped. If I didn't kill him, I guess he died of fright. Then two Filipinos sprang out of the gateway about 15 feet from us. I called "Halt!" and Miller fired and dropped one. I saw that another was left. Well, I think I got my second Filipino that time. We retreated to where our six other fellows were, and I said, "Line up, fellows, the niggers are in here, all through these yards!"

This skirmish quickly escalated into a full-scale battle. General Arthur MacArthur, commander of American forces in the region, had ordered frontline units to charge at the enemy if challenged. As soon as MacArthur heard news of the shooting, he sent reinforcements and the fighting began. By the time it ended the next evening, sixty Americans and three thousand Filipinos lay dead.

"We had a pre-arranged plan," MacArthur later told a Senate committee. "Our tactical arrangements there were very perfect indeed. Everything was connected by wire. . . . I simply wired all commanders to carry our pre-arranged plans, and the whole division was placed on the firing line."

McKinley was awoken at the White House shortly before midnight and told that Filipino insurgents had fired on American soldiers. "How foolish these people are," he said. "This means the ratification of the treaty."

The next day's papers were flooded with news of what the *New York Times* called "the insane attack of these people upon their liberators." McKinley announced that he had ordered American commanders to "crush the power of Aguinaldo in the Philippines." Opponents of the treaty felt suddenly overwhelmed.

"Time alone will tell," fumed the anti-imperialist senator Ben Tillman of South Carolina, "whether this battle was provoked by the Filipinos for purposes of their own, or by the Americans . . . to sway men in the Senate to ratify the treaty."

Senators on both sides of the debate claimed the outbreak of fighting as vindication. "The hostility of the Filipinos is due to their apprehension and belief that the United States will attempt to subjugate them," Senator Bacon reasoned. Lodge judged them more harshly: "They have violated the truce and become our public enemies, and should be treated as such." Aguinaldo, who considered himself president of the Philippine Republic, blamed the violence on Americans who were seeking to become his country's new masters.

"I have tried to avoid, as far as it has been possible for me to do so, armed conflict, in my endeavors to assure our independence by pacific means and to avoid more costly sacrifices," he wrote in a manifesto. "But all my efforts have been useless against the measureless pride of the American government."

As rhetoric became more hostile and tempers flared, one voice remained remarkably restrained: that of William Randolph Hearst. *Journal* readers were hardly told that the Senate was carrying on a momentous debate. During those days they were instead treated to breathless coverage of a murder involving poisoned Bromo-Seltzer. The other big story was Governor Roosevelt's signing of a death warrant for a murderess, Ana Place, who became the first woman electrocuted in New York.

That seems surprising. Hearst had indignantly waved the bloody shirt while demanding war in Cuba just a year earlier. Many expected him to demand war in the Philippines just as passionately. He never did. Perhaps he did not see comparable news value in the Philippines story. More likely, he was turning out not to be an imperialist at heart after all. Cheerleading for the war with Spain had been above all a business project aimed at building circulation. Now Hearst's populist impulses emerged more strongly. The *Journal* began denouncing business trusts and publishing articles favoring Bryan and his anti-imperialist ideas—in part because Hearst hoped Bryan would help him rise in Democratic politics. All of this meant the muting of what might have been a powerful voice for ratification.

On February 5, the same day that news of fighting at Manila flashed across the United States, three American newspapers—the *New York Tribune*, *New York Sun*, and *San Francisco Examiner*—published a stirring new poem by Rudyard Kipling called "The White Man's Burden: The United States and the Philippine Islands." Kipling, a renowned celebrity and his generation's pre-eminent mythologizer of empire, hoped this poem would encourage Americans to support annexation of the Philippines. He had already published it in a monthly magazine, *McClure's*, and sent copies to friends. Roosevelt forwarded his copy to Lodge with a note calling it "rather poor poetry, but good sense from the expansion point of view." It captivated readers, and has remained a definitive text in the literature of imperialism. Its opening stanza was an appeal to Americans.

> *Take up the White Man's burden—*
> *Send forth the best ye breed—*
> *Go bind your sons to exile*
> *To serve your captives' need;*
> *To wait in heavy harness,*
> *On fluttered folk and wild—*
> *Your new-caught, sullen peoples,*
> *Half-devil and half-child.*

These words captured the mood in much of America on the eve of the Senate vote. They appealed to the missionary instinct that is deeply embedded in the American psyche. Stars were aligning.

In the final hours before the vote, Senators Lodge, Aldrich, and Hanna relentlessly pressed their advantage. They intensified pressure on wavering colleagues, raising offers and dangling new emoluments. Rumors of bribery coursed through Washington. Hoar reported to Schurz that the White House was "moving heaven and earth . . . to detach individual senators from the opposition."

"McKinley himself remained unobtrusive," one historian has written. "He was not averse, however, to using all his charm and persuasive powers, as well as more solid offering of patronage, in return for votes. The genial [Vice President] Hobart, almost the President's alter ego, turned every screw with his legendary politeness."

Lobbying became so intense that Senator Pettigrew, a fervent opponent of the treaty, stormed furiously into the office of Cushman Davis, chairman of the Foreign Relations Committee, to protest.

"You are going to ratify this treaty," Pettigrew shouted, "but it is the most terrible thing that I have seen!"

"What do you mean?" Davis asked.

"I mean the open purchase of votes to ratify this treaty right on the floor of the Senate, and before the eyes of the Senators and all the world."

"They came into my office and tried to tell me about it and I said, 'Gentlemen, get out of here. You cannot open your stinkpot in my presence.'"

"Well, I can guess who came into your room and whom you ordered out," Pettigrew said. "It was Aldrich of Rhode Island."

Lodge deftly managed this campaign. The combination of his intense last-minute lobbying and news of fighting in the Philippines—coincidence or not—overwhelmed opponents of the treaty. They could see just one savior.

Only Bryan had power to swing decisive votes. In desperation, his old friends appealed to him. Rejoin us for this one moment, they begged, and you can single-handedly push the United States off the path toward empire.

Bryan was unmoved. In a cable, he told Carnegie that he still supported the treaty. "To reject it would throw the subject back into the hands of the administration, and those who prevented its ratification would be held responsible for anything that might happen," he wrote.

"I cannot wish you success in your effort to reject the treaty because while it may win the fight, it may destroy our cause."

Anti-imperialists exploded in anger. Many who had made common cause with Bryan now reviled him. Carnegie was, by one account, "beside himself with rage."

"President McKinley, our 'War Lord,' is beginning to see that he can agree to pay twenty millions for an opportunity to shoot down people only guilty of the crime of desiring to govern themselves," he wrote in an open letter to the *New York World*. "If the President gets his bargain ratified, he has Mr. Bryan alone to thank for his success. Mr. Bryan can defeat President McKinley by a word upon this question in the Senate today."

On the Sunday evening before the vote, Carnegie was at a peak of anxiety. So was Lodge, who spent hours huddled with Secretary of State Hay—presumably unaware of Hay's affair with his wife. Their friend Henry Adams, who was with them, reported that they talked ceaselessly of "Senate and Treaty." So did everyone else in Washington. Across the country and in foreign capitals, people understood that a decisive moment was at hand.

"The excitement in Washington this morning is the greatest since the news of the blowing up of the *Maine* was received," one correspondent wrote hours before the vote. "The newspapers issued extras yesterday afternoon, and so brought the news from Manila to every home. Since that time Washington has been in a ferment, and every public man has been called upon for his views four times an hour. . . . The lining up for the battle royal is, at noon today, as follows: 58 men have announced their intention of voting for the treaty. . . . The only way 60 votes can be counted today, or at any time, is by a metaphysical process. We think the minds of men in such and such conditions will take a certain bent."

February 6, 1899, dawned intensely cold in Washington. The eastern United States was in the grip of what one modern account calls "the greatest Arctic outbreak in history." Icebergs floated in the Gulf of Mexico. All-time low temperatures were recorded in twelve states. This was weather to focus the mind.

Thousands of miles away, American soldiers and Filipino insurgents were in almost continual combat. McKinley had decreed that there be "no conflict with the insurgents" and still hoped that fighting would end quickly. So did many senators. Yet the fact that American boys were under fire far away hung inescapably over the vote.

At 2:15, bells pealed and doors to the Senate chamber were pulled shut. Guards kept swarms of reporters at bay. Lodge later wrote that he was uncertain of the outcome until five minutes before the roll call began.

Several senators spoke briefly, summing up arguments all had heard before. At precisely three o'clock Vice President Hobart, who was presiding, hammered his gavel and cut off debate. Opponents had consolidated their proposed amendments to the treaty into one, declaring that the United States "relinquishes all claim of sovereignty" over the Philippines. It was defeated, but the vote—fifty to thirty-three—suggested that the sixty votes necessary to ratify the treaty had not yet been corralled.

At four o'clock a clerk began calling the roll. One by one, senators cast their votes for or against ratification. The next day's news reports were remarkably detailed.

Anxiety was due not only to the magnitude of the question at issue, but to the uncertainty which attended the matter up to the last moment. . . . The call proceeded quietly until the name of Senator [John] McLaurin [of South Carolina] was announced. He created the first stir of the occasion by a speech in explanation of his vote for the treaty. This was the initial break in the ranks. McLaurin made a brief statement in explanation of his change of position, giving the open hostilities in Manila as the reason for it. . . . This announcement created a hubbub of excitement. . . . He had hardly concluded when [Samuel] McEnery [of Louisiana] approached with words of congratulation, saying that he had decided upon the same course.

A third doubter, George Gray of Delaware, a lame duck who was looking for a new career, also voted in favor. That decided the matter.

Three pro-treaty and three anti-treaty senators had agreed to "pair" their votes rather than record them. That left eighty-four to cast ballots, with fifty-six required for ratification. They voted fifty-seven in favor, twenty-seven against. If two supporters of the treaty had voted differently, the treaty would have failed.

"At the time the Senate went into executive session, probably fifty correspondents took their places here, standing in groups," one newsman reported.

> The only sound that could be heard from the executive chamber was a somewhat sepulchral voice tone, monotonous and indistinct, which was known to be the calling of the roll. . . . The rotund form of Senator Marcus Alonso Hanna was seen coming out of the Senate chamber at a run and making its way toward the colony of correspondents. "Three [sic] votes majority!" was all he said. Then the colony turned, and in a scramble as lively as a football rush, made a "break" for the elevator. . . . In this way the news came out of one of the great events in the history of the United States Senate. Not since the impeachment proceedings of President Johnson has there been a Senate vote so close and so contested.

NO TRIFLING WITH FILIPINOS NOW, screamed the *San Francisco Call.* "Treaty of Peace Is Ratified / Carried by Just One Vote More Than Necessary Two-Thirds / Several Senators Won Over by the Clash with the Forces of Aguinaldo."

Few in Washington were surprised to learn what Lodge and his comrades had done to secure this result. Senator McEnery emerged with the power to choose a federal judge, Senator Gray became one, and Senator McLaurin took over the naming of postmasters in his home state. This disturbed some in the anti-imperialist camp but did not shock them. Others muttered about the suspiciously timed outbreak of hostilities in Manila. All agreed, however, that the fatal blade had been wielded by their own Judas.

They had reason to be bitter. Carnegie later calculated that Bryan had influenced the votes of seven senators. Hoar counted eighteen. The historian Julius Pratt has put the number at fifteen. Lodge's biographer John Garraty estimated "more than a dozen." Whatever the figure, it was more than enough to defeat the treaty.

Senator Hoar called Bryan "more responsible than any other single person" for the treaty's ratification and said it would have been defeated "but for Mr. Bryan's personal interposition in its behalf." Carnegie's lament was even more poignant: "One word from Mr. Bryan would have saved the country from disaster." Richard Olney, who had been Grover Cleveland's secretary of state and closely followed the debate in Washington, reported to his old boss, "But for Bryan and his influence with Democratic senators, the treaty would not have been ratified."

"When the Spanish Treaty was pending in the Senate," Senator Pettigrew wrote in a memoir years later, "and we believed that we had it defeated beyond a question, Bryan came to Washington . . . and urged a ratification of the treaty. . . . He was seeking political capital, and he was willing to take it where he found it, without paying too much attention to nice questions of principle."

One biographer has suggested that Bryan "let his friendliness for McKinley, his desire to do the right and good thing, and his love of peace euchre him into an embarrassing situation." But this was far more than an embarrassment. Bryan stood at a crossroads of history. His decision to support the Treaty of Paris reshaped the world. No other act in his long career had such profound long-term effect.

Bryan's decision led to precisely the expansionism he fervently opposed. Historians have puzzled over his true motives. Some conclude that they were political, stemming from Bryan's fear of seeming unpatriotic as he prepared his second presidential campaign. Others argue that he sincerely, if naively, believed that he was helping the cause of Filipino freedom.

"How could he avoid expansion by supporting a treaty that provided for the acquisition of the Philippines?" the historian Paulo Coletta has asked.

What appears to be a dichotomy in his position becomes clear upon restatement of his purpose. If the treaty were ratified, Spain would be pushed out of the picture and the United States alone would be in control of Filipino destiny. We would then take the Philippines only long enough to permit the American Congress to resolve that they should be free. . . . Bryan failed to see the incongruity of being on McKinley's side. He argued that the treaty was a solemn obligation that must be enforced. . . . He found the people still excited by the war and talking about what they would do. They would reason better once they cooled off, he said, and then talk about what they ought to do. McKinley was appealing to them while they were intoxicated with military triumph; he would appeal to them when they were sober.

Opponents of the treaty were naturally deflated by their failure to block it. Erving Winslow, secretary of the Anti-Imperialist League, declared that senators on the losing side had "lost all but honor." Senator Hoar sent a steel engraving of the Declaration of Independence to the only other Republican who voted against ratification. The dedication said: "To the Honorable Eugene Hale, who alone of my colleagues voted with me against the repeal of the Declaration of Independence."

This victory was close and came at great cost. Washington remained deeply divided. So did the country. Yet Lodge and his comrades had won a triumph for the ages. They had reason to celebrate.

"It had been a narrow thing," the historian Walter Millis wrote thirty years later, "and they owed it, by one of the singularities of history, to the baffling figure of Mr. William Jennings Bryan, who had thus delivered not only his party, but his country as well, into the hands of the skillful politicians of expansion and imperialism. It is not impossible that Mr. Bryan's inspiration will stand as one of the decisive factors in the history of the American people."

PEACE TREATY RATIFIED / AWFUL SLAUGHTER / OUR TROOPS AT MANILA KILLED THE FILIPINOS BY THE THOUSANDS / 40 AMERICANS KILLED screamed the New York Journal's front page. "The scene presented in the environs of the city of Manila as the sun went down on Sunday evening was one of terrible desolation," its correspondent reported. "The natives were confidently aggressive and wholly unprepared for the terrible punishment which the Americans inflicted on them from the outset."

Lodge basked in his epochal victory. On the morning after the Senate vote, he called on Secretary of State Hay. The two great men— one a patriarch who had been a private secretary to Abraham Lincoln, the other at the beginning of a legendary career that would last until after World War I—congratulated each other and then strolled to the White House. They were ushered immediately into McKinley's office. Upon entering, they recoiled in shock. There, sitting in warm conversation with McKinley, was none other than Lodge's nemesis, Senator Hoar. He and McKinley were old political warhorses who saw nothing odd about reconciling after a conflict, but seeing them in near-embrace drove Lodge to distraction, as he told his friend Henry Adams. Later Adams repeated the story in a letter.

> Last Tuesday morning, just the morning after the Senate vote, Hay, walking into the President's room, stood agog to see standing by the President's side, with arms about his neck, as it were, unctuous, affectionate, beaming, the virtuous Hoar! Cabot Lodge, entering at the same time, was struck dumb by the same spectacle. Only a few hours before, in the full belief that his single vote was going to defeat and ruin the administration, Hoar had voted against the treaty. And there he was, slobbering the President with assurances of his admiration, pressing on him a visit to Massachusetts, and distilling over him the oil of his sanctimony.

Lodge was in an ugly humor when he took to the Senate floor a couple of hours later. Rather than extend a hand of reconciliation—which was never his style—he bitterly attacked the senators who had opposed ratification. Most intolerable, he said, was their insinuation that American occupation of the Philippines would lead to oppression of native people.

"There has never been an act of oppression against the Filipinos by any American soldier or by the American forces of any kind in the Philippines," Lodge insisted. "Their oppression exists solely in speeches in the United States Senate. . . . They have been treated with the utmost consideration and the utmost kindness and, after the fashion of Orientals, they have mistaken kindness for timidity."

That evening the Duke of Nahant found in his mail a letter from Captain Mahan congratulating him for securing ratification of the treaty. "The country is now fairly embarked on a career which will be beneficent to the world and honorable to ourselves," Mahan wrote. "I try to respect, but cannot, the men who utter the shibboleth of self-government, and cloud therewith their own intelligence by applying it to people in the childhood stage of race development."

Lodge was the conquering hero, but the ordeal had been exhausting. In his letter to Roosevelt—he wrote one almost every day—he vividly described its intensity.

"Until the fight was over I did not realize what a strain it had been," Lodge wrote,

> but for half an hour after the vote was announced, I felt exactly as if I had been struggling up the side of a mountain and as if there was not an ounce of exertion left in any muscle of my body. We were down in the engine room and do not get the flowers, but we did make the ship move. It was the closest, hardest fight I have ever known, and probably we shall not see another in our time where there was so much at stake.

Anti-imperialists consoled themselves by lionizing their vanquished heroes. Hoar was most effusively praised. His speeches in the Senate had given him a late burst of fame. The Massachusetts poet Frances Bartlett memorialized him in verse.

> As in the Roman Senate, Cicero
> Hurled the swift javelin of his eloquence . . .
> So stands Hoar now before his fellow men,
> True to that faith for which the fathers died!
> And one day History, with iron pen,
> Shall write on Time's stale leaves his name beside,
> "Champion of Freedom's honor crucified,"
> And centuries unborn shall say "Amen."

Two days after the vote, a large cartoon in the *Journal* silently signaled the direction its coverage of the Philippine War would take. It showed a disheveled and sad-looking Uncle Sam, armed with a rifle, standing alone in a field covered by the broken bodies of slain Filipinos. The caption said simply: "I'm sorry."

Opponents of the treaty still had a chance to extract victory from their defeat. Seven resolutions related to the Philippines were pending in the Senate. One declared that American law gave the government no right to acquire overseas territory; the other six restricted American claims in various ways. By common agreement, all were withdrawn except one proposed by Senator Bacon declaring that the United States would grant independence to the Philippines as soon as "stable and independent government" was established there.

Bacon's resolution would deal the imperial project a serious if not fatal blow. Supporting it was easier than opposing the treaty, because this vote would not imply a direct rebuke of the president. The Senate convened to consider it on February 14.

By this time, rebels in the Philippines had learned that the Treaty of Paris had been ratified. Violence followed. In mid-February a large American force stormed Iloilo City, where Aguinaldo had his head-quarters, under cover of naval bombardment. When the fighting ended, according to one historian, "Iloilo City was a blackened ruin, but a ruin in American hands."

American commanders initially believed they could consolidate control over the Philippines with five thousand soldiers. By the time the Senate convened on February 14 for its last crucial vote, twenty thousand were in the Philippines and another seven thousand were under way. Senator Hale pleaded with his colleagues to realize what those soldiers were sent to do.

"More Filipinos have been killed by the guns of our army and navy than were patriots killed in any six battles of the Revolutionary War," he said. "It has become a gigantic event. The slaughter of people in no way equal to us, meeting us with bows and arrows and crawling into jungles by hundreds, there to die, has stupefied the American mind. No one has said that our mission of commerce and of the gospel was to be preceded by the slaughter of thousands of persons."

That afternoon's vote was a potential turning point, the last chance for the United States to jump off the train of Pacific empire. It was a tie. As the Constitution dictated, Vice President Hobart cast the deciding vote. With that, Senator Bacon's resolution failed, thirty to twenty-nine. In its place, the Senate approved a resolution endorsing McKinley's policy and saying that the United States would decide "in due time" what to do with the Philippines. Senator Hoar called this "a message of tyranny, of hate, of oppression, and of slaughter." The House of Representatives never adopted it, so in the end, the Treaty of Paris became law as McKinley had designed it, without any limiting amendments, reservations, or policy declarations.

Twenty inches of snow, more than ever previously recorded in Washington, blanketed streets around the White House as President McKinley emerged before dawn on the morning of February 15, 1899. He was driven along muffled streets to Union Station, and at 5:45 he boarded a private railroad car together with four members of his cabinet and several aides. The train made its way slowly northward along freshly cleared tracks. Just nine days had passed since the Senate ratified the Treaty of Paris. The *Maine* had exploded at Havana exactly one year earlier.

McKinley faced a difficult task: explain to a divided nation why taking foreign lands was no betrayal of the American idea. Most Republican leaders, along with businessmen and millions of excited voters, wanted the United States to conquer whatever it could. Yet many Democrats, along with farmers, immigrants, intellectuals, and some Republicans, were convinced that once America began trying to shape the fate of foreign lands, it would lose its moral bearings and begin spiraling down toward militarism and oligarchy.

Even before the Senate cast its decisive votes, McKinley was at work on a major speech aimed at squaring this circle. He tested phrases and paragraphs on his private secretaries. With this speech he sought to offer nothing less than an intellectual, moral, and political justification for a force that was about to reshape the world: "the large policy."

After considering several options, McKinley decided to deliver this speech in Boston, home of the Anti-Imperialist League and thus the heart of enemy territory. He assured himself a friendly audience, however, by choosing as his platform the Home Market Club, one of the country's most potent agglomerations of corporate power. New England merchants had grown rich from global trade. With their wealth they built textile mills and shoe factories that produced more than Americans could buy. Their banks prospered by financing foreign commerce. Protected access to overseas markets—taking foreign lands and then forbidding them to trade with anyone except Americans—was the key to their future prosperity. Not without reason did the Home Market Club call its monthly journal *The Protectionist*. This was the ideal audience for one of the most important speeches of McKinley's career.

When McKinley arrived at South Station in Boston, he stepped into a scene calculated to stir grandeur in any heart. South Station had opened six weeks earlier to great celebration. It was the largest train station in the world, a dazzling monument to American industry and power. Mayor Josiah Quincy and other dignitaries ushered the presidential party through the grandly pillared concourse. A nation capable of building such a stupendous civic palace, they might well have presumed, could also master the challenge of ruling a foreign people.

The waiting crowd cheered as McKinley emerged and crossed the snowy plaza, appropriately named Dewey Square. Ceremonial guards escorted him to the Hotel Touraine across from Boston Common. The next night's gala dinner, one newspaper reported, would be "a mammoth affair, with sixteen hundred or more in attendance." That proved an underestimate. Nearly two thousand guests feasted on boiled salmon, capon, beef in mushroom sauce, chicken with celery mayonnaise, half a dozen vegetable plates, sorbet, pudding, olives, nuts, and cheese while waiting for McKinley to explain why it was right for Americans to fight Filipinos who were clamoring for independence. Service, according to the official account, was executed by "two hundred and fifty colored waiters with military precision and without a hitch. . . . The waiter for the President was Sergeant Turpin of Company L, Sixth Massachusetts Regiment, who served in the Cuba and Porto Rico campaigns." This was the largest banquet ever staged in the United States.

After reportedly shaking the hand of nearly every guest in the space of just an hour—a remarkable feat if true—McKinley sat to survey the scene, half-obscured by bouquets of pink and red American Beauty roses. Mechanics Hall had been hung with two sets of paintings aimed at portraying overseas expansion as a natural step in American history. The first three paintings depicted battles: one from the Revolution, one from the Civil War, and Dewey's victory at Manila Bay. The second three were giant illuminated portraits of Washington, Lincoln, and McKinley. Beneath them was the legend "Liberators."

After dinner, doors to the Reception Hall were opened and another three thousand guests poured in. They filled the upstairs galleries. Once they were settled, and after remarks by the governor, the mayor, and the president of the Home Market Club, McKinley rose to speak. He himself had struggled with the confusion that seizes a nation born of anti-colonial revolt when it awakens to find itself fighting patriots far away. On that freezing night in Boston, he told Americans why it was the right and generous thing to do.

Members of the Home Market Club perfectly understood the economic logic of expansion. They were looking for something more: reassurance that the policies making them rich were also right and just. McKinley gave it freely and convincingly.

The United States, McKinley argued, could not possibly tyrannize faraway lands, as European powers did, because the tyrannical impulse is foreign to America's character and tradition. He said that since the United States set its foreign policies with "unselfish purpose," its influence in the world could only be benevolent. The essential goodness of the American people, he argued, is the supreme and sole necessary justification of whatever the United States chooses to do in the world.

This goodness, McKinley acknowledged, might not be clear to the "misguided Filipino" who was fighting the United States Army from "blood-stained trenches around Manila." For that rebel, McKinley had simple counsel: recognize that the United States was acting "under the providence of God and in the name of human progress and civilization"; that it had taken the Philippines "not for territory or trade or empire"; and that its sole concern was "the welfare and happiness and the rights of the inhabitants," who were about to be blessed by the rule "not of their American masters, but of their American emancipators."

> Did we need their consent to perform a great act for humanity? We had it in every aspiration of their minds, in every hope of their hearts. . . . Nor can we now ask their consent. . . . It is not a good time for the liberator to submit important questions concerning liberty and government to the liberated while they are engaged in shooting down their rescuers. . . .
>
> No imperial designs lurk in the American mind. They are alien to American sentiment, thought, and purpose. Our priceless principles undergo no change under a tropical sun. They go with the flag. If we

can benefit these remote peoples, who will object? . . . Who will regret our perils and sacrifices? Who will not rejoice in our heroism and humanity? . . . [The Filipinos'] children and children's children shall for ages hence bless the American republic because it emancipated and redeemed their fatherland, and set them in the pathway of the world's best civilization.

With these words, McKinley proclaimed principles that would guide American foreign policy for generations: the United States never goes abroad in search of selfish advantage; it seeks only to help less fortunate peoples, even if they cannot understand that they are being helped; and it always acts in accordance with noble ideals. McKinley left it to the next speaker, his trusted postmaster general Charles Emory Smith, to remind the assembled businessmen that overseas expansion would give them "outlets for the surplus" and guarantee America's "commercial supremacy."

McKinley delivered his speech in the city that gave birth to the anti-imperialist movement, so he must have expected sharp reaction. It came quickly. The philosopher William James poured out his anguished soul in a public letter. He called McKinley's speech a "shamefully evasive" attempt to obscure the fact that the United States was "now openly engaged in crushing out the sacredest thing in this great human world— the attempt of a people long enslaved to attain to the possession of itself, to organize its laws and government, to be free to follow its internal destinies according to its own ideals."

"Surely there cannot be many born and bred Americans who, when they look at the bare fact of what we are doing, do not blush with burning shame at the unspeakable meanness and ignominy," James wrote. "We are cold-bloodedly, wantonly, and abominably destroying the soul of a people who never did us an atom of harm in their lives. It is bald, brutal piracy, impossible to dish up any longer in the cold potgrease of President McKinley's cant."

McKinley had convinced himself, on the basis of nothing but ignorance, that Filipinos would happily accept "benevolent assimilation." He ignored repeated warnings that many would certainly rebel if he denied their country independence. Fighting had already been raging in the

Philippines for ten days when he spoke in Boston. In the weeks after he returned to Washington, American soldiers consolidated their control of Manila. Filipino fighters retreated to prepare for guerrilla war. McKinley asked for authority to recruit thirty thousand more soldiers. Congress quickly approved.

"This is the President's own Pandora's box, his New Year's gift to his country," Carnegie wrote angrily. "One need not wonder why he should now attempt to evade the responsibility, since he tells us that 'every red drop, whether from the veins of an American soldier or a misguided Filipino, is anguish to my heart.' His conscience smites him. No wonder. The guilty Macbeth also cried out, 'Thou canst not say I did it!'"

Bryan, disregarding the contempt in which other anti-imperialists held him following his fatal betrayal, continued to urge that the Philippines be granted independence. "If the nation would declare its intention to establish a stable and independent government in the Philippines and then leave that government in the hands of the people of the islands, hostilities would be suspended at once and further bloodshed would be avoided," he told a crowd in Ann Arbor. This was somewhere between naive and delusional. McKinley and Congress had made their choice—with considerable help from Bryan himself—and were determined to hold the Philippines at any cost.

The frigid weather that gripped much of the United States during those eventful first weeks of 1899 began to ease at the end of February. Senators and others who had faced off in the treaty debate surveyed the result. Expansionists were the clear winners. Something—momentum, history, public opinion, political skill, fortune—gave them a string of victories. In the space of just nine months, the United States had brought Cuba under American military rule and annexed Puerto Rico, Guam, Hawaii, and the Philippines.

Many anti-imperialists, however, considered these only tactical setbacks. They set themselves two clear tasks. First they would press for a negotiated end to the Philippine War—or, if the United States refused to negotiate with Aguinaldo, mobilize Americans to oppose the war. Then they would turn the next presidential election into a referendum on imperialism.

Before setting out on those missions, the anti-imperialists paused to ponder their defeats. They could fairly claim to have lost simply because they were outmaneuvered in Washington. The deeper reason may have been that they were out of step with mainstream America.

"They labored under the decided disadvantage of saying no when the great majority of Americans wanted to say yes," the historian H. W. Brands has concluded. "After a dismal decade of depression, divisive politics, labor violence, narrowing geographic and psychic horizons, and a host of other inducers of anxiety and related ill feelings, the spectacular victory in the Spanish-American War gave Americans something to celebrate. Celebrating didn't necessarily require seizing the Philippines, but insisting on rejecting the spoils of war made the anti-imperialists seem like a bunch of spoilsports. Nobody likes spoilsports."

Expansionists also succeeded in promoting their cause as a genuinely national project that would, once and for all, end the regional division that had culminated in the Civil War. Newspapers ran endless stories about former Union and Confederate officers now serving together in foreign wars. "On ship and on shore, the men of the South and the men of the North have been fighting for the same flag and shedding their blood together!" McKinley rhapsodized in one speech. Foreign wars often have unifying effects at home, but this one had the added quality of seeming to reconcile estranged brothers. The anti-imperialists offered no comparable psychic balm.

Debate over the Treaty of Paris was about the very nature of America's mission. To anti-imperialists, the essence of this mission was democracy—deepening it at home and encouraging it abroad. The imperialists, however, saw American history through the lens of conquest. They, too, claimed democracy as their ultimate end, but they believed that in most places it could be established only under American tutelage. Two fundamentally conflicting arguments—foreigners are better on their own versus foreigners need our help—were already emerging.

This debate also marked the first time that African Americans had spoken out on a major foreign policy issue. Booker T. Washington was the most prominent. Even before he tied foreign wars to the oppression of blacks at home during his bold speech in Chicago, Washington had opposed the annexation of Hawaii. "We went to the Sandwich Islands with the Bible and prayer book in our hands to win the soul of the native," he said in one speech. "We ended up taking their country without giving them the privilege of saying yea or nay."

During 1899, groups such as the Colored National Anti-Imperial League and the Negro National Anti-Imperial and Anti-Trust League emerged in several cities. Black newspapers often defended natives in Cuba and the Philippines, with whom they felt a natural kinship, and were more dubious about imperial adventures than the mainstream press. One published an editorial saying that overseas wars were being waged "to satisfy the robbers, murderers, and unscrupulous monopolists who are ever crying for more blood." Another called annexation of the Philippines "one of the most unrighteous acts ever perpetrated by any government." A third observed wryly that "the white man's burden is never so heavy that he cannot carry it out the door or window of the house he has just burglarized."

The collective memory of slavery gave African Americans a special insight into the true meaning of "the white man's burden." Several of their most important turn-of-the-century leaders were outspoken anti-imperialists. The mathematician and sociologist Kelly Miller wrote a broadside for the Anti-Imperialist League declaring, "The whole trend of imperial aggression is antagonistic to the feebler races. It is a revival of racial arrogance." In mid-1899 the anti-lynching crusader Ida B. Wells declared, "We are eternally opposed to expansion until this nation can govern at home." Around the same time, the *Boston Post* published this declaration:

> The colored people of Boston in meeting assembled desire to enter their solemn protest against the present unjustified invasion by American soldiers in the Philippines Islands. . . . While the rights of colored citizens in the South, sacredly guaranteed them by the amendment of the Constitution, are shamefully disregarded, and while frequent lynchings of Negroes who are denied a civilized trial are a reproach to Republican government, the duty of the President and country is to reform these crying domestic wrongs and not attempt the civilization of alien peoples by powder and shot.

Race played a key role in debate over American expansion. This was an era when respectable opinion held some groups of people to be inherently superior to others. Imperialists naturally made this view a central part of their argument. During 1898 the *New York Journal* featured a comic lexicon of grotesque racial caricatures called "The Coon's Alphabet." Henry Cabot Lodge supported restrictions on immigration to prevent "the lowering of a great race." Roosevelt attributed humanity's rise from barbarism to "expansion of the peoples of white, or European, blood during the past four centuries."

"It is indeed a warped, perverse and silly morality which would forbid a course of conquest that has turned whole continents into the seats of mighty and flourishing civilized nations," Roosevelt said in one speech. "All men of sane and wholesome thought must dismiss with impatient contempt the plea that these continents should be reserved for the use of scattered savage tribes whose life was but a few degrees less meaningless, squalid, and ferocious than that of the wild beasts with whom they held joint ownership."

During the Cuban war, many American soldiers and correspondents wrote of being shocked to see that the rebel army was largely non-white. They had arrived full of admiration for these brave soldiers, relentlessly drilled into them by the jingo press. This sympathy changed quickly to disdain. One reason Americans began backing away from their promise to grant independence to Cuba was their growing realization that any elected government there would be at least partly black. Newspapers that had painted the Cuban rebels as gallant patriots began describing them as a primitive, thieving rabble. Leonard Wood said their army was "made up very considerably of black people, only partially civilized, in whom the old spirit of savagery has been more or less aroused by years of warfare, during which time they have reverted more or less to the condition of men taking what they need and living by plunder."

Racism came naturally to the expansionists. It also infected the other side. The Anti-Imperialist League traced its lineage directly to the abolitionist movement, and one of its leaders, Moorfield Storey, would become the first president of the National Association for the Advancement of Colored People. Anti-imperialist senators from the South, however, came from quite a different tradition. "You are undertaking to

annex and make a component part of this Government islands inhab-
ited by ten millions of the colored race, one-half or more of whom
are barbarians of the lowest type," said Senator Ben Tillman, a white
supremacist who worked tirelessly to deny voting rights to blacks in his
native South Carolina, in a speech opposing annexation of the Philippines. "It is to the injection into the body politic of the United States of
that vitiated blood, that debased and ignorant people, that we object."
Senator John Daniel of Virginia said the United States should not be
tempted by "a mess of Asian pottage."

"They are not all one, the Filipinos, but Negritos, Malays, and all the
concatenation of hues and colors," Daniel told the Senate. "There are
people black, and white, blue, brown and gray. There are even jotted
people and a kind that I never heard of before, said to be striped. . . . Not
in a thousand years could we raise the Filipino to the level of this
country's citizenship."

Some labor leaders who joined the anti-imperial movement did so
because they feared that annexing foreign lands would bring a flood
of immigrants who would threaten nascent trade unions. The most
powerful of them, Samuel Gompers of the American Federation of
Labor, frankly admitted that this fear had led him to his militancy.

"If the Philippines are annexed, what is to prevent the Chinese, the
Negritos, and the Malays coming to our country?" Gompers asked as
the Senate debate began. "If these new islands are to become ours . . .
can we hope to close the flood-gates of immigration from the hordes of
Chinese and the semi-savage races coming from what will then be
part of our own country?"

Anti-imperialists wanted the United States to be satisfied with the
territory it had, but Americans were not in a mood to be satisfied. They
were no more inclined to sit quietly within their own borders than the
Persians, Romans, Arabs, Turks, Spanish, British, Portuguese, French,
Russians, Dutch, Belgians, Germans, Japanese, or Chinese had been
during their most dynamic epochs. The imperial idea fit perfectly with
the explosive energy of a suddenly ambitious America.

"We have hoisted our flag, and it is not fashioned of the stuff which
can be quickly hauled down," Roosevelt insisted. "There must be control!
There must be mastery!"

Lodge, Roosevelt, and Hearst both shaped and reflected the aggressive, hyper-masculine nationalism that seized hold of the United States. Their historic victory in the Treaty of Paris ratification fight led them to believe they had subdued their anti-imperialist foes. They also assumed that Aguinaldo and his insurgents would quickly surrender or be wiped out. On both counts they were mistaken.

During the treaty debate, anti-imperialists had warned repeatedly that annexing the Philippines would set off a nationalist rebellion there. In the spring of 1899, that rebellion broke out. Anti-imperialists saw this as their great chance to win over the American people. Their fellow citizens had thrilled to the cry of battle when it brought victory over decadent Spain in a matter of weeks, but they had not imagined waging colonial war. Anti-imperialists were certain Americans would not tolerate it.

"For the first time in history," a reporter for the *Manchester Guardian* wrote from Washington, "the United States will have to shoot down men of an alien race who honestly believe that they are fighting for freedom and the interests of their country."

7

I Turn Green in Bed
at Midnight

Creating an empire was exhausting. A few days after Congress convened for its new session on March 4, 1899, it adjourned for nine months. Most members returned home for rest and politicking. Two of the most aggressively expansionist crossed oceans to tour distant lands.

For Henry Cabot Lodge, as for everyone in his social class during the Gilded Age, foreign travel meant travel to Europe. Immediately after Congress adjourned, deeply satisfied with his triumph but drained by the effort it had cost, he set sail with his wife, two sons, and dear friend Henry Adams. In the Old World he immersed himself in the culture to which he felt so deeply connected. He returned to Westminster Abbey and the Louvre, strolled down Unter den Linden in Berlin, and spent a month on the French Riviera. Often in after-dinner conversation he and Adams marveled at the magnitude of what their country had just accomplished.

"America had made so vast a stride to empire that the world of 1860 stood already on a distant horizon, somewhere on the same plane with the republic of Brutus and Cato," Adams wrote. "The climax of empire could be seen approaching."

Lodge was also busy writing. During the spring and summer of 1899, *Harper's* published a series of long essays in which he framed the war with Spain as the turning of a historic page. "For thirty years the people of the United States had been absorbed in the development of their great heritage," he concluded. "Once this work was complete, it was certain that the virile, ambitious, enterprising race which had done it would look abroad. . . . The future historian will date the opening of this new epoch and of this mighty conflict, at once economic and social, military, and naval, from the war of 1898."

As Lodge, the Senate's most prominent expansionist, traveled in Europe, one of his newest colleagues, Albert Beveridge of Indiana, was on the other side of the earth. Beveridge had just taken his oath of office when the Senate began its long recess. Eager to use the time in some way that would promote the cause of empire, and not sharing the filial tie to Europe that shaped Lodge and the East Coast elite, he set off for a place no member of Congress had ever visited: the Philippines.

Officially this was a "fact-finding" tour. Beveridge, however, already knew what he believed about the Philippine War. He sought no new facts. His real goal was to add to his credibility. He wanted to be able to tell Americans that he had seen the wisdom of conquest with his own eyes. Bearing a pass from the American military governor, General Otis, he visited several islands, rode mules, and witnessed firefights. At every stop he gave rousing pep talks to the troops.

Beveridge wrote a series of patriotic dispatches for the *Saturday Evening Post* in which he refined themes that would shape his rhetoric for years to come. He asserted that American soldiers were destined to triumph because they were "the Saxon type" and had "racial virtue in their veins." Their cause was "the divine mission of America." In them he saw "manifest destiny personified and vital."

"We are the most militant nation on earth," Beveridge concluded. "We *have* more of the world; we *know* more of the world; we are better prepared to *bless* the world, and thus to bless ourselves. The great people of the American Republic, from whom flow all our large and elemental movements, feel that the day of our empire, as a sovereign force of earth, is in its first grey dawn."

The Philippine War was spreading and intensifying, but even if Beveridge had wanted to write about that, he could not have. Military censors forbade unfavorable reporting. When American newspaper correspondents protested, General Otis threatened to have them arrested for "conspiracy against the government." Several responded by sending couriers to file their dispatches from Hong Kong. "There are towns here which have been 'captured' again and again, each time with a 'glorious victory,'" according to one of the first uncensored articles. Another reported that "the American outlook is blacker than it has been since the beginning of the war."

By midsummer, General Otis, who had urged the Filipinos to "be good Indians," was conceding that they had become "bold and defiant." One of his officers wrote home from Manila: "An air of gloom prevails everywhere, and even the city is deemed unsafe. Although we have over 30,000 troops about, Otis seems to have failed entirely." Even Henry Adams, who had been Lodge's mentor at Harvard and became one of his closest friends, was heartsick at the course of the war.

"I turn green in bed at midnight if I think of the horror of a year's warfare in the Philippines," Adams wrote to a friend. "We must slaughter a million or two foolish Malays in order to give them the comforts of flannel petticoats and electric railways."

This was the rebellion anti-imperialists had predicted. They saw it as noble and patriotic, and considered Emilio Aguinaldo a liberator. Even though he was at war with the United States, they stood by him. This brought their movement into a new phase. When they had first assembled at Faneuil Hall a year earlier, there were no American soldiers in the Philippines. At that time they had only a policy goal: to ensure that war with Spain did not transform the United States into a colonial power. They lost that battle when the Senate ratified the Treaty of Paris. Now Filipinos were rebelling. In the midst of a shooting war, anti-imperialists maintained that justice was on the enemy's side.

A surprising number of Americans agreed. That propelled the Anti-Imperialist League to its peak of power and influence. Its message reverberated through dozens of cities, scores of mass meetings, hundreds of speeches, thousands of articles, and tens of thousands of pamphlets, leaflets, and broadsides. By the middle of 1899 its membership numbered in the hundreds of thousands. Not until the Vietnam era three-quarters of a century later would so many Americans rise in opposition to a foreign war.

Eager to seize the moment, two dozen anti-imperialists sent President McKinley a letter urging him to declare a cease-fire and grant independence to the Philippines "as soon as proper guarantees can be had of order and protection of property." Signers included not just movement stalwarts such as Andrew Carnegie, Carl Schurz, and Samuel Gompers, but also McKinley's own former secretary of state, John Sherman, and his predecessor in the White House, Grover Cleveland. The president did not reply.

That led the Anti-Imperialist League to call a meeting at Boston's historic Tremont Temple, which had been a center of abolitionism and had lent its stage to idealists from Abraham Lincoln to Charles Dickens. The evening's first speaker was Albert Pillsbury, a crusader for African American rights who had served as Massachusetts attorney general and president of the State Senate. "Today we are doing in the Philippines what we made war on Spain for doing in Cuba," he told the packed house. "We are laying waste to the country with fire and sword, burning villages and slaughtering the inhabitants, because they will not submit to our rule."

After other preliminaries, the star speaker strode to the podium, introduced as "that grand old man, covered with honors as a governor of this state, as a senator, as secretary of the treasury, as a citizen and a patriot, George S. Boutwell." In a long discourse that drew deeply on history, Boutwell condemned the "aggressive, unjustifiable, cruel war" being waged in the Philippines. He compared Aguinaldo to Lincoln. Then, in a few succinct words, he pronounced the movement's new and transcendent goal.

"Our demand must be this: withdraw the troops from the Philippines," Boutwell said. "Leave the islands to the inhabitants. Let them set up a government for themselves. Let it be recognized as an independent state, and without any inquiry by us as to its character."

A few weeks after the Tremont Temple meeting, anti-imperialists held another, even larger gathering in Chicago. This one was notable in part because it marked the emergence of the movement's first female leader, Jane Addams. Until then Addams had been known for the pioneering social work that would ultimately win her the Nobel Peace Prize. At the "Chicago Liberty Meeting" she tied that work to the Philippine War.

For good or ill we suddenly find ourselves bound to an international situation. The question practically reduces itself to this: Do we mean to democratize the situation? Are we going to trust our democracy, or are we going to weakly imitate the policy of other governments, which have never claimed a democratic basis? The political code, as well as the moral law, has no meaning and becomes absolutely emptied of its contents if we take out of it all relation to the world and concrete cases. . . .

Some of us were beginning to hope that we were getting away from the ideals set by the Civil War, that we had made all the presidents we could from men who had distinguished themselves in that war, and were coming to seek another type of man. That we were ready to accept the peace ideal, to be proud of our title as a peace nation, to recognize that the man who cleans a city is greater than he who bombards it, and the man who irrigates a plain greater than he who lays it waste. Then came the Spanish war, with its gilt and lace and tinsel, and again the moral issues are confused with exhibitions of brutality.

Soon after Addams delivered this speech, she became a vice president of the Anti-Imperialist League. Gender attitudes of that era inevitably circumscribed what she and other women could do for the movement. They also shaped the propaganda war. Expansionists often depicted their rivals as lacking what Roosevelt called "the essential manliness of the American character." Lodge compared them to the American president he most despised, Thomas Jefferson, who was "supple, feminine, and illogical to the last degree." Cartoonists portrayed anti-imperialists wearing women's clothing.

Addams was hardly alone in rebelling against this stereotype. A "women's auxiliary" was part of nearly every anti-imperialist group. "We, women of the United States, earnestly protest against the war of conquest into which our country has been plunged in the Philippine Islands," the Boston auxiliary declared in June 1899. Josephine Shaw Lowell, who as a young woman had lived with her husband in Civil War camps and went on to a career of social activism, became a strategist for the New York Anti-Imperialist League and one of its principal bene-factors. Humbler women framed their protests in verse, which, as one social historian has observed, "allowed these disenfranchised citizens a more conventionally accepted but still public outlet for civic participation." One homespun poet, Alice Smith-Travers, accused the United States of rushing to "free those Filipino people from the accursed rule of Spain / To put on them the shackles of a haughtier nation's reign." Another, Pauline Wesley, also placed blame on her own country: "So strong thou art, so kind, America / Yet dost thou kill to teach the aliens peace."

During that frantic spring and summer of 1899, with both Lodge and Beveridge traveling overseas and Roosevelt preoccupied with his new duties in Albany, the anti-imperialist movement gathered unprecedented momentum. Its most indefatigable propagandist was the Boston lawyer and tycoon Edward Atkinson, in whose Milk Street office the Anti-Imperialist League had been founded. Determined to reach the shapers of American opinion, Atkinson drew up an ambitious list that made him a pioneer of direct mail lobbying. On it were the names of more than twenty thousand mayors, state legislators, newspaper editors, clergymen, business and labor leaders, librarians, directors of agricultural stations, college presidents, and officers of various civic groups. Beginning in early 1899, all of them regularly received anti-imperialist tracts.

Atkinson came up with a delightfully provocative scheme to widen his audience still further. He mailed three of his diatribes—"The Hell of War and Its Penalties," "Criminal Aggression: By Whom Committed?," and "The Cost of a National Crime"—to Secretary of War Russell Alger, along with a letter saying that he wished to send copies to officers and soldiers in the Philippines. Would the War Department forward them, he asked, or, if not, could it supply him with names and addresses so he could mail them individually? When no reply was forthcoming, Atkinson announced that, in order "to test the right of citizens of the United States to free use of the mail," he had posted copies of his pamphlets to a handful of prominent Americans in Manila, including Admiral Dewey and General Otis. The postmaster general promptly declared them "seditious" and ordered them confiscated. This "rape of the mail" set off a national scandal. Requests for copies of Atkinson's tracts poured in from across the country. He was thrilled.

"I really think members of the Cabinet have graduated from an asylum for the imbecile and feeble-minded," he wrote to a friend.

To satisfy his growing audience, Atkinson began publishing a scath-
ing quasi-monthly journal called *The Anti-Imperialist*. Each issue was a
torrent of invective, atrocity stories, reports of death and disease in the
Philippines, essays by returning soldiers ("Filipinos everywhere are alike
hostile to the Americans"), transcripts of anti-imperialist speeches and
sermons, letters from anguished Filipinos ("You are a foreign people
seeking to compel us to your will by force of arms"), and colorful denun-
ciations of militarism. Atkinson also reprinted every critical news report
from the Philippines that slipped past censors, including one headlined THE WAR A COLOSSAL BOTCH AND BUNGLE and another marveling
at President McKinley's "sudden blossoming out into a merciless conqueror." Often he focused on little-known aspects of the war, such as
peace accords that American officers signed with Filipino chieftains
guaranteeing their right to continue practicing polygamy and slavery.
One edition reported that American soldiers had turned Manila into a
world center of prostitution. ("From Vladivostok, Singapore, Yokohama,
Hong Kong, Calcutta and other treaty ports, abandoned women poured
into the new and active market.") On July 4 the cover of *The Anti-Imperialist*
depicted an American flag at half-mast, "in honor of the brave soldiers of
the United States whose lives have been sacrificed in the effort to subjugate the people of the Philippine Islands and to deprive them of their
liberty."

Newspapers reflected the public's growing doubt. They closely covered the anti-imperialist movement and published a flood of anti-war
letters. Readers' ditties turned decidedly skeptical. The *New York World*
published this one:

> *We've taken up the white man's burden*
> *Of ebony and brown;*
> *Now will you tell us, Rudyard,*
> *How we may put it down?*

Leaders on both sides of this divide were looking forward to the next
year's presidential election. William Randolph Hearst had become an
anti-imperialist in part because he hoped William Jennings Bryan would
choose him as his running mate on the Democratic ticket. Politics also

preoccupied Roosevelt, the rival Hearst most detested. Just a few months after taking office as governor of New York, Roosevelt set off on a cross-country tour. Officially he was traveling to New Mexico for a reunion of the Rough Riders, "which I would not miss for anything in the world." He also wanted to see what Americans outside New York thought of him.

"It would really be difficult to express my surprise at the way I was greeted," Roosevelt wrote to Lodge. "At every station at which the train stopped in Indiana, Illinois, Wisconsin, Iowa, Missouri, Kansas, Colorado and New Mexico, I was received by dense throngs exactly as if I had been a presidential candidate."

This tour's high point came not in New Mexico but in Chicago, where on April 10, speaking from a flag-draped platform at the Hamilton Club, a Republican citadel, Roosevelt delivered what some historians consider the defining speech of his career. He called it "The Strenuous Life." In it he exhorted Americans to do the "man's work" of civilizing the Philippines, since Filipinos "are utterly unfit for self-government and show no signs of becoming fit."

> I have scant patience with those who fear to undertake the task of governing the Philippines, and who openly avow that they do fear to undertake it, or that they shrink from it because of the expense and trouble; but I have even scanter patience with those who make a pretense of humanitarianism to hide and cover their timidity, and who cant about "liberty" and the "consent of the governed," in order to excuse themselves for their unwillingness to play the part of men. Their doctrines, if carried out, would make it incumbent upon us to leave the Apaches of Arizona to work out their own salvation, and to decline to interfere in a single Indian reservation. Their doctrines condemn your forefathers and mine for ever having settled in these United States. . . .
>
> Resistance must be stamped out! The first and all-important work to be done is to establish the supremacy of our flag. We must put down armed resistance before we can accomplish anything else, and there should be no parleying, no faltering, in dealing with our foe. As for those in our own country who encourage the foe, we can afford contemptuously to disregard them; but it must be remembered that their

utterances are not saved from being treasonable merely by the fact that they are despicable.

This speech made front pages around the country and cemented Roosevelt's place among the outstanding political figures of his rising generation. "There is no man in America today whose personality is rooted deeper in the hearts of the people than Theodore Roosevelt," wrote the influential Kansas newspaper editor William Allen White. "He is more than a presidential possibility in 1904; he is a presidential probability. He is the coming American of the twentieth century."

Praise like this naturally buoyed Roosevelt. So did the enthusiasm that washed over him in the Midwest and New Mexico. After returning to New York, he took an upstate tour that further energized him. Crowds at county fairs shouted, "Three cheers for the next president!"

"No, no, none of that," he would reply with his famous toothy smile. "Dewey's not here!"

Since no one took rumors of Dewey's candidacy seriously, Roosevelt was happy to praise him. He also recognized that a great obstacle blocked his further rise. His term as governor would last two years. "Easy Boss" Platt was unhappy with his anti-corruption campaigns and seemed likely to block his renomination. The 1904 presidential election was five years away. What would he do in the meantime?

"I have never known a hurrah to endure for five years," he mused to a newspaper reporter.

Lodge was more optimistic. In mid-1899 he wrote to Roosevelt that he had "but two great desires—one, to see my country succeed in these vast problems and emerge gloriously on the great world stage where she has set her conquering foot; the other is to make you President, and I think it can be done." Neither man, though, was sure of how this could be made to happen.

McKinley was looking for a new secretary of war, and Roosevelt considered himself the ideal candidate. The deliberative McKinley, however, was hardly willing to turn the United States Army over to such an impetuous militarist. He had decided that the next phase of the imperial project should be consolidating rule over territories already captured, not capturing more. Instead of Roosevelt he chose a Wall Street

VOL. LVI. No. 1438.   PUCK BUILDING, New York, September 21, 1904.   PRICE TEN CENTS.

Copyright, 1904 by Keppler & Schwarzmann.

Entered at N. Y. P. O. as Second-class Mail Matter.

"What fools these Mortals be!"

Puck

IMPERIALISM

U.S. GRANT STYLE

A. LINCOLN HAT.

THE COLONEL

G. WASHINGTON H.A.T.

IMPORTED HAT ALL THE STYLE IN EUROPE

GRANT HAMILTON —

"I RATHER LIKE THAT IMPORTED AFFAIR."

In 1898 Americans erupted in passionate debate over a great question: Should the United States begin intervening in faraway lands? Theodore Roosevelt was the public face of America's drive toward overseas empire.

Three willful men led the campaign for conquest. Theodore Roosevelt (above left) was a New York aristocrat who posed as a warrior and frontiersman, as in this photo taken in front of a curtain at a New York studio. Senator Henry Cabot Lodge (above), a master of Washington intrigue, shaped Roosevelt's career. "Lodge is the Mephistopheles whispering poison in his ear all the time," one anti-imperialist wrote. The publisher William Randolph Hearst (below left) commanded a mighty megaphone. His sensationalist newspapers bombarded Americans with super-patriotic chauvinism that drove them wild.

President William McKinley imposed American power in Cuba, breaking a promise that the United States would allow Cubans full independence. He had more trouble in the Philippines. McKinley ordered Filipinos to accept "benevolent assimilation," but they rebelled instead.

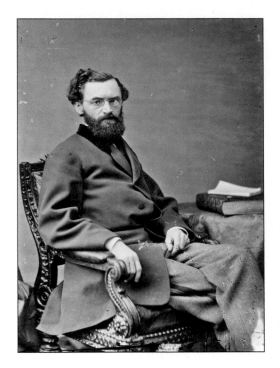

Carl Schurz, one of the most remarkable nineteenth-century immigrants to the United States, was a Civil War general, U.S. senator, and outspoken anti-imperialist. In the cartoon below, Schurz offers an engorged Uncle Sam medicine to help him "get thin again," but the tailor, President McKinley, encourages his expansion.

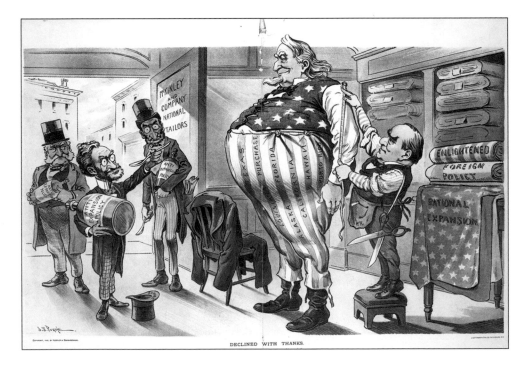

DECLINED WITH THANKS.

Two vice presidents of the Anti-Imperialist League were at opposite ends of the social and political spectrum. Andrew Carnegie, the richest man in the country, denounced America's effort to impose "triumphant despotism" over foreign peoples. The social reformer Jane Addams warned that projecting military power abroad would undermine the "democratic basis" of the United States.

"The fruits of imperialism, be they bitter or sweet, must be left to the subjects of monarchy!" cried William Jennings Bryan, the Democratic candidate against President McKinley in 1900. "It is the voice of the serpent, not the voice of God, that bids us eat!"

The most prominent African American leader of the age, Booker T. Washington, said no one had the right to rule over others "without giving them the privilege of saying yea or nay."

During the climactic Senate debate over expansion, George Frisbie Hoar of Massachusetts emerged as the most passionate anti-imperialist. By intervening in foreign countries, he said, the United States was sending them "a message of tyranny, of hate, of oppression, and of slaughter." Hoar was ridiculed for prophesying that America's foreign adventures would end badly.

THE MODERN CASSANDRA.

Emilio Aguinaldo, leader of Filipino insurgents fighting the U.S. Army, was a hero to many anti-imperialists. That outraged some other Americans, who considered it treasonous to sympathize with an enemy leader during wartime.

Mark Twain said American soldiers were doing "bandit's work" in the Philippines, and proposed a new flag with "the white stripes painted black and the stars replaced by the skull and cross-bones." He and Theodore Roosevelt were polite in public, but privately despised each other. Twain called Roosevelt "clearly insane." Roosevelt said he would like to "skin Mark Twain alive."

The first great debate over America's role in the world ended with victory for the interventionists. Each generation has re-argued it. Foreign intervention remains, as one senator called it in 1898, "the greatest question that has ever been presented to the American people."

lawyer, Elihu Root, who had spent years guiding the fortunes of the Gould, Whitney, and Harriman families.

"Thank the President for me," Root replied when one of McKinley's secretaries called to tell him of his appointment, "but say that it is quite absurd. I know nothing about war. I know nothing about the army." The secretary consulted his boss and returned to tell Root, "President McKinley directs me to say that he is not looking for anyone who knows anything about the army. He has got to have a lawyer to direct the government of the Spanish islands, and you are the lawyer he wants." Root was sworn in as secretary of war on August 1. Roosevelt, who believed he was the best man for almost any job, scorned the choice as "simply foolish."

With that prospect gone, Roosevelt found a new ambition. McKinley was looking for a new governor of the Philippines to replace the phlegmatic General Otis. That was a job big enough for Roosevelt's outsized ego. McKinley wanted an experienced officer, however, and never seriously considered naming him.

The third possibility Roosevelt considered was running for a seat in the United States Senate. That would give him the platform he wanted while bringing him even closer to his bosom friend Lodge. "Easy Boss" Platt, however, held one of New York's seats and was preparing to place his close ally Chauncey Depew in the other. In any case Platt had no interest in promoting the volatile Roosevelt. This brought Roosevelt reluctantly back to the option Lodge had begun pressing on him.

"If I were a candidate for the presidency," Lodge advised him, "I would take the vice presidency in a minute at this juncture."

Vice President Garret Hobart was a party loyalist from New Jersey whose health was failing. Whether he would seek to remain on the Republican ticket in 1900 was uncertain. Lodge determined that Roosevelt must replace him. Roosevelt was dubious. The jobs he craved were beyond his reach, yet he knew the somnolent life of a vice president would not suit him. He told Lodge he wanted "a position with more work in it."

Censorship of news from the Philippines broke down during the spring and summer of 1899. Americans began reading distressing reports about the war. In six months of fighting, the army had taken more than two thousand casualties. Some soldiers responded by abusing Filipinos. Newspaper readers learned a new phrase: "water cure."

This ingenious form of torture had been used to punish heretics during the Spanish Inquisition. Spanish soldiers brought it to the Philippines. In 1899 Filipinos passed it on to the Americans. More than a century later, versions of it would resurface at American prisons in Afghanistan, Iraq, and Guantánamo Bay.

The "water cure" became the signature torture of the Philippine War. A victim would be held to the ground while water was forced down his throat until, as one witness wrote, "his body becomes an object fright-ful to contemplate." Tormenters would stomp on his stomach and repeat the process until he talked or died.

News of this practice naturally set off protests. Mark Twain was among the outraged. "To make them confess—what?" he asked. "Truth? Or lies? How can one know which it is they are telling? For under unen-durable pain a man confesses anything that is required of him, true or false, and his evidence is worthless."

Twain had moved to London after an extended stay in Vienna. At a reception hosted by the American ambassador, he met Booker T. Wash-ington, whom he had admired from afar. This was his first encounter with an active American anti-imperialist. He was much impressed. Later he called Washington "a man worth a hundred Roosevelts, a man whose shoe-latches Mr. Roosevelt is unworthy to tie."

Living in London sharpened Twain's hatred of colonialism. His least favorite British statesman was the colonial secretary, Joseph Chamber-lain, who believed Britain must rule distant lands because "it is the duty of the landlord to develop his estate." In his private writings, Twain compared Chamberlain to "the lousy McKinley." One considered British imperialism a gift to savage peoples. The other had seized the Philippines in the name of freedom.

"I wish to God the public would lynch both these frauds," Twain fumed.

In London, Twain read many of the same reports of excesses in the Philippines that were being published in the United States. They came not only from correspondents but also in letters from soldiers, several of which were widely reprinted. "Last night one of our boys was found shot and his stomach cut open," wrote Private A. A. Barnes of the Third Indiana Artillery. "Immediately orders were received from General Wheaton to burn the town and kill every native in sight, which was done."

By late summer, McKinley and everyone else in Washington understood that ratifying the Treaty of Paris had in no way secured the Philippines. Fighting dragged on with no end in sight. McKinley's resolve stiffened. At the end of August he traveled to Pittsburgh to address a group of soldiers newly returned from the Philippines, and he used the occasion to deliver a stinging rebuke to the anti-imperialists. He asserted that insurgents represented only a small fraction of Filipinos; that they bore sole responsibility for the war because they had rebelled against America's legal authority; and that he would not rest until he had crushed them.

"They assailed our sovereignty," McKinley declared, "and there will be no useless parley, no pause, until the insurrection is suppressed and American authority acknowledged and established."

Soon after McKinley made that vow, Admiral Dewey, the hero of Manila Bay, returned home from the Philippines to a welcome the like of which no American had ever seen. Congress ordered a special medal struck with his image. In Boston, a 280-voice choir greeted him with Handel's "See the Conquering Hero Comes." New York celebrated him for three days. He circled Manhattan in the *Olympia*, his flagship during the Battle of Manila, and marched at the head of a festive parade.

The visual centerpiece of this parade was the triumphal Dewey Arch, a newly built monument intended as tribute to the conqueror—and to the idea of American conquest. Designed over a period of months by twenty-eight sculptors and architects, the arch spanned Fifth Avenue at Twenty-Fourth Street. It was modeled after the first-century Arch of Titus in Rome but was more ornate. A double colonnade led past allegorical sculpture groups, including a pair called "East Indies" and "West Indies" that showed grateful natives sitting submissively beneath towering female figures symbolizing the United States. The arch was adorned with reliefs depicting "Call to Arms," "Progress of Civilization," "Protection of Our Industries," and "Return of the Victor." It was crowned, one hundred feet above Fifth Avenue, with a statue of winged

Victory, standing tall in a vessel pulled by four steeds and holding a lau-
rel wreath above her head.

TO THE GLORY OF THE AMERICAN NAVY AND IN GREETING TO OUR
ADMIRAL, said the inscription.

For most Americans this was a grand occasion for celebration and
self-congratulation. Others were appalled. The erudite president of the
New York Anti-Imperialist League, Ernest Crosby, saw the Dewey Arch
as a symbol of militarism triumphant.

> *Build up your arch. Lay snowy stone on stone*
> *To herald to the world your glittering pride*
> *In foreign conquest. Lightly fling aside*
> *That irksome creed of liberty outgrown.*
> *Let your new toys, your ships and guns, atone*
> *For broken faith and precedent defied.*
> *Proclaim your marble goddess far and wide;*
> *Freedom no more, but Might, and Might alone!*

Dewey passed under his arch to the cheers of a vast crowd on
September 30, 1899. A couple of days later he paraded through Washington, with President McKinley at his side. Afterward the two men met
at the White House. McKinley presented Dewey with a golden sword
crafted by Tiffany & Co. When the ceremonies were over, their talk
turned to the Philippines. McKinley had written out a series of questions, with space below each one to record Dewey's replies.

SELF-GOVERNMENT—ARE THEY CAPABLE?

*No, and will not be for many, many years. The United States must control
and supervise, giving Filipinos participation as far as capable.*

WHAT DOES AGUINALDO REPRESENT IN POPULATION AND
SENTIMENT?

He has no more than 40,000 followers of all kinds out of 8 or 10 millions.

WHAT IS OUR DUTY?

Keep the islands permanently. Valuable in every way.

HOW MANY TROOPS NEEDED?

50,000

HAVE WE SHIPS ENOUGH?

Ought to send some more. Recommends that Brooklyn *go, and smaller vessels.*

SHOULD WE GIVE UP THE ISLANDS?

Never—never.

Some Americans refused to join the hero worship set off by Dewey's return. On October 17, activists from across the country gathered in Chicago to found the American Anti-Imperialist League, which was to subsume all local groups and direct a national civic uprising. Its platform was a single demand: Congress must withdraw American troops from the Philippines and "concede to them the independence for which they have so long fought and which of right is theirs."

Delegates to the Chicago convention felt a sense of surging optimism. The afterglow of Dewey's triumphal return had faded quickly. Sympathy for the Filipino cause seemed to be spreading. "These meetings recalled vividly the old slavery days," one newspaper reported. "There was the same outburst of pent-up feeling, the same settled determination to sacrifice everything to the cause of human rights, to wipe away the stain put upon the American escutcheon by this war against a people struggling for liberty."

The convention's climax was a biting speech by Carl Schurz called "The Policy of Imperialism." In ambition, conceptual scope, and rhetorical depth, it stands as a fitting counterpart and rebuttal to "The Strenuous Life," the call to imperial conquest Roosevelt had issued a few weeks before.

The Philippine War was as unnecessary as it is unjust—a wanton, wicked, and abominable war . . . and what is the answer? "No useless parley! More soldiers! More guns! More blood! More devastation! Kill, kill, kill! And when we have killed enough, so that further resistance is stopped, then we shall see." Translated from smooth phrase into plain

English, this is the program. . . . In the vocabulary of our imperialists, "order" means above all submission to their will. Any other kind of order, be it ever so peaceful and safe, must be suppressed by a bloody hand. This "order" is the kind that has been demanded by the despot since the world had a history.

"I didn't read what Carl Schurz said," Roosevelt wrote to Lodge. "I don't care what that prattling foreigner shrieks or prattles in this crisis."

Many others did. During the summer and autumn of 1899, soaring speeches like Schurz's turned many Americans against imperialism. Unhappy news from the battlefront fueled their disillusion. So did the absence of effective counter-argument.

Expansionists thought they had won their battle by securing ratification of the Treaty of Paris. They never imagined that full-scale war would explode in the Philippines. Confident in victory, they had broken camp. Lodge sailed to Europe. Beveridge left to tour the Philippines. Roosevelt immersed himself in Albany politics. He gave occasional interviews denouncing the "peace-at-any-price men" as "senile," "forces for evil," and "idiots," but that was not enough to stem the anti-war tide.

Lodge was alarmed by the public doubt he found upon his return from Europe. He and Roosevelt resolved to counterattack. On October 31 they launched their campaign at a dinner in Boston sponsored by the Republican Club of Massachusetts.

Roosevelt's speech was devoted entirely to the Philippines. He recited his familiar litany and concluded, "We have got to put down the insurrection! If we are men, we can't do otherwise!" Lodge spoke of the "vast markets" that awaited American business in the Philippines and of the "utter anarchy" that would envelop the country if the United States withdrew. Then he ventured a new argument.

Lodge accused anti-imperialists of prolonging the Philippine War by feeding Aguinaldo's hopes. Because of their encouragement, he said, Filipino fighters had "attacked our troops wantonly and without provocation" and "showed to us the blackest ingratitude." He portrayed anti-imperialists as not only defeatist, but complicit in the killing of American soldiers.

"I cannot understand, when our soldiers are in the field, face to face with an enemy, that there should be any party or any organization of men in this country ready to cry out 'Surrender!'" Lodge declared. "The soldiers of the United States in the Philippines—where they have the right to be by the laws of nations, by the laws of this country, and by the laws of sound morals—are fighting with the public enemies of the United States. . . . I vote with the army that wears the uniform and carries the flag of my country. When the enemy has yielded and the war is over, we can discuss other matters!"

For several months anti-imperialists had benefited from escalation and carnage in the Philippines, because it fed opposition to the war. Lodge's gambit turned that advantage into a trap. Once war begins, he was arguing, national unity becomes essential and questioning the war is unpatriotic. This is the impulse that later became known as the "rally 'round the flag effect." Lodge and other expansionists played to it with great success.

"A country at war is very intolerant," former president Benjamin Harrison warned his fellow anti imperialists. "The home newspapers will, while you live, make you wish you had never been born. And when you are dead, they will now and then exhume your skeleton to frighten those who live after you."

Expansionists had more than rhetoric on their side that autumn. Tens of thousands of fresh American troops—better commanded than the insurgents, more disciplined in combat, and incomparably better armed—were turning the tide of battle in the Philippines. On November 19 an American force under General MacArthur overran Aguinaldo's provisional capital, Bayambang, and sent his forces fleeing into the bush. "The so-called Filipino Republic is destroyed," MacArthur reported. That was an exaggeration, but the victory was real. It gave Americans new hope.

Roosevelt was among those cheered by improving news from the battlefield, but it did nothing to resolve his political dilemma. He was stymied. If he could not find a high-profile new job, he risked fading from view and being forced to watch from the sidelines as America reached its imperial apogee—an unthinkable prospect.

That gave Lodge another chance to press the option he favored: Roosevelt must become McKinley's running mate. Roosevelt insisted he was not interested. "In the vice presidency I could do nothing," he told Lodge. The position, in any case, was not vacant. Senator Hanna, the supreme Republican boss, made that emphatically clear when he decreed, "Nothing but death or an earthquake can stop the re-nomination of Vice President Hobart."

Then, on November 21, Hobart died.

That changed everything for Roosevelt. It set in motion a machinery of overlapping interests. Roosevelt was looking for a job with national visibility. Suddenly one had become available. Lodge could help maneuver him into it. Both men understood that Hobart's death opened a tantalizing new avenue.

McKinley never named a preferred running mate, but he recognized Roosevelt's popularity and liked the idea of a candidate who would bring youth and energy to the ticket. "Easy Boss" Platt was delighted. He wanted Roosevelt out of New York and saw the vice presidency as an elegant way to kick him upstairs. A seemingly scripted drama began unfolding.

Good news from the front, coupled with appeals for unity at home, brought a new surge of support for the Philippine War. This disconcerted the anti-imperialists. Carnegie showed his frustration in a sharp note to one negotiator of the Treaty of Paris, Whitelaw Reid, who had invited him to a banquet commemorating the first anniversary of its signing. "Unfortunately I shall be in Pittsburgh the evening of your reception to the signers of the War Treaty with Spain, not the Peace," Carnegie wrote. "It is a matter of congratulation, however, that you seem to have finished your work of civilizing the Filipinos. It is thought that about 8,000 of them have been completely civilized and sent to Heaven. I hope you like it."

The Senate reconvened in December 1899, and at one of its first sessions Albert Beveridge stood to report on his tour of the Philippines. This was the third of that year's three great speeches on the burning question of the age. It was every bit as passionate as Roosevelt's "The Strenuous Life" and Schurz's "The Policy of Imperialism," with a flashy prop.

"Thanksgiving to Almighty God that He has marked us as His chosen people!" Beveridge cried as he began. Then, methodically and persuasively, he crystallized essential arguments for taking the Philippines. "No land in America surpasses in fertility the plains and valleys of Luzon," he said, referring to the largest island in the archipelago. He talked of rice, coffee, sugar, coconuts, hemp, tobacco, "mountains of coal," forests that "can supply the furniture of the world for a century to come," and "great deposits" of gold.

As he reached this rhetorical peak, Beveridge pulled a rock from his pocket and waved it above his head. It glistened. "I have a nugget of pure gold picked up in its present form on the banks of a Philippine creek!" he cried. Here was the ideal symbol of what awaited Americans overseas.

Beveridge went on to assert that the Philippines would become America's base for China trade, "the mightiest commercial fact in our future"; that its harbors and ports would make "military and naval operations" possible over a vast area; and that the entire archipelago would become "a fortress thrown up in the Pacific, defending our Western coast, commanding the waters of the Orient, and giving us a point from which we can instantly strike and seize the possessions of any possible foe." Then, in a rising crescendo, he argued that the imperative was not simply commercial and strategic but spiritual; to rule people of "a barbarous race" was America's right and duty.

> God has not been preparing the English-speaking and Teutonic peoples for a thousand years for nothing but vain and idle self-contemplation and self-admiration. No! He has made us the master organizers of the world to establish system where chaos reigns. He has given us the spirit of progress to overwhelm the forces of reaction throughout the earth. He has made us adepts in government that we may administer government among savage and senile peoples. Were it not for such a force as this the world would relapse into barbarism and night. And of all our race, He has marked the American people as His chosen nation to finally lead in the regeneration of the world. This is the divine mission of America, and it holds for us all the profit, all the glory, all the happiness possible to man. We are trustees of the world's progress, guardians of its righteous peace.

Beveridge spoke for two spellbinding hours. When he was finished, the Senate gallery erupted in applause. Newspapers around the country reported his words under banner headlines. Young, radical, uncompromising, and blessed with a rare rhetorical gift, he became a national figure almost overnight. Columnists and editorial writers praised him. Imperialism had a dynamic new champion.

"I have heard much calculated to excite the imagination of the youth seeking wealth, or the youth charmed by the dream of empire," Senator Hoar groused in his reply to Beveridge, "but the words Right, Justice, Duty, Freedom were absent, my young friend must permit me to say, from that eloquent speech."

Beveridge had struck a chord. He personified, as the *Chicago Times-Herald* observed the next day, "the psychological moment in the tide of our national affairs." The Republican National Committee printed a million copies of his speech. Congratulatory letters flooded into his office.

"If his Americanism is now the true brand," the anti-imperialist *Springfield Daily Republican* warned its readers, "then indeed the Republic is no more."

8

What a Choice
for a Patriotic American!

Scion of political royalty in Ohio, obese and widely admired, William Howard Taft enjoyed a remarkable rise. At Yale he had been a heavy-weight wrestling champion. Back home, partly through the influence of his father, a former attorney general and secretary of war, he was named a prosecutor and then a judge. At the age of thirty-two he became the youngest-ever solicitor general of the United States. A decade later, in January 1900, he was serving on the United States Court of Appeals in Cincinnati and dreaming of a seat on the Supreme Court when he received an enigmatic telegram from President McKinley.

"I would like to see you in Washington on important business within the next few days," it said.

The dramatic escalation of the Philippine War had shocked McKinley. By the time he wired Taft, seventy thousand American soldiers were in the Philippines, fighting a war that anti-imperialists had foreseen but few others expected. He had to decide how to govern the islands while "rebellion" raged. The United States was new to the business of ruling foreign lands, and McKinley asked one of his confidants, Senator John Spooner of Wisconsin, for advice. Spooner studied various options and recommended that McKinley do what Jefferson had done after purchasing the Louisiana Territory: appoint a civilian governor to rule alongside the military commander. McKinley liked the idea.

"Judge, I'd like you to go to the Philippines," he told Taft as soon as their White House chat began.

Taft was taken aback. Later he wrote that McKinley "might as well have told me that he wanted me to take a flying machine." He was at heart a jurist, not adventurous by nature, and he worried that the tropics might not suit a man of his constitution.

"Why, I am not the man you want," Taft protested. "To begin with, I have never approved of keeping the Philippines."

McKinley surprised him by saying he agreed. "But we have them," the president reasoned, "and in dealing with them, I think I can trust the man who didn't want them better than the man who did."

An awkward silence followed. Sensing Taft's reluctance, Secretary of War Elihu Root, who had been listening quietly, offered a different kind of nudge. He appealed to Taft's sense of patriotism and manly duty.

"You have had an easy time of it, holding office since you were twenty-one," Root said. "Now your country needs you. This is a task worthy of any man. This is the parting of the ways. You may go on holding the job you have in a humdrum, mediocre way. But here is something that will test you, something in the way of effort and struggle. And the question is, will you take the harder or the easier task?"

Still Taft resisted. To close this deal, McKinley had to produce the high card he had been saving.

Everyone in the room knew of Taft's desire for promotion to the Supreme Court. Go to the Philippines, McKinley promised, and "if I last and the opportunity comes, I will appoint you." That sealed the deal.

McKinley and Taft set out on a mission that neither had sought but that both considered an inescapable responsibility. Mark Twain, watching from London, was disgusted. He could not countenance the idea of American rule over the Philippines, and he began saying so publicly.

"When the United States sent word that the Cuban atrocities must end, she occupied the highest position ever taken by a nation since the Almighty made the earth," Twain said in one after-dinner speech. "But when she snatched the Philippines and butchered a poverty-stricken, priest-ridden nation of children, she stained the flag. That's what we have today—a stained flag."

Twain had seen enough of colonialism around the world to realize that the ugly war the United States was fighting in the Philippines was hardly unique. Other Americans were beginning to reach the same conclusion. The Philippine War was one of three colonial conflicts that raged as the nineteenth century turned into the twentieth. All were in countries about which Americans knew nothing. Most disconcertingly, they were not being fought in familiar ways. Raids, ambushes, torture, and mass killing replaced set-piece battles. This was the emergence of guerrilla warfare and the harsh field tactics later called "counterinsurgency."

Early in 1900, Britain sent 180,000 soldiers, the largest force it had ever deployed anywhere, to suppress Dutch settlers in South Africa, the Boers. Under the famously ruthless Lord Kitchener, British commanders applied a scorched-earth policy that included burning farms, poisoning wells, salting fields, and killing livestock. In large regions, civilians were herded into camps where thousands died from disease and malnutrition. Anyone found outside a camp was considered an enemy and hunted down.

Thousands of miles away, fighting in China also reached a terrifying peak. For decades foreigners had been picking at the entrails of China's decaying sovereignty. Britain extracted a host of special privileges from the supine monarchy. American warships patrolled the Yangtze River. Nearly a dozen outside powers, including France, Germany, Italy, Belgium, and Russia, established quasi-independent trading enclaves. Opium and Christian missionaries flooded in. By 1900 it seemed that China might collapse and be carved up by outside powers. To prevent this, the empress dowager made common cause with nationalist militias that became known as the Boxers. Their depredations led eight foreign governments to send soldiers to China. Thousands were killed, making for gory reading in Europe and the United States.

The Boer War and the Boxer Rebellion provided a psychic backdrop for Americans as they followed the progress of their own army in the Philippines. So did reports of other imperial atrocities. During this period the first stories about Belgian brutality in the Congo reached American readers, as did reports of British and French bombardments of coastal towns in Africa. In many minds these faraway conflicts blended into one another. Americans could tell themselves that the United States was not the only honorable nation being forced to use extreme measures against uncooperative natives. This helped soothe consciences.

War in the Philippines also gave President McKinley the chance to take an audacious step whose effects have reverberated through history. In June 1900, provoked by stories of barbarities inflicted on priests and nuns and by threats to American diplomats, McKinley ordered five thousand American soldiers from the Philippines to join the multinational force in China. Never before had a president sent a large force to a country with which the United States was not at war, to fight an army supported by that country's legal government. Even more remarkable, McKinley took this step solely on his own authority, without consulting Congress. This signaled the arrival of the United States Army as a decisive force in world affairs. It was also the birth of what came to be called "presidential war power."

Although many Americans believed their country was speeding too quickly toward empire, Henry Cabot Lodge found the pace maddeningly slow. Lodge knew that the grandiose imperial project he imagined would become real only if a president fully supported it. Roosevelt must be that president—but what was his most likely route to the White House? Lodge remained adamant: Roosevelt must seek nomination as McKinley's vice president.

"I have thought it over a great deal and I am sure I am right," he wrote to his dear friend. Roosevelt fretted in reply that the vice presidency was "about the last thing for which I would care."

In Albany, though, Roosevelt had burned his political bridges. "Easy Boss" Platt was determined to be rid of him. The barren vice presidency seemed an ideal dumping ground. It was known as a dead-end job; no vice president had been elected president since Andrew Jackson had arranged to be succeeded by Martin Van Buren generations before. Platt began telling friends, as Roosevelt reported in a letter to Lodge, "that I would undoubtedly have to accept the vice presidency; that events were shaping themselves so that this was inevitable." Then Platt went public, telling reporters that Roosevelt "ought to take the vice presidency, both for national and state reasons."

That sobered Roosevelt. "It is quite on the cards that I shall be beaten for Governor this fall," he wrote to one friend. He continued to feign lack of interest in the vice presidency, but no alternative presented itself. For months he wavered in almost comical indecision.

"Under no circumstances could I or would I accept the nomination for the vice presidency," he told the *New York Herald* on February 12. A few weeks later he wrote to Lodge, "I did not say on February 12 that I would not under any circumstances accept the vice presidency." In April he said he "would rather be in private life than vice president." In May he told a friend, "If the convention nominates me, I will accept."

As the Republican convention in Philadelphia approached, McKinley let it be known that he would leave the choice of his running mate to the delegates. Lodge immediately arranged to be named chairman of the convention. Not for nothing was he called "the wily one."

The 1900 presidential election turned out to be a replay of the one four years earlier. The staid, reassuring McKinley faced off against the prairie firebrand William Jennings Bryan. For a time, anti-imperialists hoped that this election would produce their supreme triumph.

In the two years since America's anti-imperialist movement was born at Faneuil Hall, it had lost all of its great campaigns. It had failed to persuade McKinley that he should allow the Cubans, Puerto Ricans, and Filipinos to shape their own fates; failed to block ratification of the Treaty of Paris; and failed to prevent war in the Philippines. Anti-imperialists saw the presidential election as a golden chance to end their losing streak. Many were still furious with Bryan for his past betrayals, but his campaign seemed to represent their last great hope. He was their vessel, the supreme political embodiment of their ideals. If he would agree to make imperialism his main issue, this election would become a referendum on the transcendent question of the age. Bryan's victory would mean withdrawal of American troops from the Philippines and death for "the large policy." This was a contest the anti-imperialists believed they could win.

Bryan encouraged them with a series of speeches rejecting "the divine right of the American people to rule distant and subject races." Republicans bitterly attacked him. Their most popular magazine, *Judge*, published a bitingly ingenious cover posing the question, "What Is Behind Aguinaldo, That Fiend Who Has Slain Many American Soldiers?" The cover had a flap that, when opened, revealed a portrait of Bryan with a sappy grin.

Anti-imperialists were never fully comfortable with Bryan. They appreciated his stirring support for their cause but knew that the issue of foreign expansion was not closest to his heart. He remained obsessed with "free silver," the proposal that terrified businessmen and many other Americans. Their fears had helped ensure Bryan's defeat four years before. The phrase "free silver" took on a symbolic meaning. In many minds it became code for dangerously populist economic policies that threatened the new prosperity. This confronted Bryan with a historic choice.

The emotional power that drove "free silver" to the forefront of national debate in 1896 had subsided by 1900. Times were better, even for debt-ridden farmers. The discovery of gold in the Klondike region of Canada had made the gold standard less onerous to the poor. Anti-imperialists begged Bryan to ease away from "free silver" and focus his campaign on the issue of foreign expansion. They were ready to forget the past and support him, but only if he would meet this essential demand.

"Twice you have failed us: once when you justified the war with Spain, and once when you advised the ratification of the Treaty of Paris," David Starr Jordan, the president of Stanford University, wrote to Bryan. "If imperialism is an issue, it is the sole issue possible. If you cannot make it so, it is your duty to stand aside for someone else who can."

Carnegie, who was convinced that "free silver" would shatter the American economy, also begged Bryan to drop it. This would allow him to revive his idea of an odd-couple alliance that might propel Bryan to the White House. His hopes were raised by a highly encouraging letter from the anti-imperialist leader Edward Atkinson reporting a conversation with "a personal friend of Bryan who has his entire confidence." According to this informant, "it is possible and even probable that Bryan is big enough to come out and declare that while he still thinks his crusade on unlimited silver is right, the country and the world have decided against him; he therefore puts it aside as a back number and proposes to enter the field on the present great issues."

This was precisely what Carnegie and his fellow anti-imperialists wanted Bryan to do. It was also what the Republicans most feared. They recognized that if Bryan were to distance himself from "free silver" and turn the campaign into a referendum on the Philippine War, his prospects for victory would improve. At stake was nothing less than "the large policy" itself. Lodge understood the scope of the threat. On March 7, with the election still eight months away, he took to the Senate floor and delivered a methodical three-hour attack on Bryan that was also a trenchant defense of the imperial idea. This speech was later included in an anthology called *Masterpieces of American Eloquence*.

It has been stated over and over again that we have done great wrong in taking these islands without the consent of the governed, from which, according to American principles, all just government derives its powers. The consent of the governed! It is a fair phrase and runs trippingly upon the tongue, but I have observed a great lack of definite meaning in those who use it most. The Declaration of Independence was the announcement of the existence of a new revolutionary government upon American soil. Upon whose consent did it rest? Was it upon that of all the people of the colonies duly expressed? Most assuredly not. . . .

We took Louisiana without the consent of the governed, and ruled it without their consent so long as we saw fit. . . . Then came the Mexican war, and by the treaty of Guadalupe Hidalgo we received a great cession of territory from Mexico, including all the California coast. . . . There were many Mexicans living within the ceded territory. We never asked their consent . . .

To abandon the islands or to leave them now would be a wrong to humanity, a derogation of duty, and in the highest degree contrary to sound morals. As to expediency, I should regard their loss as a calamity to our trade and commerce, and to all our business interests, so great that no man can measure it. . . .

I do not believe that this nation was raised up for nothing. I have faith that it has a great mission in the world—a mission of good, a mission of freedom. I would have it fulfill what I think is its manifest destiny.

Speeches like this were the public side of Lodge's campaign to keep the United States on course toward empire. The private side was his insistent effort to persuade Roosevelt to seek the vice presidency. Inevitably the time for decision came. Republicans were to open their convention on June 19. Lodge tartly advised his friend that if he wanted to avoid being nominated, he needed only to "stay away, with your absolute declination." He well knew that declination was not in Roosevelt's nature.

"You are the only man whom, in all my life, I have met who has repeatedly and in every way done for me what I could not do for myself, and what nobody else could do, and done it in a way that merely makes me glad to be under obligation to you," Roosevelt replied.

No candidate campaigned openly for the vice presidential nomination. There was talk that Secretary of the Navy John Long might be a good choice—and in fact the shrewd Lodge appeared in Philadelphia wearing a gilt-lettered badge reading FOR VICE PRESIDENT—JOHN D. LONG. All understood, however, that the nomination was Roosevelt's if he wanted it.

On the train ride from New York to Philadelphia, Roosevelt shared a car with "Easy Boss" Platt. Neither admitted what both understood: they were about to become partners in shaping a McKinley-Roosevelt ticket. Platt had brought several other political bosses, notably the Pennsylvania kingmaker Matthew Quay, into the plot. Roosevelt willingly played his role.

Soon after the convention was gaveled to order, a rear door opened and Roosevelt entered, wearing a hat that looked like his old Rough Riders sombrero. One biographer calls this "the most famous of all his delayed entrances." Thousands of delegates applauded. Streamers rained down. Roosevelt took a full two minutes to find his place. Then he stood at attention as a band struck up "The Star-Spangled Banner," holding his sombrero over his heart.

This wild welcome suited Platt, but it horrified Senator Mark Hanna, whose backroom fundraising had paved McKinley's way to the White House four years earlier. Hanna considered Roosevelt's fascination with war and conquest to be the symptom of a deranged mind. The two had crossed swords several times. In 1898, when Hanna was trying to stop the rush to war in Cuba, Roosevelt had turned to him angrily at a Gridiron Club dinner in New York and shouted, "We will have this war for the freedom of Cuba, Senator Hanna, in spite of the timidity of the commercial classes!" Soon afterward, during a speech in which Roosevelt demanded an end to British power in the Western Hemisphere, Hanna called out, "You're crazy, Roosevelt! What's wrong with Canada?"

Now, as the Republican convention prepared to nominate Roosevelt for the vice presidency, Hanna exploded.

"Do whatever you damn please!" he shouted at a group of delegates after Roosevelt made his triumphant appearance on the convention floor. "I'm through! I won't have anything more to do with the convention! I won't take charge of the campaign! I won't be chairman of the national committee again!" One delegate, alarmed at this tirade, asked him what was the matter with Roosevelt.

"Matter?" he cried in reply. "Matter? Why, everyone's gone crazy! What is the matter with all of you? Here is this convention going headlong for Roosevelt for vice-president. Don't any of you realize that there's only one life between this madman and the presidency? Platt and Quay are no better than idiots! What harm can he do as Governor of New York compared to the damage he will do as President if McKinley should die?"

Few shared these fears. Hanna realized he could not stop the stampede, and he passed word that since the result was certain, the vote for Roosevelt should be unanimous. So it was, with a single abstention; Roosevelt announced that he could not vote for himself. Delegates erupted when the tally was declared official. Roosevelt made his way through the tumult, ascended the podium, and shook Lodge's hand. When the cheering finally subsided, he delivered an acceptance speech devoted mainly to America's global destiny. He seemed almost overcome. By one account he spoke "at torrential speed unusual even for him, his body trembling with the force of his gestures."

> We stand at the threshold of a new century big with the fate of mighty nations. It rests with us now to decide whether in the opening years of that century we shall march forward to fresh triumphs or whether at the outset we shall cripple ourselves for the contest. Is America a weakling, to shrink from the work of the great world powers? No! The young giant of the West stands on a continent and clasps the crest of an ocean in either hand. Our nation, glorious in youth and strength, looks into the future with eager eyes.

A couple of days after the convention, one of Roosevelt's oldest friends, Winthrop Chandler, sent him a clever note. "Long ago, when you first got the nomination for Governor, the astute Cabot told me that he wanted you to be Vice President, and enumerated all the advantages therein for you and for the country," he wrote. "The Wily One has won the day, in spite of your titanic struggles to disappoint him. It is the first time you have been beat, old man."

Lodge promoted Roosevelt because he understood that this was the best way to advance his life project: turning the United States permanently and irrevocably toward "the large policy." His success in engineering Roosevelt's nomination for vice president was a giant step. As soon as it was secured, he turned to the next challenge: making sure Roosevelt would handle the campaign properly. After returning to Nahant he wrote to his friend suggesting how they should proceed. He urged Roosevelt to submit himself fully to McKinley and "not permit the President or any of his friends, who are of course in control of the campaign, to imagine that we want to absorb the leadership and the glory."

"My purpose in this is to secure for you by every righteous means the confidence and support for you of the President and his large following," he wrote. "There is today no one who could stand against you for a moment for the nomination of the Presidency, but no one can tell what will happen in four years. I believe that by judicious conduct we can have it just as surely within our grasp four years hence as it would be today, but we should make no mistakes."

Two weeks after the Republicans nominated McKinley and Roosevelt, the Democrats opened their convention in Kansas City. Bryan's nomination for the presidency was a foregone conclusion. Delegates did not seriously consider William Randolph Hearst as a vice presidential possibility, and chose instead a former vice president, Adlai Stevenson of Illinois. This convention, though, had an importance far beyond the routines of coronation. It marked a decisive turning point in American history, one of those fork-in-the-road moments that determine the fate of nations. No decision ever made by a presidential candidate at a national convention shaped America and the world more profoundly than the one William Jennings Bryan made in 1900 at Kansas City.

Anti-imperialist delegates had reason for optimism as the convention convened. The American people seemed genuinely torn by the idea of overseas empire, powerfully drawn to it but increasingly aware of its dangers. News from the Philippines was bad. Eminent figures were arguing eloquently against expansion. The press had lost some of its passion for foreign wars, thanks in part to Hearst's reinvention as a Democratic populist. Anti-imperialists dreamed of a presidential campaign in which Bryan would tell voters, "In this election we decide whether the United States should rule other nations—McKinley and Roosevelt say yes, I say no."

The coalition that awaited Bryan was formidable. His base was among midwestern farmers and immigrants. Democrats also dominated the South, a political legacy of the Civil War. Anti-imperialists were strong in the Northeast. Andrew Carnegie's interest held out the possibility of an alliance between prairie populist and icon of capitalism that could change the face of American politics. Here was a chance to abort "the large policy."

A single key had to be turned to open this historic door. In order to make the 1900 presidential election a referendum on imperialism, no other issue could be allowed to muddy the debate. In practical terms, that meant one thing: Bryan must soften his "free silver" policy, which was abhorrent to the country's most powerful political and economic interests and to many voters in key states.

This was the second time Bryan stood at a crossroads of world history. Eighteen months earlier, he had been decisive in securing ratification of the Treaty of Paris. Now he had a chance to change course. He faced a choice that was moral and strategic but also overwhelmingly practical. Jettisoning "free silver" was his surest path to the presidency.

The fateful day was July 4, 1900. Democratic delegates convened at Kansas City Convention Hall to adopt the platform on which the forthcoming presidential campaign would be waged. Bryan, as unchallenged leader of the party, had the final word on what the platform would say. During the morning, a stream of delegates visited his hotel suite. Many urged him to drop or soften the "free silver" plank. Their arguments were: (1) discovery of new gold deposits in the Klondike made principled opposition to the gold standard obsolete; (2) imperialism was the great question of the age; and (3) a campaign against overseas expansion could win, while "free silver" was a proven loser.

During the French wars of religion in the late sixteenth century, Henry of Navarre, a Protestant, concluded that his best hope of gaining the French throne was to convert to Catholicism. After doing so, he became King Henry IV and supposedly explained, "Paris is well worth a mass." Bryan faced a comparable imperative. He needed only to conclude that the White House was worth dropping "free silver."

In the end, Bryan found himself unable to make King Henry's leap. The platform he sent to delegates on that decisive July 4 contained the fatal plank: a Democratic president would adopt a "bi-metallic price-level" and allow "the free and unlimited coinage of silver." These were code words for economic policies that terrified the political and economic elite much as Bolshevism would a generation later.

"Bryan threatened to withdraw his candidacy unless a silver plank was included in the platform," according to one historian. "The silver plank was accepted without protest by the delegates."

The irony of this decision is that while the "free silver" plank took up just a single dry sentence in the platform, long and passionate paragraphs were devoted to "the burning issue of imperialism." Never before or since has a major party candidate for the American presidency run on a platform so passionately opposed to overseas expansion. The words, dictated by Bryan himself, are stirringly poetic, couched in evangelical appeals to conscience and patriotism.

—We denounce the Porto Rican law [that] imposes upon the people of Porto Rico a government without their consent, and taxation without representation.

—We demand the prompt and honest fulfillment of our pledge to the Cuban people and the world that the United States has no disposition nor intention to exercise sovereignty, jurisdiction, or control over the Island of Cuba.

—We condemn and denounce the Philippine policy of the present administration. It has involved the Republic in an unnecessary war, sacrificed the lives of many of our noblest sons, and placed the United States, previously known and applauded throughout the world as the champion of freedom, in the false and un-American position of crushing with military force the efforts of our former allies to achieve liberty and self-government.

—We are unalterably opposed to seizing or purchasing distant islands to be governed outside the Constitution.

—We oppose militarism. It means conquest abroad and intimidation and oppression at home. It means the strong arm which has ever been fatal to free institutions.

Senator Ben Tillman, who read the platform to delegates, reached a mighty crescendo when he came to a sentence declaring imperialism "the paramount issue of the campaign" because it "involves the very existence of the Republic and the destruction of our free institutions." Delegates cheered with what one reporter called "a deluge of shouting that was as wild as the untamed spirit of the West." What a historic question American voters would have been able to decide in November 1900 if Bryan had chosen to pose it! Instead, the platform's ringing anti-imperialism was overwhelmed by the "free silver" plank.

Here lies the great conundrum of Bryan's career. He was profoundly anti-imperialist, not simply as a political choice but on deeply moral grounds. His speeches on the subject are some of the most stirring in American history. Yet when fate offered him the chance—twice!—to stop the train of American empire, he turned away. First he gave crucial support for Senate ratification of the Treaty of Paris, which brought the United States far-flung territories. A year and a half later at Kansas City, he had his second chance. Again he shrank from the challenge of history.

By obstinately clinging to his "free silver" dogma, Bryan made it impossible for many anti-imperialists to support his presidential campaign. That not only guaranteed his defeat at the polls, it also deprived Americans of the chance to cast a clear-cut vote on the question of overseas expansion. Bryan delivered the nation into the hands of the very imperialists against whom he so eloquently railed.

Bryan might have set the United States on a profoundly different course as it entered the twentieth century. Instead he decided that he would, as Speaker Reed put it, "rather be wrong than president." That consigned him forever to the margins of history.

"He is his own best opponent," Secretary of State John Hay observed.

In campaign speeches, Bryan promoted "free silver," railed against banks, and denounced trusts—but always returned to the issue of imperialism. He vowed to oppose every "war of conquest" and uphold the principle of self-government for all. These are the most passionately anti-imperialist speeches ever delivered by a major party nominee for president.

"We cannot set a high and honorable example for the emulation of mankind while we roam the world like beasts of prey seeking whom we may devour," Bryan declared as the campaign began. In another speech he asked, "Can it be our duty to kill those who, following the example of our forefathers, love liberty well enough to fight for it?" Often his appeals were laced with Christian pacifism: "It was God himself who placed in every human heart the love of liberty. He never made a race so low on the scale of civilization or intelligence that it would welcome a foreign master."

Bryan's insistence on clinging to his "free silver" platform proved just as self-defeating as many had predicted. It terrified millions of voters, among them leaders of the American Anti-Imperialist League who were well-to-do easterners and "sound money" men. Bryan's choice ensured that this campaign would be fought mainly on economic issues. It would not be a referendum on imperialism after all.

"This appears to have been a colossal blunder," the historian Thomas Bailey wrote a generation later. "It completely ruined whatever chances the Commoner may have had of carrying the gold-standard east. . . . The silver plank was a godsend to the harassed Republicans. Driven into a defensive position by the embarrassing Philippine insurrection, they promptly and joyously assumed the offensive with the very weapon Bryan had thrust into their hands. They could scarcely have asked for anything better."

Anti-imperialists found this especially frustrating because they sensed public opinion shifting to their side. Many Americans seemed fatigued with the idea of empire. One of the clearest signs came from New York City, where the spectacular Dewey Arch, constructed to welcome the conquering hero just a year earlier, was already falling into disrepair. Soon after Bryan was nominated, the *New York Evening Post* ran a story calling the arch an "eyesore and disgrace." It had been built of wood and plaster with the expectation that, like Washington Square Arch nearby, it would later be replaced with stone and become a permanent part of the cityscape. The cost would be half a million dollars. A much-publicized fundraising campaign produced less than half that sum. Plans to raise the remainder by selling medallions from the plaster remains fell flat. Finally the City Council decided that demolition was the only option and, as the *New York Times* reported, "One morning the work lay on the ground in a hundred pieces." Yet despite clues like these to changing public attitudes, neither presidential candidate questioned the need for annexing the Philippines.

This sent the American Anti-Imperialist League into crisis. Hastily its leaders called an emergency National Liberty Congress in Indianapolis. It would consider a single question: For whom should we vote?

The first and most radical proposal was to form a third party with an anti-imperialist presidential candidate. Carl Schurz and a handful of others favored the idea, but only if a major political figure could be recruited to run. Grover Cleveland refused. So did Speaker Reed. Lew Wallace, the seventy-three-year-old retired Civil War general and author of *Ben-Hur,* flirted with the idea and then demurred. The third-party idea failed for lack of a candidate. That failure, in turn, reflected a sharp generation gap: nearly every anti-imperialist leader was over sixty, while all of the most prominent expansionists were under fifty.

A second option was for the league to stay out of the presidential race entirely. Since neither candidate supported its central demands, the argument ran, neither should be endorsed. That had the ring of moral purity. Many delegates, however, saw it as a form of retreat. They wanted to fight one last time, not sit out the campaign and watch from the sidelines. George Boutwell, one of their founding leaders, roused them to battle.

> I am for Bryan in spite of what he has said, and in spite of what he may believe concerning the currency or the finances of this country. The question is one of life or death for the Republic. . . . I believe Mr. Bryan is as honest in his purpose to redeem the country from its degradation

and its policy of imperialism as any man who sits on this platform or in this audience today. Therefore, for one, I am in favor of supporting Mr. Bryan in spite of his belief in things concerning which he has not my concurrence. . . . Thus it may come to pass that next March you may have an inauguration to be followed by a policy which will bring our troops out of the islands of the sea; a policy that will bring the boys back to their mothers' arms; a policy in which the death-roll will be diminished; and a policy by which the massacre of innocent people who never did us any harm will come to an end.

This appeal swayed delegates. In its final resolution, the Liberty Congress declared that voting for Bryan was "the most effective means of crushing imperialism." Large groups within the league disagreed and publicly rejected this advice. Rival factions emerged. They could not reconcile. This crack-up was the beginning of the end for the American Anti-Imperialist League.

"The 1900 election might have marked its triumph, but Bryan's decisions made that impossible," one historian has written. "His recalcitrance left anti-imperialists feeling deeply cheated."

As he had done four years earlier, McKinley waged a "front porch" campaign from his home in Canton, Ohio. He made no formal speeches. The only voters he saw were well-wishers who congregated on his lawn; he waved benevolently to them from his rocking chair on the veranda. His greatest asset was the nation's rising prosperity. Mark Hanna coined a slogan to embody it: "Four More Years of the Full Dinner Pail."

While McKinley cultivated a fatherly image, Roosevelt was the campaign's public face. That suited him perfectly. As soon as summer turned to fall, he hit the campaign trail. In every speech he denounced Bryan's economic policies, calling them "criminal," "communistic and socialistic," "vicious," and "fundamentally an attack on civilization." He compared Bryan's supporters to the Paris Commune rebels of 1871. In a letter to a friend he listed the pillars of the Bryan coalition: "All the lunatics, all the idiots, all the knaves, all the cowards, and all the honest people who are slow-witted."

Roosevelt's other campaign theme was America's global destiny, which Bryan could not grasp because he was "a small man."

"I wish to see the United States the dominant power on the shores of the Pacific Ocean," Roosevelt said in one campaign speech. In another he declared, "We are for expansion and anything else that will tend to benefit the American laborer and manufacturer." Overseas expansion, he insisted in a third, was "only imperialistic in the sense that Jefferson's policy in Louisiana was imperialistic, only military in the sense that Jackson's policy toward the Seminoles or Custer's toward the Sioux embodied militarism." Often he described Filipino insurgents as Apache or Comanche. He called them "Chinese half-breeds" and "Malay bandits" and compared their leader, Aguinaldo, to the traitorous Benedict Arnold.

That autumn, by one count, Roosevelt made 567 campaign stops in twenty-four states. He traveled more than twenty thousand miles and delivered 673 speeches to a total of three million people. Crowds gathered wherever he appeared. He fed off their cheers. In Iowa an admirer, after watching in amazement as Roosevelt greeted hundreds of voters with wildly gesticulating energy, asked if he was drunk. "Oh no," came the reply, "he needs no whiskey to make him feel that way—he intoxicates himself by his own enthusiasm."

Bryan could hardly compete. His base among immigrants and farmers remained strong, but he could not broaden it. Many anti-imperialists despised him for his fatal equivocation. Eastern businessmen found his "free silver" plan abhorrent and contributed generously to McKinley's campaign. Bryan ran on a shoestring. His campaign was a tired reprise of the previous one.

"If thayse annywan r-runnin' in this campaign but me friend Tiddy Rosenfelt, I'd like to know who it is," Mr. Dooley mused. "It isn't Mack, f'r he wint away three weeks ago, lavin' a note sayin' that he'd accept the nummynation if twas offered to him, and he ain't been heered fr'm since. It ain't Bryan . . .'Tis Tiddy alone that's runnin', and he ain't runnin', he's gallopin'."

Roosevelt stayed away from some states. Mark Hanna, who had overcome his anger and ran the Republican campaign, sent him only to places where his tough-talking bluster would play well. Massachusetts was not one of them. Hanna shrewdly turned that state's campaign over to an anti-imperialist hero, Senator George Frisbie Hoar. In speeches across the state, Hoar insisted that the two candidates' views on overseas expansion were not very different, but that anti-imperialist Democrats were fatally tainted by their alliance with racism. Their true intent, he warned, was to "strangle Booker Washington with one hand and wave the flag over the head of Aguinaldo with the other."

Before select audiences, Roosevelt made the same case. "The leading argument against our holding the Philippines is that based upon the 'consent of the governed' theory," he said in one campaign speech. "Nothing but indignation can be felt for such an argument, in view of the fact that it is made by or on behalf of the very men who are at this moment either suppressing or willing to benefit from the suppression of the colored vote in certain southern states."

Bryan refused to distance himself from the racists who formed an important part of his southern base. This cost him anti-imperialist votes in Massachusetts, New York, New Jersey, and other northern states. As the election approached, many anti-imperialists fell from despair into anguish. To lose would be painful enough. Having no one to vote for was worse.

Many voters were unhappy with both candidates. McKinley had brought good times but was unimaginative and tainted by the blood of empire. Bryan was passionate but seemed frighteningly radical. Rarely have partisans of opposing presidential candidates voted with less enthusiasm.

One newspaper endorsed McKinley with an editorial headlined THE NATION'S CHOICE—OF EVILS. Benjamin Harrison, the most recent Republican president, refused to endorse McKinley, leading newspapers to note his "masterly inactivity" and "brilliant flashes of silence." Grover Cleveland went duck hunting rather than vote, muttering before he set out, "Bryanism and McKinleyism! What a choice for a patriotic American!" Carl Schurz lamented being "forced by two rotten old party carcasses to choose between two evils." In the end he voted for Bryan, calling it a "horrible duty" and "the most distasteful thing I ever did." Carnegie could not.

"McKinley stands for war and violence abroad," he reasoned, "but Mr. Bryan stands for those scourges at home."

The only great enthusiasm in this campaign, other than that generated by Roosevelt, came from insurgents in the Philippines. They knew enough about American politics to realize that the fate of their infant republic hung in the balance. A couple of weeks before the election, a delegation of Aguinaldo's supporters quietly approached the Bryan campaign with an offer they thought might turn the election in his favor. Aguinaldo, they reported, was ready to announce publicly that if Bryan won, Filipino insurgents would immediately lay down their arms. Some of Bryan's partisans wanted to pursue the offer. Others feared it would expose them to charges of collaboration with enemies. Their internal debate weakened a movement already rent by factional strife. Yet Filipino leaders looked to Bryan as their last possible savior.

"On this day there is a struggle in America: On this day is decided our life," a pro-independence newspaper in Manila proclaimed as Americans went to the polls. "Glory to Bryan. . . . Grief to Imperialism and McKinley. . . . Mother Philippines—Blessed be Thou. Mr. Bryan—Triumphant be Thou."

Bryan never made a real race of it. On November 6 voters resoundingly re-elected McKinley. He won 292 electoral votes to just 155 for Bryan, with the greatest popular plurality since Ulysses S. Grant. It was, Mark Hanna said, "a clear mandate to govern the country in the interests of business expansion." Bryan lost his own state, Nebraska, his hometown of Lincoln, and his home precinct. Roosevelt's campaigning may not have been decisive, but he brought votes to the ticket.

"After McKinley and Hanna," he wrote to Lodge, "I feel that I did as much as anyone in bringing about the result—although after all, it was Bryan himself who did most."

Lodge's strategy had worked perfectly. He had maneuvered the nation's most popular expansionist into the position of virtual president-in-waiting. If all went well, the world would soon be their plaything. Roosevelt told friends that he planned "to be a dignified nonentity for four years."

Many doubted that voters would ever promote Roosevelt to the White House. The vice presidency was a notorious burial ground for politicians. "Easy Boss" Platt was among those who believed it would be so for Roosevelt.

"We're off to Washington," he said mischievously as he departed for the inauguration, "to see Teddy take the veil."

9

The Constitution Does Not Apply

Reporters swarmed around the end of a New York pier as the liner SS *Minnehaha* docked on October 15, 1900. Mark Twain was coming home. He was among the most beloved of all Americans, and newspapers treated his return as epochal.

Twain appeared at the top of the gangplank in his mature persona, complete with bow tie, thick mustache, and unkempt shock of curly white hair. Correspondents shouted questions. Several pressed Twain about his recent criticism of the Philippine War. Before leaving London he had told a reporter for the *New York World* that the war was "a quagmire," that the islands should be ruled "according to Filipino ideas," and that the United States should "not try to get them under our heel" or intervene "in any other country that is not ours."

"You've been quoted here as an anti-imperialist!" one reporter cried out.

"Well, I am," Twain replied. "A year ago I wasn't. I thought it would be a great thing to give a whole lot of freedom to the Filipinos. But I guess now that it's better to let them give it to themselves."

With those words, Twain plunged into the great debate. Quickly he became its brightest celebrity. He gave a stream of interviews that filled many anti-imperialists with new hope and zeal. After a string of disappointments, they had a new champion. Twain happily explained his conversion to the *New York Herald*.

"I left these shores, at Vancouver, a red-hot imperialist," he said.

I wanted the American eagle to go screaming into the Pacific. It seemed tiresome and tame for it to content itself with the Rockies. Why not spread its wings over the Philippines, I asked myself? And I thought it would be a real good thing to do. I said to myself, "Here are a people who have suffered for three centuries. We can make them as free as ourselves, give them a government and country of their own, put a miniature of the American constitution afloat in the Pacific, start a brand new republic to take its place among the free nations of the world!" It seemed to me a great task to which we had addressed ourselves. But I have thought some more since then, and I have read carefully the Treaty of Paris, and I have seen that we do not intend to free, but to subjugate the people of the Philippines. We have gone there to conquer, not to redeem. . . . And so I am an anti-imperialist. I am opposed to having the eagle put its talons on any other land.

Twain refused to endorse either candidate in the upcoming presidential election. Later he told the City Club of New York that he had stayed home on Election Day, paralyzed by the same dilemma that frustrated many anti-imperialists.

"Bryan was all wrong on the money question, so I didn't vote for him," Twain said. Then, slipping into his most disarming drawl, he added that he knew enough about the Philippines "to have a strong aversion to sending our bright boys out there to fight with a disgraced musket under a polluted flag, so I didn't vote for the other fellow."

Those strong words disturbed some in the City Club audience. They liked the easygoing, joke-cracking Twain, but not this one. As soon as his speech was over, one club member stood to denounce him. "Candidly and absolutely," he said, "I protest against his estimate of the able and dignified soldier and statesman who is the President of the United States, and I believe that our gallant Army is fighting behind no dishonored muskets and under no polluted, but a glorious flag." Others called out their agreement. Twain listened in silence but could not avoid recognizing how unpopular his views were in some circles.

"The standard of honor is shrinking pretty fast everywhere," he wrote afterward. "I find but few men who disapprove of our theft of the Philippines & our assassination of the liberties of the people of the Archipelago."

Soon after Twain's speech at the City Club, he visited Carl Schurz, whom he considered his "political channel-finder." Schurz urged him to spend the next phase of his career fighting "the new un-American policy." Twain agreed to do so.

"I dropped into his wake and followed," the sage recalled years later in a tribute to Schurz. "Followed with perfect confidence. Followed, and never regretted it."

Over the next few weeks, Twain composed a series of devastating critiques of the expansionist ethos. Two became the best-selling items ever offered for sale by anti-imperialist leagues.

First was the brief but savage "Salutation Speech from the Nineteenth Century to the Twentieth, Taken Down in Shorthand by Mark Twain." It appeared in the *Minneapolis Journal* on December 29, 1900, as part of a collection of such salutations composed by famous men. The others were banal clichés. Twain's was so delightfully sardonic that the New England Anti-Imperialist League printed it as a New Year's card and sold thousands.

"I bring you the stately matron named Christendom, returning bedraggled, besmirched, and dishonored, from pirate raids in Kiaochow, Manchuria, South Africa, and the Philippines, with her soul full of meanness, her pocket full of boodle, and her mouth full of pious hypocrisies," Twain wrote. "Give her soap and towel, but hide the looking glass."

One of Twain's biographers has called this his "most perfect single piece of persuasive writing." A New England anti-imperialist, the lawyer and historian Abner Goodell, compared it to the Gettysburg Address. On the card version, anti-imperialists added a couplet—probably written by Twain himself—encouraging the stately matron:

> Give her the glass; it may from error free her
> When she shall see herself as others see her.

With these few lines, Twain secured his position as the movement's eviscerating bard. The New York Anti-Imperialist League invited him to become one of its vice presidents. "Yes, I shall be glad to be a vice president of the League," he wrote back, "a useless because non-laboring one, but prodigiously endowed with sympathy for the cause." Twain proudly held this post for the rest of his life.

Encouraged by the success of his "salutation speech," Twain decided to set down his anti-imperialist creed in a full-length essay. The result was one of his most powerful pieces, "To the Person Sitting in Darkness." It is a slashing attack on the so-called civilized powers: Britain for its brutality in South Africa, others for their dismemberment of China, and "the blessings-of-civilization trust" for dealing in "glass beads and theology, and Maxim guns and hymn books." Twain especially rues the "bad mistake" the United States made in annexing the Philippines.

"It was a pity; it was a great pity, that error; that one grievous error, that irrevocable error," he wrote.

For it was the very place and time to play the American game again. And at no cost. Rich winnings to be gathered in, too; rich and permanent; indestructible; a fortune transmissible forever to the children of the flag. Not land, not money, not dominion—no, something worth many times more than that dross: our share, the spectacle of a nation of long harassed and persecuted slaves set free through our influence; our posterity's share, the golden memory of that fair deed. The game was in our hands. If it had been played according to the American rules, Dewey would have sailed away from Manila as soon as he had destroyed the Spanish fleet . . . and [allowed] the Filipino citizens to set up the form of government they might prefer.

At the end of this essay, Twain imagines himself explaining annexation of the Philippines to an ignorant "person sitting in darkness." This is the wickedest paragraph in the literature of American anti-imperialism.

There have been lies; yes, but they were told in a good cause. We have been treacherous; but that was only in order that real good might come out of apparent evil. True, we have crushed a deceived and confiding people; we have turned against the weak and the friendless who trusted us; we have stamped out a just and intelligent and well-ordered republic; we have stabbed an ally in the back and slapped the face of a guest; we have bought a Shadow from an enemy that hadn't it to sell; we have robbed a trusting friend of his land and his liberty; we have invited our clean young men to shoulder a discredited musket and do bandit's work under a flag which bandits have been accustomed to fear, not to follow; we have debauched America's honor and blackened her face before the world; but each detail was for the best. . . . And as for a flag for the Philippine Province, it is easily managed. We can have a special one—our States do it: we can have just our usual flag, with the white stripes painted black and the stars replaced by the skull and cross-bones.

This essay, which appeared in the February 1901 issue of the *North American Review*, was one of the most popular Twain ever wrote. The American Anti-Imperialist League published it as a pamphlet and distributed 125,000 copies. It was reprinted across the country. Some newspapers ran editorials about it day after day. "Mark Twain," the *Springfield Daily Republican* reported, "has suddenly become the most influential anti-imperialist, and the most dreaded critic of the sacrosanct person in the White House, that the country contains." Andrew Carnegie sent him an admiring note.

"There's a new Gospel of Saint Mark in the *North American* which I like better than anything I've read for many a day," Carnegie wrote to Twain. "I am willing to borrow a thousand dollars to distribute that message in proper form, & if the author don't object, may I send that sum, when I can raise it, to the Anti-Imperialist League, Boston, to which I am a contributor, the only missionary work I am responsible for? Just tell me you are willing & many thousands of the holy little missals will go flying out."

The strong response to Twain's essay encouraged him to press on. Some of the pieces he wrote during these months were so inflammatory that even he agreed they should not be published. He began sketching a history of the world told from the future, including a revisionist view of George Washington.

He did not write the Declaration of Independence, as some historians erroneously believe, but excused himself on the plea that he could not tell a lie. It was the intention of the Americans to erect a stately Democracy in their land, upon a basis of freedom and equality before the law for all; this Democracy was to be the friend of all oppressed weak peoples, never their oppressor; it was never to steal a weak land or its liberties; it was never to crush or betray struggling republics, but aid and encourage them with its sympathy. The Americans required that these noble principles be embodied in their Declaration of Independence and made the rock on which their government should forever rest. But George Washington strenuously objected. He said that such a Declaration would prove a lie . . . that as soon as the Democracy was strong enough it would wipe its feet on the Declaration and look around for something to steal—something weak, or something unwatched— and would find it; if it happened to be a republic, no matter; it would steal anything it could get.

Twain emerged as an anti-imperialist much as freethinking writers such as Thoreau and Emerson had become abolitionists half a century before. Characters in his books were often unconventional. He had a distinct contrarian impulse. His instinctive skepticism, however, was not enough to explain the intensity of his opposition to American expansion. His life experiences drove him to it.

Partly as a result of his foreign travel, Twain's view of race was more enlightened than that of most Americans. Often he wrote admiringly about anti-colonial rebels. He even admired the Boxers in China, who were portrayed in the United States as savages dedicated to slaughtering Christian missionaries. "The Boxer is a patriot, he is the only patriot China has and I wish him success," Twain wrote in one letter. In another he said, "My sympathies are with the Chinese. They have been villainously dealt with by the sceptered thieves of Europe, and I hope they will drive all of the foreigners out and keep them out for good."

Twain was always iconoclastic, but his pen never dripped as poisonously as when he skewered American imperialism. During his first year back in the United States it was his favorite theme. In speeches, interviews, letters, and pamphlets, he scorned and condemned the expansionist idea.

"We find a whole heap of fault with the war in South Africa, and feel moved to hysterics by the sufferings of the Boers, yet we don't seem to feel very sorry for the natives in the Philippines," he told one reporter. In a letter to a friend he confessed "that I am distressed because our President has blundered up to his neck in the Philippine mess, and that I am grieved because this great big ignorant nation, which doesn't even know the ABC facts of the Philippine episode, is in disgrace before the sarcastic world." When the War Department began placing patriotic poems in newspapers to recruit volunteers, he sent a note to one of the authors: "Will you allow me to say that I like these poems of yours very much? Especially the one which so vividly pictures the response of our young fellows when they were summoned to strike down an oppressor and set his victim free. Write a companion to it and show us how the young fellows respond when invited by the Government to go out into the Philippines on a land-stealing and liberty-crucifying campaign." Twain even rewrote "The Battle Hymn of the Republic" to fit what he saw as the tenor of the time:

> Mine eyes have seen the orgy of the launching of the Sword,
> He is searching out the hoardings where the stranger's wealth
>   is stored;
> He hath loosed his fateful lightnings, and with woe and death is
>   scored,
> His lust is marching on.

Twain did not confine his comments to the printed page. He spoke freely with the guests he entertained at his rented estate in Riverdale, on the outskirts of New York City—by lovely coincidence an estate where Theodore Roosevelt had lived during the summers of 1870 and 1871, when he was eleven and twelve years old. Often he was invited to speak at formal dinners. He developed a pattern: compliment the guests, tell a witty story or two, and then, once the audience was in his grasp, finish with a barbed attack on imperialism. It was a delicate balance. He had to take special care when he introduced Winston Churchill at the Waldorf-Astoria Hotel on December 12, 1900.

Churchill was just twenty-six years old, but he had become famous in Britain for his exploits as a correspondent covering the Boer War and then as an officer in the South African Light Horse. Anti-imperialists detested him, and some, among them Twain's friend William Dean Howells, boycotted the dinner. Twain agreed to be the toastmaster. He offered his usual mix of sweet and bitter. First came a rambling salute to the history and shared values that bind Great Britain and the United States. Then, at the end, Twain pulled out his rhetorical dagger.

"I think that England sinned when she got herself into a war in South Africa which she could have avoided, just as we sinned in getting into a similar war in the Philippines," he said. "England and America—yes, we are kin. And now that we are also kin in sin, there is nothing more to be desired. The harmony is complete, the blend is perfect."

A few months later Twain was toastmaster at another dinner, this time at his preferred New York club, the Lotos, and discovered that among the guests was none other than Vice President Theodore Roosevelt. He could not allow this chance to pass. Roosevelt was the era's pre-eminent imperialist. Twain was the fieriest zealot on the other side, and he had the speaker's platform. True to form, he began with a fanciful story, about his effort to enact a law creating a police force made up of authors. Slowly he came to his climax. While he was lobbying the legislature for his proposal, he told Roosevelt and the other guests, a "reverend gentleman" had accused him of treason for his attacks on the Philippine War and said "that if I had my just deserts I would not be a guest there, I should be a guest somewhere else maybe, or be dangling from a lamp-post somewhere."

> He hadn't anything personal against me, except that I was opposed to the political war, and he said I was a traitor and didn't go to fight in the Philippines. That doesn't prove anything. That doesn't prove a man is a traitor. . . . It would be an entirely different question if the country's life was in danger, its existence at stake. Then—that is one kind of patriotism— we would all come forward and stand by the flag, and stop thinking about whether the nation was right or wrong. But when there is no question that the nation is in any way in danger, but only some little war away off, then it may be that on the question of politics the nation is divided, half patriots and half traitors—and no man can tell which from which.

Twain's writings and public speeches during 1900 and 1901 made him the anti-imperialist movement's highest-profile star. They are conspicuously absent from many anthologies of his work, due in part to a censorious impulse that began with his wife. "Does it help the world to always rail at it?" she asked him in one letter. "There is great & noble work being done, why not sometimes recognize that? Why always dwell on the evil until those who live beside you are crushed to the earth & you seem almost like a monomaniac?"

Twain agreed that some of his rants were too extreme for public consumption. Privately he looked forward to the day when he could be "as caustic, fiendish and devilish as possible" and publish tirades that would "make people's hair curl." Some fragments later found among his papers, according to one scholar, are "as savage as Fuller's poetry."

Henry Blake Fuller laced his poems with such harsh personal attacks that no publisher would accept them. He appealed to anti-imperialists for contributions, and raised enough money to pay for a volume called *The New Flag*. One of his poems calls Roosevelt "a cut and thrusting bronco-busting / Megaphone of Mars." Another is addressed to McKinley: "Thou sweating chattel slave to swine / Who dost befoul the holy shrine / Of liberty with murder!"

Twain's essays and Fuller's purple verse were part of a new genre, anti-imperialist literature, that began emerging almost immediately after the Senate voted to take the Philippines. Stories, fables, poems, fantastical essays, and even a couple of hastily composed novels gave the movement a new jolt of energy. As anti-imperialists were struggling to recover from a string of defeats, these writers inspired them.

Twain is one of the few who left work of enduring literary value. Another is the poet William Vaughn Moody. His elegiac "An Ode in Time of Hesitation" is a lament that America's "ignoble battle" in the Philippines requires him to point "a slow finger at her shame."

Among the lesser literary products of this debate was a slim novel called *Captain Jinks, Hero*, by the anti-imperialist leader Ernest Crosby, a former New York assemblyman who had traveled to Russia to meet Tolstoy and admired his vision of world peace. *Captain Jinks, Hero* tells the story of an American officer who fights "to free the downtrodden inhabitants of the Cubapine Islands from the tyranny of the ancient

Castalian monarchy." Jinks rails against the "ungrateful Cubapinos," bans the publication of a "clearly seditious" broadside without realizing that it is the Declaration of Independence, approves killing prisoners, witnesses atrocities ("The river was more full of corpses than ever"), and launches a punitive expedition with the order "Exterminate the vermin!" When he returns home, he bathes in glory and is urged to run for president.

The humorist George Ade took a different tack with sixteen witty sketches that he published in the *Chicago Record* and later collected as "Stories of Benevolent Assimilation." Ade's hero is a missionary named Washington Connor, who considers himself a "traveling representative of the civilization of the United States." Connor moves in with a Filipino family, intending to Americanize them, but instead slowly adopts their ways. He discards his coat and starched collar, acquires a tan, discovers the pleasures of smoking, and begins to doubt the wisdom of his mission.

Most of the anti-imperialist poetry published in daily newspapers was, like much of the prose, long on passion but short on quality. Nearly one hundred of the better efforts, with titles such as "The Pirate Flag," "What Would Lincoln Say?," and "To Our Betrayed Allies," were collected into a volume called *Liberty Poems Inspired by the Crisis of 1898–1900*. Katharine Lee Bates, author of "America the Beautiful," wrote a vividly antiwar companion piece called "In the Philippines":

> *We've set the torch to their bamboo town,*
> *And out they come in a scampering rush,*
> *Little brown men with spears.*
> *Shoot!*
> *Down they go in a crush.*

Literary works like these expressed the passion that filled anti-imperialist hearts during 1900 and 1901. Most of them sprung, however, from the social and political elite, and found their audience in that same elite. Ordinary people—the unpersuaded—did not read them. They preferred the irascible bartender Mr. Dooley. He doubted that Americans would ever manage to rule Filipinos, and his monologues resonated with the masses in ways poetry never could.

We say to thim: "Naygurs," we say, "poor, dissolute, uncovered wretches," says we, "ye mis'rable, child-minded apes, we propose f'r to larn ye th' uses iv liberty. . . . We can't give ye anny votes, because we haven't more thin enough to go round now; but we'll threat ye th' way a father shud threat his children if we have to break ivry bone in y'er bodies. So come into our arms," says we. But glory be, 'tis more like a rasslin' match than a father's embrace. . . .

An' there it stands, Hinnissy, with th' indulgent parent kneelin' on the stomach iv his adopted child while a dillygation fr'm Boston bastes him with an umbrella. There it stands, an' how it will come out I din-naw. I'm not much iv an expansionist mesilf.

Taking the Philippines required an act of Congress, a presidential sig-nature, and a war. Taking Cuba posed a different problem: America had promised not to do it. In the Teller Amendment, passed during the frantic spring of 1898, the United States pledged that it would never seek "sovereignty, jurisdiction, or control over said island," and that as soon as fighting ended Americans would "leave the government and control of the island to its people." That sounded noble and fine in the heady days of *Cuba Libre*. It no longer did. American troops were in absolute control of Cuba. Some in Washington asked: Why bring them home? Why not keep Cuba for ourselves?

Expansionists began complaining about the restrictions imposed by the Teller Amendment. The publisher and diplomat Whitelaw Reid, one of McKinley's close advisers, called it a "self-denying ordinance possible only in a moment of national hysteria." Senator Beveridge said it reflected "impulsive but mistaken generosity." General William Shafter, who had commanded American forces in Cuba, pronounced Cubans "no more fit for self-government than gunpowder is for hell." American statesmen faced a dilemma. The *New York Evening Post* framed it well: "Given a solemn and unmistakable promise of independence to Cuba, how can I lie out of it and still go to church and thank God that I am not as other men are?"

Fears that Cuba was not ready for self-government had some basis. Most Cubans were illiterate peasants. A middle class had emerged in

Havana and several provincial towns, and the rebel force had an ordered hierarchy, but few people had any experience with political or civic democracy. Behind the Americans' argument that Cuba was unprepared for independence, however, lay other concerns.

One was racial. American political and military leaders had come to realize that a large portion of Cuba's population, and an even larger portion of its rebel army, were black. Few Americans believed blacks capable of responsible civic life. Senators who wished to discard or evade the Teller Amendment raised the specter of Haiti, which they said was corrupt and anarchic because it was ruled by blacks, and warned that the United States must not tolerate the rise of another "slave republic" in the Caribbean.

The main reason Americans were reluctant to allow Cuban independence, however, transcended race. Lodge, Roosevelt, and their friends had come to realize that Cuban revolutionaries wanted not just independence but also sweeping social reform. If they were allowed to rule Cuba, they would not do what the Americans wanted. Three of their main goals were anathema to the United States: they proposed to limit the amount of land foreigners could own in Cuba, seize large plantations and parcel them out to peasant families, and impose tariffs on imported goods to encourage local business. The biggest landholders in Cuba were American fruit and sugar companies. American investors were digging mines, building railroads, and establishing power companies in Cuba. Exporters counted on the Cuban market. If *Cuba Libre* meant an end to all that, *Cuba Libre* could not be.

The greatest anti-imperialist fear—that the United States would find a way to take Cuba despite the promise of independence it made in the Teller Amendment—seemed to be coming true. Carl Schurz was among those who howled in protest. Only by scrupulously complying with the Teller Amendment, he argued, could America maintain its national honor.

> If this democracy, after all the intoxication of triumph in war, conscientiously remembers its professions and pledges, and soberly reflects on its duties to itself and others, and then deliberately resists the temptation of conquest, it will achieve the grandest triumph of the democratic

idea that history knows of. It will give the government of, by and for the people a prestige it never before possessed. It will render the cause of civilization throughout the world a service without parallel. It will put its detractors to shame, and its voice will be heard in the council of nations with more sincere respect and more deference than ever.

That kind of idealism sounded outlandish to expansionists in Washington. They were looking for a way to wriggle out of the Teller Amendment so the United States could keep control of Cuba. Some suggested formally repealing the amendment, but that seemed likely to provoke another angry battle in Congress. General Leonard Wood, the military governor of Cuba, suggested that the United States simply extend its rule indefinitely and pretend that the amendment did not exist, "while saying as little as possible about the whole thing." Another American officer in Havana, General James Wilson, came up with a more elegant solution. In letters to Lodge and other influential senators, Wilson proposed that Cuba be granted independence, as required by the Teller Amendment, but under a treaty that would "practically bind Cuba, hand and foot, and put her destinies absolutely within our control." This would be a deft way to wipe away the promise of the Teller Amendment while seeming to keep it. McKinley appreciated the sleight of hand.

"The new Cuba yet to arise from the ashes of the past must needs be bound to us by ties of singular intimacy," McKinley said in his second inaugural address, on March 4, 1901. "We must see to it that free Cuba be a reality, not a name, a perfect entity, not a hasty experiment bearing within itself the elements of failure. Our mission, to accomplish which we took up the wager of battle, is not to be fulfilled by turning adrift any loosely framed commonwealth to face the vicissitudes which too often attend weaker States whose natural wealth and abundant resources are offset by the incongruities of their political organization and the recurring occasions for internal rivalries to sap their strength and dissipate their energies."

General Wood set to work designing a singularly powerless Republic of Cuba. He arranged for the election of delegates to a constitutional convention, but even though he sharply circumscribed the electorate, many of the thirty-one delegates turned out to be what he called "political jumping-jacks." One of their first proposals was that the constitution should begin with this declaration: "To Cuba, independence and self-government were assured in the same voice with which war was declared, and to the letter this pledge shall be performed." Wood rejected that out of hand. On the contrary, he said, the constitution would have to guarantee an American "right of intervention."

As the Cuban delegates were realizing the limits of their power, Congress worked to legalize this peculiar form of independence. On February 25, 1901, Senator Orville Platt, chairman of the Senate Committee on Cuban Relations, introduced a bill to make Cuba a new kind of colony, not officially annexed like Hawaii, Puerto Rico, Guam, and the Philippines, but just as fully under Washington's control. Until its repeal more than thirty years later, the Platt Amendment set the paradigm by which the United States dominated Central America, the Caribbean, and many lands farther away: formal independence, rule by natives who cooperated with American businessmen, and military intervention as necessary. This was a giant conceptual leap beyond the classic colonialism that European powers had practiced for centuries, based on direct rule by foreigners. It became a template for American dominance of weak countries. Latin Americans called it *Plattismo*.

The Platt Amendment was actually the work of Lodge, Roosevelt, and Root. It is one of their masterpieces, a pillar of "the large policy." The Platt Amendment affirms Cuba's right to independence, but only under conditions "substantially as follows":

—The government of Cuba shall never enter into any treaty or other compact with any foreign power or powers which will . . . permit [them] to obtain by colonization or for military or naval purposes, or otherwise, lodgment in or control over any portion of said island. . . .

—The government of Cuba consents that the United States may exercise the right to intervene for the preservation of Cuban independence. . . .

—The government of Cuba will sell or lease to the United States lands necessary for coaling or naval stations at certain specified points, to be agreed upon with the President of the United States.

The U.S. Senate approved the Platt Amendment on February 27, in a party-line vote. All forty-three votes in favor came from Republicans and all but three of the opposing votes came from Democrats. The *New York Herald* reported that several senators had been "soothed into acquiescence" with the addition of new projects to the pending River and Harbor bill and extra money for the St. Louis World's Fair, scheduled to open in the summer of 1904. Four days later the House of Representatives voted 161 to 137 in favor of the Platt Amendment, again along party lines. On March 2, when McKinley signed the Army Appropriations Act, to which it was attached, the Platt Amendment became law.

"There is, of course, little or no independence left Cuba under the Platt Amendment," Wood wrote in a letter from Havana.

Wood had prepared for this moment by carefully dispersing veterans of Cuba's independence war. He placated officers with cash payments, plots of land, or jobs as postmasters. For a time he relied on one of them, Juan Rius Rivera, to advise him on agriculture, but after Rius was discovered to have written what Wood called "a very silly letter" advocating Cuban independence, Wood fired him. Later Wood learned that a rebel hero, Máximo Gómez, was living off the charity of friends, and he offered Gómez a sinecure with an annual salary of $5,000. Gómez turned it down, adding poignantly that he wished he had never agreed to American intervention in Cuba.

"None of us thought that it would be followed by a military occupation of the country by our allies, who treat us as a people incapable of acting for ourselves, and who have reduced us to obedience, to submission, and to a tutelage imposed by force of circumstances," Gómez wrote. "This cannot be our fate after years of struggle."

It was indeed their fate. Wood presented delegates at his "constitutional convention" with a stark choice: accept the highly restricted version of independence offered under the Platt Amendment or reject it and trust themselves to the not-so-tender mercies of the United States Congress, where many favored outright annexation. On May 28 the delegates decided, by a margin of fifteen to fourteen, to ratify the constitution Wood had designed.

With that, the Republic of Cuba was born. Wood considered Cubans "as ignorant as children" and resolved to choose their first president for them. He settled on an American citizen, Tomás Estrada Palma, who had been the director of a private school in Central Valley, New York. Wood called an election. Since the result was preordained, Estrada Palma remained in New York instead of campaigning. The sole opposition candidate withdrew.

Cuba had been a colony of Spain for two and a half centuries. In 1901 it became nominally independent but remained securely under American control. The promise of Cuban independence was made to evaporate. That pacified Cuba. Expansionists were now free to focus on their more troublesome task: subduing the Philippines.

A tropical squall was drenching Manila when Brigadier General Frederick Funston kissed his wife goodbye on the morning of February 6, 1901. From his bungalow he made his way to United States military headquarters. The new military governor, Arthur MacArthur, was waiting. MacArthur had approved Funston's mission, but his parting words were hardly encouraging.

"Funston, this is a desperate undertaking," he said. "I fear I shall never see you again."

With that, Funston saluted, took his leave, and headed toward the harbor. Four of his handpicked men and eighty-one native scouts were waiting aboard the USS *Vicksburg*, a newly built navy gunboat. When all was prepared, they set sail. Only then did Funston tell the captain their destination. They were off on a madly daring mission aimed at ending the Philippine War in a single stroke.

American commanders were frustrated by the tenacity of Aguinaldo's force. By the end of 1900 he commanded tens of thousands of guerrillas spread across the archipelago. Aguinaldo had given up hope for a peaceful settlement after Bryan's defeat—"We have failed to waken the lethargic American conscience"—and resolved to wage war without quarter.

General MacArthur wrote in a dispatch that the insurgency represented "almost complete unity of action of the entire native population."

McKinley, ever sensitive to politics, waited until the day after the 1900 election to respond. He summoned his cabinet and reviewed the bad news from the Philippines. All agreed that it was time for a change of strategy. That afternoon, Secretary of War Root sent a stark order to MacArthur: "Start a vigorous campaign at once, pressing the remnants of the Filipino army to the last extremity."

Root told reporters in Washington that the United States Army would henceforth follow a "more rigid policy" in the Philippines. One commander announced ominously that he had ordered his officers to begin using "European methods." Reports of this change in strategy filled front pages around the country.

"Forbearance has ceased to be a military virtue in the Philippines, according to news that came from the War Department today," wrote a correspondent for the *San Francisco Call.*

> Lord Kitchener's plan of operations in South Africa, harsh though it appears to be, appeals to the officials of the War Department, and during the coming campaign in the Philippines, no mercy is to be extended to those in active rebellion or who give aid and comfort to the insurgents. The administration, according to a high official, has become weary of the long-drawn-out war. It has been conciliatory in dealing with insurgents, and efforts to accomplish peace by this means have been met by contempt. It is now proposed to give them a taste of real war, although many innocent may suffer. It is only by this means, it is believed, that the guilty can be reached.

Filipinos soon learned what the Americans meant by "real war." Army units across the archipelago began applying fierce anti-guerrilla tactics, including the torture and killing of civilians, that had previously been used only by especially zealous commanders. This was the first time American soldiers had systematically brutalized a civilian population overseas.

Distribution of rice was tightly controlled to prevent it from reaching rebel fighters. Farmers and their families were herded into camps where many suffered and died. Naval patrols prevented supplies from moving among islands. The Americans also learned to exploit ethnic differences among Filipinos. Most guerrillas were Tagalog, and the Americans recruited men from a rival group, the Macabebe, to serve as scouts and guides. Together they found and captured several guerrilla bands.

Early in 1901 a New York magazine, *The Outlook*, sent one of its star correspondents, the explorer George Kennan—a distant cousin of the later-famous diplomat with the same name—to report on America's newly forceful campaign in the Philippines. His dispatch confirmed much of what anti-imperialists knew and feared.

> The Spaniard used the torture of water, throughout the islands, as a means of obtaining information; but they used it sparingly, and only when it appeared evident that the victim was culpable. Americans seldom do things by halves. We come from here and announce our intention of freeing the people from three or four hundred years of oppression, and say "We are strong and powerful and grand." Then to resort to inquisitorial methods, and use them without discrimination, is unworthy of us and will recoil on us as a nation. It is painful and humiliating to have to confess that in some of our dealings with the Filipinos we seem to be following more or less closely the example of Spain. We have established a penal colony; we have burned native villages near which there has been an ambush or an attack by insurgent guerillas; we kill the wounded; we resort to torture as a means of obtaining information.

None of this bothered General MacArthur. Following direction from Washington, he ordered his officers to pursue a "more rigid policy." No longer should they seek "to avoid all appearance of harshness." Instead they should treat as enemies all Filipinos not explicitly allied to the American cause and hold them "responsible for their actions." Those captured "are not entitled to the privileges of prisoners of war."

"Whenever action is necessary," MacArthur wrote in his orders, "the more drastic the application, the better."

The new strategy had its desired effect. Many Filipinos supported the insurgency, but they could not resist the Americans' scorched-earth tactics.

MacArthur, sensing momentum on his side, issued a proclamation granting amnesty to guerrillas who surrendered, plus a bonus for turning in
a firearm. Thousands accepted. They recognized the overwhelming superiority of American military power. Besides, their leaders had told them
they were destined for victory because Bryan would win the American
presidency, and they were devastated when Bryan lost.

"McKinley, our mortal enemy, who aims at our subjugation, whose
announced plan is to convert us into servants of his servants," one of
Aguinaldo's aides wrote after hearing the news, "McKinley, we repeat,
he who calls us bandits, savages and uneducated, has been re-elected."

Though the guerrillas were weakened, however, the war was by no
means over. American soldiers were still dying almost every day. Despite
renewed efforts at press censorship, news about excesses committed by
soldiers appeared regularly in American newspapers. That fed the war-
weariness that was fodder for Mr. Dooley, Mark Twain, and other doubters. General MacArthur was under pressure to end the conflict quickly.
This was preoccupying him when General Funston turned up at his
headquarters.

Funston brought an outlandish boast accompanied by an irresistible
offer: *I know where Aguinaldo is hiding, and I can capture him.*

Short, compact, and muscular, with red hair and a thin beard, Funston was a romantic adventurer who became the most flamboyant
hero—or villain—of the Philippine War. As a young man he had left
Kansas to test himself against extreme environments in Death Valley and
Alaska. He made his own way to Cuba to fight alongside the insurgents in
1896, before most Americans even knew that a rebellion was under way
there. A year later he returned home to Kansas and joined the state militia after the sinking of the *Maine* in 1898. He was commissioned as a colonel and sent with his regiment to the Philippines, where he quickly won
a reputation for reckless bravery and the nickname "Fearless Freddie."
Just a few months after arriving, he led an amphibious attack that
destroyed a guerrilla position, and for his "most distinguished gallantry"
he was awarded the Medal of Honor. He considered Filipinos "a semi-
savage people" and said his mission was to "rawhide these bullet-headed
Asians until they yell for mercy."

Now, at the age of thirty-five, this swashbuckler was leading a commando raid that he believed would change the course of the Philippine War.

Early in February, while Funston was at an outpost north of Manila, one of his men brought in a prisoner who had been captured carrying encrypted messages and was thought to be a rebel courier. In short order the prisoner was induced to talk; Funston later said his cooperation was voluntary, but some suspected otherwise. From the interrogation, Funston learned that Aguinaldo was in a remote outpost called Palanan awaiting reinforcements. Funston developed an astonishing Trojan horse plan: assemble a force of Macabebe scouts, dress them as insurgents, sail with them to the American base closest to Palanan, lead them on a hundred-mile trek inland, take them into Palanan pretending to be the expected reinforcements, and then surprise and capture Aguinaldo.

With MacArthur's reluctant blessing, Funston and his men set sail as planned. They landed safely and then hiked for two weeks through overgrown mountains, often in heavy rain. At several guerrilla checkpoints, sentries asked the Macabebe why they were traveling with Americans. They had a well-rehearsed answer: *These are prisoners we are delivering to Aguinaldo.*

At three o'clock on the afternoon of March 23, 1901, the disguised force finally reached Palanan. Aguinaldo had assembled an honor guard to receive the "reinforcements" and their American "prisoners."

"The poor little 'Macs' were in such a nervous state," Funston wrote afterward. "They were pretty badly rattled."

Had their ruse been discovered, the "Macs" would certainly have been killed, perhaps along with Funston and his men. To avoid surprises, Funston gave his prearranged signal quickly. Gunfire broke out. One of Aguinaldo's bodyguards fell dead. Aguinaldo reached for his pistol, but one of the Macabebe scouts threw him to the ground before he could draw, and sat on him.

"You are now a prisoner of the Americans!" the scout shouted. Then, to Funston: "We have him!" Aguinaldo was stunned. After a few moments he sputtered, "Is this not some joke?"

News of Aguinaldo's capture astonished the world. Americans

exploded in jubilation. Funston leaped to heroic status overnight. Thomas Edison made a film based on his exploit. There was talk of his running for governor of Kansas, or for president in 1904. Mr. Dooley was not so sure. Aguinaldo's only mistake, he suggested, was that he hadn't known when to quit.

> Th' consul at Ding Dong, th' man that r-runs that end iv th' war, he says to Aggynaldoo: "Go," he says, "where glory waits ye," he says. "Go an' sthrike a blow," he says, "f'r ye'er counthry," he says. . . . He was a good man thin—a good noisy man. Th' throuble was he didn't know whin to knock off. He didn't hear th' wurruk bell callin' him to come in fr'm playin' ball an' get down to business. . . .
>
> Aggynaldoo didn't hear th' whistle blow. He thought th' boom was still on in th' hero business. If he'd come in, ye'd be hearin' that James Haitch Aggynaldoo 'd been appointed foorth-class postmasther at Hootchey-Kootchey; but now th' nex' ye know iv him 'll be on th' blot-ther at th' polis station.

By capturing Aguinaldo alive, Funston deprived Filipinos of a martyr. He also gave Americans the chance to persuade Aguinaldo that his cause had become hopeless and that he should ask his fighters to surrender. Aguinaldo had good reason to consider this offer. His country was ravaged. While he was in custody in Manila, one American commander, General Franklin Bell, casually mentioned to a newspaper reporter that in two years of warfare one-sixth of Luzon's population had either been killed or died of disease. That was probably an exaggeration—it would have amounted to more than half a million people—but it reflected the scale of the conflict.

"The loss of life by killing alone has been very great, but I think than not one man has been slain except where his death has served the legitimate purposes of war," General Bell said. "It has been necessary to adopt what in other countries would probably be thought of as harsh measures."

Bell was awarded the Congressional Medal of Honor for his actions in the Philippines. Newspapers were awed by his zeal. "Our men have been relentless, have killed to exterminate men, women, children, prisoners and captives, active insurgents and suspected people, from lads of ten and up, the idea prevailing that the Filipino, as such, was little better than a dog, a noisome reptile in some instances, whose best disposition was the rubbish heap," wrote a reporter for the *Philadelphia Ledger* who covered Bell's campaign. "It is not civilized warfare, but we are not dealing with civilized people. The only thing they know and fear is force, violence, and brutality, and we give it to them."

Aguinaldo spent his captivity in a comfortable suite at American military headquarters. From his window he could watch soldiers playing football. His family visited. General MacArthur came several times to explain the wonderful future Americans had planned for the Philippines—and also to make clear to Aguinaldo the futility of further resistance. Other Americans also called. Some took him to dinner. Several former guerrilla leaders were brought to counsel him. Finally he gave in. On April 19 he issued a manifesto that was at once a surrender, a call to end the fighting, and a cry of pain in defeat

> The Filipinos have never been dismayed at their weakness, nor have they faltered in following the path pointed out by their fortitude and courage. The time has come, however, in which they find their advance along this path to be impeded by an irresistible force. . . .
>
> There has been enough blood, enough tears, and enough desolation. . . . I cannot refuse to heed the voice of a people longing for peace, nor the lamentations of thousands of families yearning to see their dear ones enjoying the liberty and the promised generosity of the great American Nation. By acknowledging and accepting the sovereignty of the United States throughout the Philippine Archipelago, as I now do, and without any reservation whatsoever, I believe that I am serving thee, my beloved country.

This thunderbolt shattered all assumptions. Millions of Americans celebrated. Army commanders in Manila realized that although more fighting might lie ahead, the tide had turned decisively in their favor. They had converted the enemy leader to their cause, a rare triumph in war.

"The pacification of the Philippines gives a market of ten millions of people," exulted Senator Chauncy Depew of New York. "It will grow every year as they come into more civilized conditions and their wants increase."

Anti-imperialists were stunned to the point of paralysis. Many had imagined Aguinaldo as a resolute patriot who would resist the invader forever and by all means. They had made his cause their own. When he abandoned it, they were bereft. Aguinaldo's capture and conversion made the process of "benevolent assimilation" seem truly inexorable.

Although the United States was on the brink of consummating its conquest of the Philippines, bothersome legal questions remained. What law applied in America's new colonies? What rights should subject peoples enjoy? Newspapers put the dilemma simply: Does the Constitution follow the flag?

Certainly not, argued the McKinley administration. Terms of the military rule that Americans imposed on Cuba, Puerto Rico, Guam, and the Philippines approximated those of martial law. Subject peoples had no right to due legal process, no guarantee against cruel and unusual punishment, no right to choose their own leaders, no right to assemble, and no free speech or free press. Anti-imperialists found this repugnant to America's democratic principles and patently unconstitutional. They presented their argument in a series of lawsuits collectively known as the "insular cases."

On May 27, 1901, the Supreme Court decided the first of these cases, *Downes v. Bidwell*. Justice Edward White, who five years earlier had joined the majority in *Plessy v. Ferguson*, which sanctioned racial segregation, wrote the opinion. Once again he ruled that American law need not protect everyone equally. "The Constitution does not apply to foreign countries," he wrote. "There may be territories subject to the jurisdiction of the United States which are not *of* the United States."

> If those possessions are inhabited by alien races, differing from us in religion, customs, laws, methods of taxation, and modes of thought, the administration of government and justice, according to Anglo-Saxon principles, may for a time be impossible; and the question at once arises whether large concessions ought not to be made for a time, that ultimately our own theories may be carried out, and the blessings

of a free government under the Constitution extended to them. We decline to hold that there is anything in the Constitution to forbid such action.

The vote in this case was as close as could be: five justices to four. The dissent, written by Chief Justice Melville Fuller, reads like a dirge for the death of something sacred.

> Monarchical and despotic governments, unrestrained by written constitutions, may do with newly acquired territories what this government may not do consistently with our fundamental law. To say otherwise is to concede that Congress may, by action taken outside of the Constitution, engraft upon our republican institutions a colonial system such as exists under monarchical governments. Surely such a result was never contemplated by the fathers of the Constitution. . . .
>
> The idea that this country may acquire territories anywhere upon the earth, by conquest or treaty, and hold them as mere colonies or provinces—the people inhabiting them to enjoy only such rights as Congress chooses to accord to them—is wholly inconsistent with the spirit and genius, as well as with the words, of the Constitution.

In 1899 the Senate had ratified the Treaty of Paris by one vote more than the required majority. Its vote on an amendment requiring the United States to free the Philippines as soon as "stable and independent government" emerged there was a tie, forcing the vice president to cast the decisive vote against. The Supreme Court decided the "insular cases" by a one-vote margin. In each of these instances, the change of a single person's mind would have made American overseas expansion effectively impossible.

These excruciatingly narrow margins, however, obscure a larger political reality. Americans were eager for the adventure of conquest. They had been convinced that the stability of their economy, and of the United States itself, depended on taking foreign lands. Neither Congress nor the Supreme Court would stand in their way. "A false step at this time might be fatal to the development of what Chief Justice Marshall called the 'American Empire,'" Justice White reasoned in his opinion.

He was acknowledging that laws are not made or applied in a vacuum. Even Mr. Dooley noticed the political tint of his ruling.

"Some say it laves the flag up in th' air and some say that's where it laves th' constitution. Annyhow, something's in the air. But there's wan thing I'm sure about."

"What's that?" asked Mr. Hennessey.

"That is," said Mr. Dooley, "no matter whether th' constitution follows th' flag or not, th' supreme coort follows th' election returns."

The anti-imperialist movement, already disheartened by McKinley's re-election, suffered three heavy blows in that spring of 1901. First Aguinaldo was captured. Then he issued a proclamation giving up his struggle and accepting American power. Finally, the Supreme Court ruled in the "insular cases" that it was legal for the United States to rule foreign lands indefinitely by decree.

Anti-imperialists held only a couple of public meetings during those disheartening months. They faced an obvious question: What can we do now? The Chicago lawyer and civic reformer Edwin Burritt Smith proposed an answer. Since the United States had acquired new territories, Smith argued, anti-imperialists should dedicate themselves to two goals: moving the new territories toward independence as quickly as possible and ensuring that the United States seized no more.

These seemed goals to which President McKinley might be amenable. On July 4 he declared the end of military rule over the Philippines and gave William Howard Taft the gentle-sounding new title of civil governor. Taft had said repeatedly that he wanted to work with America's "little brown brothers," not fight them.

Many American soldiers felt differently. They had become accustomed to scorched-earth campaigns and other "European methods." One composed a drinking song that became an unofficial anthem:

I'm only a common soldier in the blasted Philippines.
They say I've got brown brothers here but I don't know
*   what that means.*
I like the word fraternity but still, I draw the line.

*He may be a brother of Big Bill Taft, but he ain't no
brother of mine.*

On the same day Taft took office as civil governor of the Philippines—July 4, 1901—the American Anti-Imperialist League issued its first major statement since McKinley's re-election eight months earlier. It was endorsed by six of the league's most active chapters and also by movement stalwarts including Carl Schurz, Charles Eliot Norton, George Boutwell, William Dean Howells, and Mark Twain. The old lions were not ready to surrender. Many had been schooled on inspiring stories about the decades-long struggle to outlaw slavery, or had participated in the struggle itself, with all its reverses and disappointments. They had reason to hope that anti-imperialism would also triumph in the end.

> The Anti-Imperialist Leagues of the United States have been silent since the presidential election, but not because they have lost faith in their cause or believe the battle lost. They had hoped that those who voted for Mr. McKinley, while disapproving his policy in the West Indies and the Philippines, would see that their votes were misinterpreted, and would make their disappointment known and felt. They had hoped that Congress would claim its place in our government, and would insist that the principle of freedom must be recognized and applied wherever our country holds sway. They had hoped that the Supreme Court would with no uncertain voice declare that no human being under our control could be without the rights secured by our Constitution. . . . These hopes have not been realized [and] the war in the Philippines has been prosecuted with unrelenting cruelty until the resistance of the unhappy islanders seems to have been crushed. . . .
>
> The incoming Congress is not yet committed to the policy of incorporating the island peoples into our system without rights. Let it resume its position in the government in defense of the inalienable rights of man.

Those were brave words, but the anti-imperialists had every reason to be discouraged. Despite more than three years of ceaseless work, they had achieved none of their major goals. The interests that defeated them were rich and powerful, but many of the movement's leaders took the blame upon themselves. They admitted that their arguments had been too abstract and moralistic. Some concluded that the very name of their movement was wrong because it sounded negative, whereas the imperial project sounded dynamic and positive. In Boston, several prominent activists quit the New England Anti-Imperialist League and formed a new group, the Philippine Information Society. The movement was fragmenting, searching for a new course in an America that had, Mark Twain groused, "gone to hell."

During the summer of 1901, several newspapers reported that American soldiers in the Philippines were operating under unwritten orders to take no prisoners. Casualty figures showed that five times as many Filipinos were being killed as wounded, the opposite of the usual case in war. Asked about these reports, General MacArthur said that while Governor Taft might be inclined toward benevolence, soldiers in the field were still under orders to use "very drastic" tactics.

As autumn approached, anti-imperialist leaders bravely announced that they had come up with a new strategy. It embodied what Edwin Burritt Smith had recommended in Chicago: political action to elect more anti-imperialists to Congress, coupled with public campaigns encouraging McKinley to free America's new wards as quickly as possible. McKinley had been reluctant to take foreign territories in the first place; it seemed reasonable to believe that, once they were pacified, he would consider granting them independence. Persuading him to do so would be slow work, but there was plenty of time. He had just been re-elected. Anti-imperialists hoped that over the next three and a half years, if self-governing institutions emerged on captured islands, he would see the wisdom of their cause.

As the great events of 1901 captivated Americans, one familiar voice was notably absent. Theodore Roosevelt had disappeared into the vice presidency just as completely as his enemies had hoped. After being sworn in with McKinley on March 4, he presided over the Senate for parts of the next four days. Then the Senate declared its customary nine-month recess. Most lawmakers left Washington. Roosevelt retired to Oyster Bay.

Before leaving, Roosevelt approached Justice White of the Supreme Court with an odd request: Would the justice tutor him in law? White was taken aback. Finally he agreed to give the new vice president a list of books to read during the summer, after which the two men would discuss them. Roosevelt was preparing for the future. He recognized that by the time his term ended in 1904, the public might well have forgotten him and his political career would be over. A law license would help him find work.

That summer all New Yorkers, and many people around the country, were fixated on the dazzling Pan-American Exposition in Buffalo. Years in the making, it was intended as a celebration of "commercial well-being and good understanding among the American Republics." The 350-acre fairground was a sprawling carnival featuring shaded colonnades, a stadium modeled after one in ancient Greece, twenty-six towering sculptures, grandly domed Beaux-Arts exhibit halls, a mile-long Grand Canal complete with gondola rides and "mirror lakes," a Temple of Music, and a Court of Fountains "brilliantly and fantastically illuminated" with hydroelectric power from nearby Niagara Falls. New inventions on display ranged from an X-ray machine to a Kodak Brownie camera. The most popular attractions were forty-two "foreign villages" intended to showcase the lives of lesser peoples. Among them were Darkest Africa, where visitors could stare at "the largest and most interesting company of blacks that has landed in America since slavery days"; Indian Congress, presenting "long-haired painted savages in all their barbaric splendor"; Old Plantation, "introducing 150 Southern darkies in their plantation songs and dances"; and Philippine Village, where performers "wash their clothes tropical fashion by slapping them on stones, hold cock-fights, ride about on awkward water-buffalo, and give you every opportunity to see them live."

An event of this magnitude required inauguration by the president. McKinley duly accepted the honor, but at the last moment his wife, who was nervous and sickly, fell ill. McKinley decided to stay with her in Washington and announced that Vice President Roosevelt would open the exposition in his place. He promised that he and his wife would visit later. Roosevelt welcomed the chance to appear in the president's place. He was a great proponent of unity among Western Hemisphere states—under United States hegemony, of course—and had done much to promote the Pan-American Exposition. A short film shot on May 20 shows him leading a parade around the fairground, looking proud.

Opening the Pan-American Exposition was Roosevelt's only official duty during that quiet spring and summer. He had plenty of time to read his law books. Twice he traveled to western states. Occasionally he made speeches, always returning to familiar themes. He warned students at Clark University in Massachusetts not to develop "that kind of idealism which makes you filled with vague thoughts of beneficence for mankind." At the Minnesota State Fair he asserted, "It is our duty toward the people living in barbarism to see that they are freed from their chains, and we can only do it by destroying barbarism itself." On September 5 he told an audience in Burlington, Vermont, that American rule was "giving to the Philippines a degree of freedom which they could never have attained had we permitted them to fall into anarchy or under tyranny."

The day after delivering that speech, Roosevelt decamped to Isle La Motte, near the Canadian border in Lake Champlain, where his friend Nelson Fisk, a former lieutenant governor of Vermont, had an estate. There he spent a long afternoon eating and drinking with more than a thousand guests invited by the Vermont Fish and Game League. His speech was short and refreshingly non-political.

"I am interested in all furred, finned, and feathered inhabitants of the woods and waters," he said. "These things prevent the tameness and monotony that sometimes comes into life."

After Roosevelt's speech, it was announced that he would retire briefly and then return for a reception so guests could greet him. He was walking into Fisk's home when a telephone rang. Fisk answered, listened for a moment, then silently beckoned Roosevelt inside. He locked the door behind them. Soon the mansion's other doors were being locked. Guards sprang up in front of them. Murmurs rippled through the crowd. After a few minutes, Senator Redfield Proctor emerged.

"Friends, a cloud has fallen over this happy event," Proctor told the uneasy crowd. "It is my sad duty to inform you that President McKinley, while in the Temple of Music at Buffalo, was this afternoon shot by an anarchist, two bullets having taken their effect. His condition is said to be serious, but we hope that later intelligence may prove the statement to be exaggerated."

At Proctor's words, according to the next day's *Burlington Free Press*, "a moan of sorrow went up from the entire assemblage, and women and strong men burst into tears." Roosevelt was escorted onto a yacht and taken to Burlington. There, after reading a sheaf of messages, he boarded a special train for Buffalo.

10

You Will Get Used to It

Dawn had not yet broken when a crowd began gathering outside the entrance to the Pan-American Exposition on Thursday, September 5, 1901. It swelled to thousands by the time the gates opened at six o'clock. All were there to cheer President McKinley, who had reached a peak of popularity. Lusty applause broke out when he stepped onto the exposition's main stage at mid-morning. In his speech he returned to a theme that had become one of his favorites. Subduing foreign lands so they must trade with the United States, he said, was the way to sell "our increasing surplus."

"Our capacity to produce has increased so enormously, and our products have so multiplied, that the problem of more markets requires our urgent and immediate attention," McKinley declared. "The expansion of our trade and commerce is the pressing problem."

After speaking, the president toured several of the exposition's main attractions and then retired to a hotel. Later he and his wife watched a fireworks display culminating in a burst that spelled out "Welcome to McKinley, Chief of our Nation."

The next day's schedule called for McKinley to appear at the cavernous Temple of Music and shake the hand of any paying customer willing to wait in line. This worried his personal secretary George Cortelyou. A violent strain of anarchism had seized some radical minds in Europe and set off a rash of political assassinations. Victims had included President Sadi Carnot of France, Prime Minister Antonio Canovas of Spain, Empress Elisabeth of Austria-Hungary, and King Umberto of Italy. The thought of uncontrolled thousands filing past McKinley at the Palace of Music disturbed Cortelyou, and he ordered the event canceled. McKinley restored it to the schedule. Cortelyou then asked him personally to reconsider.

"Why should I?" McKinley replied. "No one would wish to hurt me."

McKinley spent Friday morning touring Niagara Falls. By midafternoon he was ready for his meet-and-greet. He was briskly efficient at such events, reportedly able to shake fifty hands per minute with a two-handed technique that allowed him to move the line quickly along. Soon after the doors were opened, a young girl asked him for the red carnation that he habitually wore in his lapel as a good luck charm. He gave it to her. Bunting was draped behind him. An organist played Bach.

At 4:07, an unshaven young man with his right hand wrapped in a bandage came to the head of the line. As McKinley reached toward him, he thrust the bandaged hand forward. Inside he had concealed a .32 caliber pistol. He fired twice, and McKinley fell.

After a moment's shock, McKinley looked up and said, "My wife— be careful, Cortelyou, how you tell her. Oh, be careful." Then, seeing security agents subduing the gunman, he pleaded, "Go easy on him, boys. He could not have known."

What followed was a tragic comedy of errors. McKinley was rushed to a clinic on the grounds of the exposition. There it was determined that one of the bullets had glanced away, but the other was lodged in his abdomen. Surgery did not begin until 5:20. It was carried out by a gynecologist who had never before operated on a traumatic wound. Despite much poking he could not find the bullet, which was ominous because it was lead and could cause infection. Medical personnel might have found it with the X-ray machine that was conveniently on display nearby, but no one knew how to use it. Nonetheless, doctors issued an encouraging bulletin.

"Condition at the conclusion of the operation was gratifying," they reported. "The result cannot be foretold. His condition at present justifies hope of recovery."

By the time Roosevelt arrived the next morning from Vermont,

McKinley had rallied. A couple of days later the president's advisers asked Roosevelt to leave Buffalo in order to allay public fears. Roosevelt traveled to the Adirondacks, in northeastern New York, where his wife, children, several friends, and two park rangers were waiting. He had long wanted to conquer Mount Marcy, the tallest peak in the range. Early on Friday, September 13, facing the extreme weather he loved most—cold rain and swirling fog—he and his companions set out. They climbed over rocks and along wet trails for several hours, reaching the summit at midday. The sun broke briefly, giving them a spectacular vista.

From the peak, Roosevelt and his party descended to a lake called Tear-of-the-Clouds. They found a spot by the shore and unpacked sandwiches. At 1:25 a ranger appeared from the woods. He was carrying a yellow telegram. McKinley's condition had suddenly worsened.

Back at base camp, Roosevelt waited through the evening for news. It came at eleven o'clock in a brief message from one of McKinley's aides: "Lose no time coming." A buckboard was waiting outside. Roosevelt rode through the night, with two changes of driver and horse team, to the train station at North Creek, New York. The third driver knew McKinley had died, but said nothing because "I did not want to add to Mr. Roosevelt's anxiety." Roosevelt was told when he arrived at North Creek.

The assassin was a twenty-eight-year-old former steelworker named Leon Czolgosz. According to one of his friends, Czolgosz had been angered by "outrages committed by the American government in the Philippine Islands." He became an anarchist. When the murderer of King Umberto declared that it was time for common people to take history into their own hands, he decided to strike against McKinley. At his trial, lawyers argued that he was innocent by reason of insanity. He refused to testify in his own defense, was convicted in short order, and was electrocuted on October 29. His last words were "I killed the President because he was the enemy of the good people—the good working people. I am not sorry for my crime." After electrocution his body was destroyed with sulfuric acid.

No one else was tried for the assassination, but when it turned out that Czolgosz had met the anarchist leader Emma Goldman, police in Chicago arrested her. She was vilified in the press. Her portrait appeared in the *Chicago Daily Tribune* with the headline EMMA GOLDMAN, HIGH

PRIESTESS OF ANARCHY, WHOSE SPEECHES INCITED CZOLGOSZ TO HIS CRIME. The ordeal stunned her. She was released after two weeks and retreated into a period of seclusion.

In the search for culprits, some angry Republicans turned their sights on William Randolph Hearst. During 1901 Hearst had pursued politics more directly than ever. He traveled the country organizing his network of Democratic Clubs, which he hoped to build into a base for a future presidential campaign, and ingratiated himself to Bryan by making him a "special correspondent" and sending him on a tour of Europe. In the pages of the *New York Journal* he attacked McKinley ever more stridently. After governor-elect William Goebel of Kentucky was murdered in 1900, the *Journal* ran a ditty by Ambrose Bierce suggesting that since no bullet had been found in Goebel's body, it might be "speeding here / To stretch McKinley on his bier." Later the *Journal* published an editorial oddly sympathetic to the idea of political murder. "If bad institutions and bad men can be got rid of only by killing," it concluded, "then the killing must be done."

Under other circumstances these lines might have been dismissed as typically overblown, and quickly forgotten. After McKinley's assassination they were used to paint Hearst as a virtual accomplice. "The verses," Bierce wrote later, "variously garbled and mostly made into an editorial, or a news dispatch with a Washington dateline but no date, were published all over the country as evidence of Mr. Hearst's complicity in the crime." Death threats flooded in. Hearst began keeping a revolver in his desk. He refused to open packages addressed to him. That spring his picture had appeared on the cover of *Editor and Publisher* with the title "The Foremost Figure in American Journalism." By autumn he found himself pilloried by Republicans who had been waiting for a chance to strike at him.

"His reclamation and elevation to the plane of honorable men is not to be thought of," one wrote. "He will always remain the degraded, unclean thing that he is."

Henry Cabot Lodge was among the incensed. On September 7, when it still appeared that McKinley would recover from his wounds, he wrote to Roosevelt, "Every scoundrel like Hearst and his satellites, who for whatever purposes appeals to and inflames evil human passion, has made himself accessory before the fact to every crime of this nature." As public and private attacks mounted, Hearst's reputation, never unblemished, suffered seriously. He still owned newspapers in New York, Chicago, San Francisco, and Los Angeles, and remained a powerful figure. Yet he was thrown so fully off balance that he felt compelled to reassure his mother, who was also his principal financier.

"All that distresses me," he wrote, "is the fear that you will be hurt by the wicked assertions in hostile newspapers."

In such tragic circumstances, no one would speak ill of the murdered McKinley. Mark Twain, however, reacted by writing a remarkable poem called "My Last Thought" in which he imagines what might have flashed through McKinley's mind in his last hours. Twain immediately filed this poem in his thick do-not-publish folder, and it remained unknown for more than half a century. "I was only weak, not bad," it begins. In verse after verse, the tormented McKinley pleads for forgiveness. He confesses that he was unfit for the presidency, "a lost & wandering atom in that vast seat / which only Lincolns & their like compactly fill." The climax is poignant.

> *Overborne by sordid counsels,*
> *Base ambitions, from my head I took*
> *The precious laurel I had earned, & in its place*
> *I set this poor tin glory, now my wear,*
> *Of World-Power, Conqueror of helpless tribes,*
> *Extinguisher of struggling liberties! . . .*
> *Sleep & forget, sleep and forget—*
> *If that dear boon might be mine!*

For Roosevelt the turn of events was shocking beyond description. He had been placidly studying his law books, hoping for a political break but realistic enough to realize that it was uncertain. Now, at the age of forty-two, he was the youngest-ever president of the United States. With astonishing suddenness, the world had been laid at his feet. It was not precisely his to command, but the moment at which he rose to power, combined with the forcefulness of his personality and beliefs, made him the first American president with global ambition and global power.

A judge administered the oath of office to Roosevelt at a private home in Buffalo. He promised to "continue absolutely unbroken the policy of President McKinley for the peace, prosperity, and honor of our beloved country." Roosevelt, though, was never one to continue what anyone else did. In some ways he was strikingly different from his slain predecessor. Most important, he believed passionately in "the large policy" that McKinley had promoted only halfheartedly.

"I told William McKinley that it was a mistake to nominate this man in Philadelphia!" Senator Hanna ranted on the funeral train from Buffalo to Washington. "I asked him if he realized what would happen if he should die. Now look! That damned cowboy is President of the United States!"

Roosevelt's ascension to the presidency dealt a deadly blow to the anti-imperialist movement. It seemed to end the battle fully and finally. Those who plotted to make the United States a global military power had won. Czolgosz's bullet was the coup de grâce that killed America's first anti-imperialist movement.

Thirty-nine months passed between the birth of the movement at Faneuil Hall on June 15, 1898, and Roosevelt's inauguration on September 14, 1901. At several points during that period, the anti-imperialists had come tantalizingly close to triumph. They lost Senate votes and Supreme Court cases by narrow margins, and might have taken the White House in 1900 if their hero Bryan had not turned his back on them. Now their last hope—to convert the president to their cause—was dashed. McKinley might one day have lost interest in occupying foreign lands. Roosevelt, however, considered overseas expansion to be America's providential mission, and he had risen to ultimate power.

Roosevelt had every reason to be thrilled by his rise, despite the circumstances. Lodge could feel even more satisfied. He directed this drama brilliantly. Years before, he had realized that the United States would fully adopt "the large policy" only if it was led by a president who embraced it without reservation. For years he methodically groomed Roosevelt for the role. His last move was the wiliest: maneuvering Roosevelt into the vice presidency. It was risky, but it produced the desired result sooner than he had imagined possible.

Lodge was in Paris when he learned that McKinley had been shot. He was uncertain about details until Roosevelt sent him a reassuring cable. Lodge replied with a witty note warning Roosevelt to stay away from anarchists. When McKinley died, both men were subdued. Lodge had been denied the chairmanship of the Senate Foreign Relations Committee in a bitter seniority battle, and some thought he would leave the Senate to become his best friend's secretary of state. He did not seek the job, though, and on September 19 he wrote to Roosevelt saying he had heard that Secretary of State Hay was to remain at his post and adding, "I hope it is so."

Immediately after returning to the United States a couple of weeks later, Lodge visited the White House. He and Roosevelt talked until late at night. They soon became closer than ever. "Hardly a day passed, at least during the earlier years of Roosevelt's administration, which did not see the two men in consultation," one biographer has written.

> The Senator had a door cut into his library and a stairway built from the courtyard of his Massachusetts Avenue home to give direct access from the outside, so that the President could call upon him without the formality of using the front door and going through the house. Even when the two did not ride together, Roosevelt as likely as not would pop in for a drink and talk in the late afternoon. Most of Roosevelt's messages were written only after consultation in the Lodge library.

The Roosevelt administration began with a period of good feeling. People were shocked by McKinley's assassination and eager to give their new leader time to settle into his job. American investors acquired interests in Cuba, Puerto Rico, Hawaii, and the Philippines.

Anti-imperialists said nothing because there was nothing for them to say. A group of them met in New York soon after Roosevelt ascended to the presidency. Carl Schurz and Mark Twain offered a resolution proposing that "the Anti-Imperialist League should for the time being confine itself to disseminating knowledge and sound opinion on the subject of the Philippines, keeping itself in the background as much as possible." All agreed. Twain, according to minutes of the meeting, said he believed "an aggressive policy was not wise now."

Proceeding methodically to consolidate "the large policy," Lodge and Roosevelt decided that their first diplomatic priority must be to secure

Senate ratification of the Hay-Pauncefote Treaty between the United States and Great Britain, which set conditions for construction of a canal across Central America. It was duly ratified on February 21, 1902. Before the empire builders could move on to planning the canal, however, they were suddenly distracted by a new crisis that was also an old one. American soldiers in the Philippines had been implicated in savage crimes. The war was not over after all. Some anti-imperialists saw an unexpected chance to break out of the sarcophagus into which their movement was being sealed.

The scandal broke from Samar, an island in the eastern Philippines whose people were known for rebelliousness. American troops had sought to break their resistance with the familiar tactics of burning crops, killing livestock, taking hostages, forcing civilians into guarded camps, and capturing or sinking vessels approaching the coast. They succeeded in reducing much of the island to hunger and disease. At their base in the river town of Balangiga, they learned on September 26 of McKinley's assassination and held a memorial service. The next morning they awoke as usual to six o'clock reveille. Twenty minutes later, scores of villagers threw off disguises and others burst from hiding places. They attacked the Americans, many of whom were unarmed, with knives and axes. More than forty fell dead. Twenty-six survivors, most of them seriously wounded, staggered to boats and, keeping the insurgents at bay with rifle fire, managed to flee.

Reports of the "Balangiga massacre" gripped the United States. Newspapers presented it as an unprovoked attack by crazed savages on those who had come to civilize them. Outraged editorials ranked it among the most disastrous military engagements Americans had ever suffered, along with the Alamo and Custer's Last Stand.

Mark Twain spat back into the public eye with an essay defending Filipino rebels as "not worse than were our Christian Ku-Klux gangs of a former time, nor than are our churchgoing negro-burners of today." His volley was drowned out by thunderous cries for revenge. In the Philippines they were led by General Adna Chaffee, who had replaced Arthur MacArthur as military governor. Chaffee had clashed several times with his civilian counterpart, Governor Taft, who was still preaching cooperation with America's "little brown brothers." He blamed the Balangiga attack on Taft's "silly talk of benevolence" and vowed to subdue Samar by "shot, shells, and bayonets." For the task he chose a sixty-two-year-old veteran of the Civil War and Indian campaigns, Brigadier General Jacob "Hell-Roaring Jake" Smith.

Americans had no way of learning about General Smith's campaign in Samar as it was happening. Over the next few months, though, disturbing reports began filtering back to the United States. They were accompanied by a new wave of evidence, much of it provided by returning soldiers, that the torture and killing of civilians remained common in the Philippines despite impressions that the war was ending. Anti-imperialists, sensing an opportunity, demanded an investigation. Ultimately the Senate reached a compromise. It accepted Senator Hoar's proposal to establish a special investigating committee, thrilling anti-imperialists, who believed they could use it as a platform to attack the war and reawaken the nation's civic conscience. Soon afterward, though, Lodge maneuvered to be named the committee's chairman. This guaranteed that its investigation would be forgiving.

Lodge gaveled his new Senate Committee on the Philippines to order for the first time on January 26, 1902. Over the next six months he convened it irregularly. Most hearings were closed to journalists. This was necessary, Lodge explained, because "the committee room was totally inadequate for their accommodation."

Acting behind the scenes as usual, Lodge shaped a witness list heavy with stalwarts including Governor Taft, Admiral Dewey, and General Otis, all certain to wave the flag and defend the war's nobility. No anti-imperialists were invited. Lodge turned down an application from the Boston propagandist Edward Atkinson on the grounds that since Atkinson had never visited the Philippines, his testimony would be hearsay. Democrats on the committee wanted to call Aguinaldo and other Filipino leaders, but Lodge refused. Nor would he accept testimony from newspaper correspondents who had covered the war. By one account he guided the hearings with "all the power of a judge, and there was no question where his sympathies lay."

While Lodge presided over the hearings, Albert Beveridge took the role of aggressive prosecutor. He browbeat soldiers who testified about abuses and scorned critics of annexation as apologists for terror. At one session he had a sharp exchange with Governor Taft over Taft's proposal to convene an advisory council of Filipino notables, which he warned would cause "all sorts of trouble for us." On the delicate question of the army's conduct in the Philippines, however, Taft was as effusive as Beveridge could have wished. He testified, according to one account, that "never had a war been conducted in which more compassion, more restraint, and more generosity had been exhibited than in connection with the American war in the Philippines." Under questioning from a skeptical senator, Taft admitted that there had been "some retaliation on the part of small bands of Americans," along with "some cases of unnecessary killing, some cases of whipping, and some cases of what was called the water cure." He said this was to be expected. Senator Thomas Patterson, a Democrat from Colorado, asked him to elaborate.

"When war is conducted by a superior race against those whom they consider inferior in the scale of civilization," Patterson asked, "is it not the experience of the world that the superior race will almost involuntarily practice inhuman conduct?"

"There is much greater danger in such a case than dealing with whites," Taft agreed. "There is no doubt about that."

Lodge had decided that the best course for promoters of the Philippine War to pursue at this point was to admit isolated abuses but insist that the war was being fought humanely and with exemplary restraint. Secretary of War Root took this line of argument to an extreme. In a letter to the committee, he said he had investigated all reports of misconduct in the Philippines and found that "in substantially every case . . . the report has proved to be unfounded or grossly exaggerated."

"The war on the part of the Filipinos has been conducted with the barbarous cruelty common among uncivilized races," Root asserted. "[It] has been conducted by the American Army with scrupulous regard for the rules of civilized warfare, with careful and genuine consideration for the prisoner and the non-combatant, with self-restraint and with humanity never surpassed, if ever equaled, in any conflict, worthy of praise and reflecting credit on the American people."

Language like this was so clearly exaggerated that it seemed calculated to provoke critics of the war. If so, it had the desired effect. Anti-imperialists in Congress were already seething at Lodge's success in winning the chairmanship of the Committee on the Philippines. After the first couple of hearings, an angry Senator Hoar demanded to know why the committee was not investigating "the killing of prisoners, the shooting without trial of suspected persons, the use of torture, the use of savage allies, the wanton destruction of private property, and every other barbarous method of waging war which this Nation from its infancy has ever condemned."

Tensions in the Senate rose steadily. On February 23 they exploded. One newspaper called it "a thrilling and sensational scene."

The Senate was debating the Philippines that day, and speeches were full of rancor. Senator John Spooner, a supporter of the war, needled his anti-imperialist colleagues by reminding them that they had not even been able to hold the loyalty of their supposed champion William Jennings Bryan. This was still a sore spot for the anti-imperialists. One of them, Ben Tillman, rose to take the bait.

"I have many friends on the Republican side," Tillman said. "Personally, you are a nice, clean-hearted set of men, but politically you are the most infamous cowards and hypocrites that ever happened."

Nervous laughter rippled through the chamber. Spectators in the galleries fell silent. Tillman pressed further. Corruption, not Bryan's betrayal, he said, had been the key to ratifying the Treaty of Paris. He knew of the corruption firsthand, since he had spent more than a year watching the other senator from South Carolina, John McLaurin, run the rewarding federal patronage machine in their state after deciding at the last moment to vote for ratification.

"You know how those votes were secured!" Tillman cried, angrily shaking a forefinger at the Republican side.

"How were they secured?" Spooner innocently asked.

"I know, if the Senator does not," Tillman replied. "I know that improper influences were used in getting those votes."

"Name the man!"

"I know that the patronage, the federal patronage of a state, has been parceled out to a Senator since the ratification of that treaty."

"What state?"

"South Carolina."

"Then I leave you to fight the matter out with your colleague."

"Well, I never shirk the responsibility for a statement I make. I know that he voted for the treaty. I know that improper influences were brought to bear. I know what I believe."

"You simply believe what you do not know."

McLaurin was not in the chamber, and the colloquy ended there. Tillman went on with his speech. He read letters from veterans, including one reporting 160 cases of "water cure" in the Philippines that had caused 134 deaths. Moments after he finished, the man he had impugned burst in. A *New York Times* correspondent vividly reported the scene.

> Scarcely had [Tillman] resumed his seat when there was enacted one of the most sensational scenes ever witnessed in the history of the United States Senate. Pale to the lips, and trembling with the emotion which in vain he endeavored to control, Mr. McLaurin rose and addressed the Senate, speaking to a question of personal privilege. Instantly a hush fell over the Senate and over the people in the thronged galleries. The very atmosphere seemed surcharged with excitement. With breathless interest, the auditors, both on the floor and in the galleries, hung upon every word uttered by the Senator from South Carolina. . . . All seemed to realize that a portentous event was about to happen.

McClaurin was a lawyer and former South Carolina attorney general who, on the day the Treaty of Paris was to be ratified, had seen a political opportunity and taken it. Now he was called to play the role of outraged innocent. He performed well.

"During my absence a few moments ago from the Senate chamber in attendance upon the Committee on Indian Affairs, the Senator who has just taken his seat said that improper influences had been used in changing the vote of somebody on that treaty, and then went on later and said that it applied to the Senator from South Carolina," McLaurin told the hushed chamber. "I now say that the statement is a willful, malicious, and deliberate lie."

At that Tillman leaped from his seat, lunged at McLaurin, and punched him above his left eye. McLaurin struck back. Blood spilled

from Tillman's nose. The two senators flailed at each other until colleagues and a sergeant-at-arms finally pulled them apart. "The Senate
never in its history had received such a shock," the *Times* reported.

Both combatants were later censured. There were no more fistfights
in the Senate, but Washington remained tense as the Philippine hearings
continued. Though supposedly closed, they made great newspaper copy.
Stories about testimony by the first witnesses, Dewey and Otis, ran alongside reports of a cholera epidemic in the Philippines that ultimately
killed more than a hundred thousand people. Lodge summoned a handful of veterans, carefully selected from a War Department "safe list,"
and was embarrassed by their frank talk. No fewer than six said they had
witnessed the "water cure," other tortures, or reprisal killings. All said,
however, that these were reasonable tactics when fighting an enemy who
showed what one called "inability to appreciate human kindness."

General Robert Hughes, who had commanded units in several parts
of the Philippines, testified that he routinely ordered the burning of
Filipino villages in order to deny shelter to insurgents. Senator Joseph
Rawlins of Utah drew him out.

> *Rawlins:* If these shacks were of no consequence, what was the utility
> of their destruction?
>
> *Hughes:* The destruction was a punishment. They permitted these
> people to come in there and conceal themselves, and they gave
> no sign.
>
> *Rawlins:* The punishment in that case would fall, not upon the men,
> who could go elsewhere, but mainly upon the women and little
> children.
>
> *Hughes:* The women and children are part of the family, and where
> you wish to inflict a punishment, you can punish the man prob-
> ably worse in that way than in any other.
>
> *Rawlins:* But is that within the ordinary rules of civilized warfare?
> Of course you could exterminate the family which would be still
> worse punishment.
>
> *Hughes:* These people are not civilized.

Rawlins: But is that within the ordinary rules of civilized warfare?

Hughes: No, I think it is not.

Weeks of this kind of testimony focused public attention back on the Philippine War. Once again it was looking misbegotten. The anti-imperialists had warned that it would lure Americans into political and moral quagmires. They felt vindicated.

"It is most provoking, we know, for anti-imperialists to pretend they are still alive," observed the *New York Evening Post*. "They have been killed so often. After 1899 we were to hear no more of them. In 1900 they were again pronounced dead, although like the obstinate Irishman, they continued to protest that if they were dead, they were not conscious of it. Last year the slain were slaughtered once more, and that time buried as well, with all due ceremony. Yet the impudent creatures have resumed activity during the last few months as if their epitaphs had not been composed again and again."

President Roosevelt was worried. In two years he would have to run for election in his own right, and he did not want to face charges that he tolerated atrocities in the Philippines. Seeking to prove his rectitude, he approved the court-martial of several American officers implicated in war crimes.

This began as a standard prosecution of scapegoats, which happens often in war, but it soon spiraled out of control. Under questioning, one defendant, Major Anthony Waller, revealed what became the war's most shocking scandal. He said that while he was serving in a reprisal campaign on Samar, General Smith had given him extermination orders.

"I want no prisoners," Smith had told him. "I wish you to kill and burn. The more you kill and burn, the better you will please me. I want all persons killed who are capable of bearing arms in actual hostilities against the United States."

Waller asked for an age guideline, and Smith replied, "Ten years."

"Persons ten years and over are those designated as being able to bear arms?"

"Yes."

Smith then ordered that Samar "be made a howling wilderness." His officers and men complied. According to their own testimony, they razed every village they found, usually massacring civilians.

Newspapers covered this new scandal with horror and delight. "If we are to 'benevolently assimilate' Filipinos by such methods, we should frankly so state, and drop our canting hypocrisy about having to wage war on these people for their own betterment," wrote the New Orleans *Times Picayune*. Thrilled anti-imperialists awoke from their slumber and leaped into action.

Public outrage at news of General Smith's tactics became so intense that Roosevelt had no choice but to order him court-martialed as well. This was a rash but necessary measure. Defending the conduct of soldiers in the Philippines had become untenable after so much abuse was revealed in testimony at courts-martial and before the Senate committee. Next best was to follow Lodge's strategy: admit that war crimes had been committed but insist that they were aberrations and would be punished.

General Smith turned out to be an ideal villain. Newspapers called him "Howling Wilderness" Smith. In his first appearance before the Committee on the Philippines, he denied that he ever gave orders to kill. Later testimony showed that this was a lie. Once caught, Smith reveled in the truth. He was quietly advised that the charges could be dropped if he testified that he had not expected his orders to be taken literally, but he defiantly refused to do so. Instead he proclaimed loudly that he had meant every word. That guaranteed his conviction. Secretary Root let him off with a reprimand on the grounds that he had been driven to excess by "cruel and barbarous savages." Major Waller was acquitted. Many cheered.

By countenancing three years of intense counterinsurgency in the Philippines, Americans lost whatever national innocence had survived slavery, anti-Indian campaigns, and the Mexican War. News of atrocities did not set off anti-war protests. In fact, it stirred patriotic backlash. Republican newspapers and magazines defended the war and the honor of the United States Army.

"Having the devil to fight, it has sometimes used fire," reasoned *Harper's*. "Having liars to fight, it has sometimes used lies. Having semi-civilized men to fight, it has in some instances used semi-civilized methods. That was inevitable, and will be inevitable as long as soldiers are men."

Even more direct words came from General Funston, whose capture of

Aguinaldo had made him a national hero. Funston was disgusted by the prosecution of his fellow officers. During a speaking tour at the beginning of 1902 designed to drum up support for the war, he was free with his opinions. "I personally strung up thirty-five Filipinos without trial, so what was all the fuss over Waller's dispatching a few treacherous savages?" he mused in one interview. Asked his view of anti-imperialists, he said they "should be dragged out of their homes and lynched."

Upon reading this interview, Mark Twain volunteered to be lynched first. Then he wrote a sardonic "Defense of General Funston" in which he concluded that Funston's character "took as naturally to moral slag as Washington's took to moral gold. . . . His conscience leaked out through one of his pores when he was little." Twain was especially disgusted by the "forgeries and falsehoods" Funston had used to capture Aguinaldo.

> Funston is not to blame for his fearful deed; and, if I tried, I might also show that he is not to blame for our still holding in bondage the man he captured by unlawful means, and who is not any more rightfully our prisoner and spoil than he would be if he were stolen money. He is entitled to his freedom. If he were a king of a Great Power, or an ex-president of our republic, instead of an ex-president of a destroyed and abolished little republic, Civilization (with a large C) would criticize and complain until he got it.

Twain's published essays and public speeches were sharp but leavened by humor or satire. In his private writing, much of which remained unknown for generations, he poured out his despair. One of his pieces reads like an obituary for the United States. "It was impossible to save the Great Republic," he wrote. "She was rotten to the heart. Lust of conquest had long ago done its work. Trampling upon the helpless abroad had taught her, by a natural process, to endure with apathy the like at home; multitudes who had applauded the crushing of other people's liberties, lived to suffer for their mistake in their own persons. The government was irrevocably in the hands of the prodigiously rich and their hangers-on, the suffrage was become a mere machine, which they used as they chose. There was no principle but commercialism, no patriotism but of the pocket."

Other anti-imperialists were just as heartbroken. Many agreed with Twain that their failure meant the end of the America they loved. "She has lost her unique position as a potential leader in the progress of civilization," Charles Eliot Norton wrote, "and has taken up her place simply as one of the grasping and selfish nations of the present day."

The United States Army was completing its "pacification" of the Philippines. Its last large campaign, waged south of Manila in the first months of 1902, pitted four thousand American soldiers under General Franklin Bell against five thousand insurgents loyal to Miguel Malvar, a legendary commander. Bell's orders were among the most extreme of this war: all natives must be forced from their homes into fortified camps; "neutrality should not be tolerated," so natives not actively aiding the U.S. force must be killed; crops must be burned and livestock destroyed; and a native would be selected by lot for execution every time an American was killed. These tactics worked. The rebel force went hungry and ran out of ammunition. Starvation and diseases spread. On April 14, Malvar staggered out of the jungle and surrendered. That marked the effective end of Filipino resistance. Fifty-four thousand civilians died during Bell's three-month campaign.

Five days after this campaign ended, Twain delivered a speech at Princeton University. He was in peak form. First he cited the staggering casualty figures. Then he read an American decree making it a crime for any Filipino to advocate independence.

"If I were in the Philippines, I could be imprisoned a year for publicly expressing the opinion that we ought to withdraw and give those people their independence—an opinion which I desire to express right now," he said. "On these terms I am quite willing to be called a traitor— quite willing to wear that honorable badge—and not willing to be affronted with the title of Patriot and classed with the Funstons, when so help me God I have done nothing to deserve it."

As Twain recognized, though, few Americans were listening anymore. Many welcomed the end of fighting in the Philippines as a chance to turn away. People were tired of hearing about that faraway place and the unpleasant things that were done there. Lodge brought his hearings to a desultory close. The Senate Committee on the Philippines remained in existence but never issued a report. Its "investigation" unfolded just as Lodge planned. Every story of abuse was countered by indignant denials punctuated by pro forma prosecution of a few officers. Public anger passed. Appeals to patriotism proved effective. The idea of overseas empire had taken root in the American soul.

"The American public," observed an editorial writer for the *New York World* in early 1902, "sips its coffee and reads of its soldiers administering the 'water cure' to rebels . . . and remarks, 'How very unpleasant!' It then butters its bread. . . . It cracks an egg and reads of the orders of General Smith 'to kill and burn,' 'to take no prisoners,' 'to kill everything over ten,' and 'to make Samar a howling wilderness.' 'Rather extreme,' is the comment of the American people, with a feeling of mild disapproval, not unmingled, perhaps, with disgust."

On July 1, 1902, Congress passed the Philippine Organic Act, providing a legal structure by which the United States could rule the islands indefinitely. Three days later, on July 4, President Roosevelt issued a proclamation declaring the Philippine War officially over and thanking American soldiers for their "self-control, patience, and magnanimity." With these two acts, the United States consummated its conquest of the Philippines.

The Philippine War lasted forty-one months. A total of 120,000 American soldiers participated. Commanders later estimated that they killed about twenty thousand Filipino insurgents. Hundreds of thousands of civilians also perished. The population of water buffalo, the essential article of rural life in the Philippines, fell by 90 percent. Americans suffered 4,234 dead and 2,818 wounded. During those forty-one months, far more Filipinos were killed or died as a result of mistreatment than in three and a half centuries of Spanish rule.

Twain was in a foul mood on that Fourth of July. He hated the idea of colonialism, and now his own country was beginning formal rule over a distant nation. As his bile rose, he scribbled his vision of what the 1902 Independence Day parade should look like.

—Waving from a float piled high with property—the whole marked with Boodle. To wit: 12,000 islands

—Crowd of slaughtered patriots—called "rebels"

—Filipino Republic—annihilated

—Crowd of deported patriots—called "rebels"

—A Crowned Sultan—in business with the United States and officially-recognized member of the firm.

—Motto on the Flag: "To what base uses I have come at last"

—The Pirate Flag. Inscribed: "Oh, you will get used to it, brother. I had sentimental scruples myself at first."

Twain's bitterness became more intense as he and other anti-imperialists came to recognize, during that summer of 1902, that their cause was truly lost. The United States had seized the Philippines, crushed the incipient Philippine Republic, and begun ruling seven million Filipinos. Hawaii, Guam, and Puerto Rico had also been annexed. Cuba was an American protectorate. A vast commercial empire began to open, guarded by an army and navy with global reach.

This was precisely what anti-imperialists had fought to prevent. Some hoped that overseas expansion would resurface as a campaign issue on the off-year election of 1902, but it did not. Republicans held their majorities in both houses of Congress. Roosevelt focused on building the coalition he would need to win election to a full term in 1904.

The most intriguing result of the 1902 election was William Randolph Hearst's emergence as a politician. Hearst won a seat in Congress from Manhattan and immediately began campaigning for the 1904 Democratic presidential nomination. The combination of his scandalous private life and immoderate politics—he favored Irish independence and "equitable distribution of wealth" at home—doomed his candidacy. Democrats instead nominated Alton Parker, chief judge of the New York Court of Appeals. Roosevelt crushed him.

For four intense years, Americans were locked in one of their most profound and passionate debates. They were given a clear choice. In the end they made a clear decision.

"Well, we are defeated for the time," admitted Charles Eliot Norton, whose 1898 speech in Cambridge had set the anti-imperialist movement in motion. "But the war is not ended, and we are enlisted for the war."

11

The Deep Hurt

A brisk wind blew across the East Portico of the United States Capitol as Theodore Roosevelt raised his right hand to be sworn in for a full term as president on March 4, 1905. His ascent had been meteoric. Just as astonishing had been his ability to carry the American imperial project along with him to the pinnacle of triumph. He had won a landslide victory at the polls and looked forward to four more years of immense power. Woe to every land upon which the United States had ever cast a covetous eye!

Days after the election, leaders of the American Anti-Imperialist League met at the Twentieth Century Club in Boston for what one speaker called "a very cheerful sort of a funeral." Another speaker was brutally realistic: "Theodore Roosevelt represents today the temper and point of view of the American people, as to armies, navies, world power, Panama republics, and American police duty in the Western hemisphere. That is as undeniable as the rising of the sun."

Mark Twain also accepted the new reality. He and President Roosevelt crossed paths a few times, including at a White House dinner that Twain attended to lobby for changes in copyright law. They appreciated each other as personalities, but each continued to despise what the other represented. Twain pronounced Roosevelt "one of the most likeable men that I am acquainted with" and also "far and away the worst president we have ever had."

"We have never had a President before who was destitute of self-respect & of respect for his high office," Twain wrote. "We have had no President before who was not a gentleman; we have had no President before who was intended for a butcher, a dive-keeper or a bully."

Twain's opinion, as he well understood, now mattered little. The United States was poised to enter the period of Roosevelt Empire. Led by Theodore Rex, it had the power to absorb territory around the world. It could have annexed Cuba, Guatemala, or Nicaragua or claimed slices of Mexico, China, Africa, or South America. In his inaugural address, however, Roosevelt hardly mentioned the rest of the world. This most ambitious of nation grabbers was no longer interested in grabbing nations. His burst of conquest had sated him. Finally armed with the weapons of state, he turned away. Henceforth he would focus on domestic affairs, specifically his campaigns to protect America's natural environment and curb the power of business monopolies.

"Our forefathers faced certain perils, which we have outgrown," Roosevelt said in his address. "We now face other perils."

Part of the explanation for this turnaround lay with Roosevelt's personality. He was too restless to devote an entire career to a single cause. For years he had felt driven to prove, to the world and to himself, that he could lead the United States toward world power. Once he had proved it, subjugating another group of countries would have been repetitive. He wanted to move on. So did most Americans.

After the Philippines debacle, the United States reduced the scope of its imperial ambition. Its attempt to take a distant archipelago, though ultimately successful, had been traumatic. Anti-imperialists had warned that any attempt to annex the islands would set off rebellion. They were proven right. This left a deep impression on public opinion. By pushing the question of overseas expansion so insistently to the center of national debate, anti-imperialists led many Americans to doubt the idea of conquest. Their movement, it turned out, had not completely failed. Its arguments did not carry the day when they were first made, but they left an imprint. Anti-imperialists decisively influenced American history by helping to ensure that the first burst of American annexation would be the last.

They even affected Roosevelt himself. Slowly but palpably he lost enthusiasm for the idea of conquest. Soon after taking office he engineered a bogus revolution in Panama to secure a strip of land for his interoceanic canal, but that was his only major intervention. For the rest of his life he liked to point out that he had never ordered a foreign engagement in which a single life was lost. He even came to recognize presciently—though not presciently enough—that annexing the Philippines might have been a mistake because the archipelago could become a "heel of Achilles" for the United States.

Roosevelt charged into the White House as an aggressive expansionist. As president, he had to live with the effects of his interventions, including long and costly occupations, periodic rebellions, and criticism at home and abroad. That experience sobered him. He did not truly change a deeply held opinion, but he harbored opposing views simultaneously: the United States should intervene to help other people, but should not oppress them. It is the dichotomy that torments our national psyche. From it springs the question we have never managed to answer: Does intervention in other countries serve our national interest and contribute to global stability, or does it undermine both?

More than a century has passed since American hearts were first seized by the grand debate about overseas expansion. During that period, much of what anti-imperialists predicted has come to pass. The United States has become an actively interventionist power. It has projected military or covert power into dozens of countries on every continent except Antarctica. In many places, these interventions have set off anti-American resistance movements, insurgencies, rebellions, or terror campaigns. George Frisbie Hoar was right when he warned that intervening in distant lands would turn the United States into "a vulgar, commonplace empire founded upon physical force."

Anti-imperialists also predicted that an aggressive foreign policy would have pernicious effects at home. In this, too, history has vindicated them. Military budgets have soared to levels that would have seemed unbelievable to even the most fervent expansionists of 1898. The weapons industry wields inordinate power. Government is highly centralized. A wealthy elite dominates politics. Martial values are exalted over peaceful ones. Earth-shaking decisions to wage distant wars are made in private by a handful of people. Charles Ames was right when he warned that militarism would lead to "trampling on the principles of free government."

Those who first pushed the United States toward global military power—the expansionists of 1898—may also claim a measure of vindication. They believed that taking Cuba, the Philippines, and other island nations would be the first steps toward a world largely dominated by American power. That world emerged much as they imagined. Entire regions fell under the formal or informal control of the United States. This gave Americans almost unlimited access to the world's markets and resources. In the space of just a few generations, the United States reached levels of national wealth unmatched in human history. This prosperity helped propel Americans to victory in two world wars and the Cold War. Henry Cabot Lodge was right when he predicted that overseas expansion would bring "enormous material benefits to our trade, our industry, and our labor."

Imperialists believed that American influence would benefit the whole world. This, they argued, would happen in two ways. First, Americans who intervened in foreign countries would bring the material blessings of civilization: good schools, orderly systems of justice, modern transport networks, new jobs, control of tropical diseases. Second, even in places where such tangible benefits did not take hold, rising American power would be good for everyone simply because it meant strengthening the world's most beneficent nation.

Within a few years after the United States assumed control of Cuba, towns were cleaner, roads were safer, and the plague of yellow fever was under control. Much the same happened in parts of the Philippines. Over the century that followed, Americans imposed arbitrary rule and suppressed dissent in countries they dominated, but also saved and improved many lives. Senator Knute Nelson was half right when he predicted that these idealists would be "ministering angels, not despots."

A truism holds that any story can be happy or sad depending on where you end it. That perfectly describes the history of American intervention. Overwhelming power has allowed the United States to impose its will on many peoples. Often, however, these successes have been short-lived. Americans have been forced to learn an ancient lesson: nations dominated by foreign power eventually seek to throw it off.

The expansionists of 1898 understood that rebellions had shaken and destroyed past empires, but they dared to believe the United States was immune to this pattern of history. America's inherent benevolence, they insisted, made it unlike every previous great power. From this illusion they leaped to another: that America's benevolence would quickly become clear to people in subject nations and would lead them to welcome American power. The opposite happened. Teaching half-free people the value of freedom made them want more of it. Carl Schurz was right when he warned that dominating foreigners would ultimately force Americans to "shoot them down because they stand up for their independence."

One reason for this backlash, paradoxically, is the idealism that lies near the heart of America's expansionist impulse. Convinced that we have been granted providential access to secrets that can produce free and prosperous societies anywhere, Americans seek to share those secrets with others. Sometimes we take on the mission of fundamentally changing foreign societies—"destroying barbarism," as Roosevelt put it. People in those societies, though, often see such projects as efforts to rip them away from their deepest social and cultural roots. William Graham Sumner was wise to observe that although Americans presume their rule over foreigners is "a welcome blessing," many foreigners "like their own ways, and if we appear amongst them as rulers, there will be social discord."

In the face of profound new challenges, Americans are once again debating the role of the United States in the world. Should it intervene violently in other countries? This remains what Senator William V. Allen called it in 1899: "The greatest question that has ever been presented to the American people."

Spasms of interventionist passion convulse the American body politic every generation or so. Sometimes the United States steps away from conflict and allows history to take its course. At other times it seeks to shape history. Its choices have shaken the world.

Roosevelt left office in 1909, secure in the conviction that his chosen successor, William Howard Taft, would exercise restraint in foreign policy and crack down on corporate abuses. Taft did neither. Soon after taking office, he directed the overthrow of President José Santos Zelaya of Nicaragua, whom Roosevelt had called "my great and good friend." Then he used American power to depose a similarly independent-minded regime in Honduras. Both of these interventions were aimed at protecting American business interests. Taft's embrace of those interests angered Roosevelt and led him to declare his candidacy for another term as president in 1912. Denied the Republican nomination, he ran as an independent. That split the Republican vote and allowed an ardent pro-moter of peace, Woodrow Wilson, to win the presidency.

Wilson preached the supreme value of self-determination, which he called the right of all people "to choose the sovereignty under which they shall live." In office, though, he sent American troops to intervene in Cuba, Haiti, the Dominican Republic, Mexico, and Russia. No other president invaded as many countries as this sworn promoter of self-determination. Like his predecessors—and successors—Wilson insisted that he was doing it for the good of the target countries. Americans would leave them alone, he promised, as soon as they learned "to elect good men."

Roosevelt, Lodge, and other interventionists of 1898 had urged the United States to expand overseas in order to gain economic and strategic advantage. Wilson preached a different gospel. He considered the human-itarian motive supreme because it embodied the democratic mission of the United States. "America is the only idealistic nation in the world," he liked to say. Yet this most compassionate of presidents not only invaded countries that defied the United States, but studiously ignored appeals from colonized people outside Europe, notably in Egypt, India, Korea, and Indochina. His hypocrisy set the stage for generations of war and upheaval.

Wilson hoped to keep the United States out of World War I. So did many other Americans. The original anti-imperialist movement had faded away, but in its place a new political force emerged. Nativists, Ger-man Americans, and many who had been influenced by anti-imperialist ideas joined to oppose American entry into the war. Among their leaders were Governor Hiram Johnson of California, who had been Roosevelt's running mate when he ran as a third-party candidate for president in 1912, and Senator Robert La Follette of Wisconsin, who a decade later would launch his own third-party presidential campaign. This war, they argued, was just another European conflict like those that had shaken the Continent for centuries, motivated by lust for territory and profit, and no business of the United States. Only after German submarines sank American ships in the Atlantic, and the German government was found to be encouraging Mexico to take its side and attack the United States, did Congress approve entry into the war.

Kaiser Wilhelm's eagerness to expand the German navy, which terrified British leaders and helped set off World War I, was fueled by Captain Mahan's book *The Influence of Sea Power Upon History*. The kaiser was deeply impressed with its arguments and ordered it translated into German. "It is on board all my ships and constantly quoted by my captains and officers," he told a visitor. Later the book was translated into Japanese. More recently a Chinese version has appeared. After giving shape to America's imperial dreams, Mahan's naval militarism fueled those of America's rivals.

Debate over entry into World War I profoundly affected the course of anti-imperialism in the United States. Opponents of American involvement became known by a new name: isolationists. Once they lost their battle and the United States entered the war, "isolationism" became a pejorative term. It still is. Just as those who want to use American military power around the world no longer call themselves imperialists, those who oppose military intervention fear the isolationist label. It has come to imply not prudent restraint but blindness to the nation's interests and the world's problems. In the battle of semantics, proponents of "the large policy" have won. They are called globalists or internationalists rather than imperialists or neo-colonialists, and are said to promote not war, occupation, and coercive power, but economic growth, human rights, and democracy.

America's appetite for foreign wars ebbed dramatically after World War I. Wilson's three successors, all Republicans, rejected utopian visions. None believed the United States could remake the world or was called to do so. All three were classic conservatives. They were drawn to anti-imperialism because it is at heart a conservative doctrine.

Warren Harding was the first president to take office after the end of World War I. In his inaugural address, he made clear that he considered American involvement in that conflict to have been a onetime exception, and that he wished the United States never again to fight a foreign war. "We do not mean to be entangled," he declared. "America, our America, the America built on the foundation laid by the inspired fathers, can be party to no permanent military alliance. . . . We do not hate; we do not covet; we dream of no conquest, nor boast of armed prowess."

Another president might have ordered a postwar military buildup to secure American superiority. Harding feared that any buildup would set off a new global arms race, and did the opposite. He proposed a treaty to limit every major country's naval power, and even offered to scrap fifteen American warships as a sign of good faith. A coalition of shipbuilders, steelmakers, and arms manufacturers managed to block the treaty. Harding's successor, Calvin Coolidge, tried again. He summoned world leaders to a disarmament conference in Geneva, but it, too, failed.

Coolidge sent American troops to impose "stability" on Cuba, Haiti, the Dominican Republic, and Nicaragua. His defense of American oil companies in Mexico almost led to war and set off protests across the hemisphere. Taken aback, Coolidge sent a new ambassador to Mexico with instructions to improve relations. Then he traveled to Havana for a conference of Latin American leaders. In his speech, he said he had come to believe in "resolving international differences without resort to force." Coolidge, like Theodore Roosevelt, became more dubious about the value of foreign wars as he gained experience in the White House.

The high-water mark of American restraint in foreign affairs came during the presidency of Coolidge's successor, Herbert Hoover. Historians fault Hoover for his inaction after the stock market crash of 1929, but he was a genuine humanitarian who became the most resolutely anti-imperialist president in modern American history. His background was highly unusual. He was shaped by strong Quaker beliefs, extended stays in a dozen countries on engineering projects, and work directing food relief programs in Europe during and after World War I. As president he pursued modest and respectful foreign policies. In one speech

he asserted that conflict in the world was the result not of the rebelliousness of ignorant natives, but of "the great inequalities and injustices of
centuries." He brought Americans the unwelcome news that in "a large
part of the world," the United States was seen as "a new imperial power
intent upon dominating the destinies and freedoms of other people."
Soon after taking office he declared, "It ought not to be the policy of
the United States to interfere by force to secure or maintain contracts
between our citizens and foreign states." No previous president had
spoken like that. None has since.

Immediately after his election in 1928, Hoover set out on a tour of
Latin America that lasted an astonishing seven weeks, accompanied
by his wife, who spoke fluent Spanish. Later he withdrew United States
Marines from Nicaragua, where they had been fighting nationalist guerrillas for twenty years. He signed a treaty that led to the withdrawal of
American troops from Haiti. When Japan seized part of Manchuria in
the fall and winter of 1931–32, he announced that the United States would
not recognize the conquest—but would not send troops to reverse it.
During his four years in office, he turned down appeals to intervene on
behalf of American companies in Mexico, Cuba, Honduras, El Salvador,
Panama, and Peru. His successor, Franklin Roosevelt, is often credited
with proclaiming the "good neighbor" policy toward Latin America, but
both the idea and the phrase were originally Hoover's. He is the sterling
exemplar of the Republican Party's rich anti-imperial tradition.

Hoover was not alone in proclaiming this creed. Senator William
Borah, the Republican "Lion of Idaho" who succeeded Henry Cabot Lodge
as chairman of the Senate Foreign Relations Committee when Lodge
died in 1924, was an outspoken opponent of U.S. intervention abroad.
So was Senator Huey Long of Louisiana, a Democrat who was assassi-
nated in 1935 while preparing his campaign for the presidency. Long had
promised that if elected he would name the country's most contrarian
military hero, General Smedley Butler, as secretary of war.

Butler had spent decades leading invasions of other countries. He
commanded troops in Cuba and the Philippines, fought the Boxers in
China, helped overthrow the governments of Nicaragua and Honduras,
directed occupations of the Dominican Republic and Haiti, secured the
Panamanian regime that gave Americans the right to build their canal,

and won a Medal of Honor—the first of two—for valor in suppressing Mexican resistance at Veracruz. By the 1920s he was a living legend, a personification of "the large policy." The Marine Corps decided to use his popularity as a recruiting tool and sent him on a speaking tour. It did not unfold as planned. Butler strayed far from his script. He not only failed to defend the policies for which he had fought, he denounced them. Marine commanders called him back to Washington and, by mutual agreement, he resigned from active duty. Freed from constraint, he began barnstorming the country on his own. In passionate speeches and articles, he said that serving as a marine commander had made him "a high-class muscle man for big business" and "a gangster for capitalism."

> I helped make Mexico and especially Tampico safe for American oil interests in 1914. I helped make Haiti and Cuba a decent place for the National City Bank boys to collect revenues in. I helped in the raping of half a dozen Central American republics for the benefit of Wall Street. I helped purify Nicaragua for the International Banking House of Brown Brothers in 1902–1912. I brought light to the Dominican Republic for the American sugar interests in 1916. I helped make Honduras right for the American fruit companies in 1903. In China in 1927 I helped see to it that Standard Oil went on its way unmolested. Looking back on it, I might have given Al Capone a few hints. The best he could do was to operate his racket in three districts. I operated on three continents.

By the time Butler reached his rhetorical peak, Franklin Roosevelt had won the presidency. Roosevelt turned out to be a halfhearted good neighbor to Latin America. In 1934 he signed a treaty with Cuba that annulled the hated Platt Amendment, which had provided a legal fig leaf for repeated interventions in the region. Later he resisted pressure to declare war on Mexico after President Lázaro Cárdenas nationalized the Mexican oil industry. He also, however, generously supported the hemisphere's most repressive dictators, including Rafael Trujillo in the Dominican Republic, Fulgencio Batista in Cuba, and Anastasio Somoza in Nicaragua. Like most other American presidents, Roosevelt was unable or unwilling to see that his foreign interventions were planting the seeds of anti-American rebellion.

Franklin Roosevelt's presidency was dominated by the cataclysm of World War II. In the early years of the war he, like Wilson a generation earlier, sought to keep American troops out, largely in response to public sentiment. Many Americans believed that the United States had no business joining the war. Senator Gerald Nye of North Dakota spoke for them when he railed against the "rotten commercialism" that led American corporations to push their country into foreign wars. Congress passed resolutions opposing American intervention in conflicts that broke out in China, Spain, and Ethiopia. Ernest Hemingway, who had seen World War I, wrote that Americans "were fools to be sucked in once on a European war, and we should never be sucked in again." This ethos remained strong, in Washington and across the United States, until Japan's attack on Pearl Harbor gave Roosevelt the excuse he wanted to enter the war.

With the nation mobilized, anti-interventionist passion naturally faded. It weakened further as Americans learned of horrific crimes committed by Japan and Germany. Intervention in foreign conflicts came to seem right and just.

Franklin Roosevelt, who had maintained a decent working relationship with the Soviet dictator Joseph Stalin during World War II, died as the war was ending. Historians have speculated whether he might have been able to maintain that relationship, possibly averting the Cold War. Instead the inexperienced Harry Truman came to the presidency. He told Americans that they faced a new and relentless enemy bent on world domination, the Soviet Union, and had no choice but to fight back.

According to this narrative, Communism posed such a mortal threat to humanity that all means to resist it, anywhere in the world, were justified. The global economy had become heavily transnational, meaning that American business relied more than ever on access to global markets and resources. A new crop of leaders in Washington, both Democrats and Republicans, saw the entire world as a battleground. This was "the large policy" for a modern age.

"The 20th century, if it is to come to life in any nobility of health and vigor, must be to a significant degree an American century," the publisher Henry Luce famously wrote in 1941. "It now becomes our time to be the powerhouse."

Not all Americans immediately accepted this worldview. During the late 1940s and early '50s, an extraordinary array of dissenters from left and right shouted into the intensifying Cold War wind. They saw the Soviet Union as a shattered nation eager to control its own borderlands, not a relentless enemy of the United States. If Americans sought to project power everywhere in the world, they warned, the Soviets would respond by doing the same.

On what is normally considered the left of the American political spectrum, these iconoclasts included the journalists Walter Lippmann and I. F. Stone, the scientists Leo Szilard and Albert Einstein, a few members of Congress led by Senator Claude Pepper of Florida and Representative Vito Marcantonio of New York, and African American leaders including W. E. B. DuBois and Paul Robeson. Their most prominent leader was the remarkable heretic Henry Wallace.

Wallace's father had been secretary of agriculture under two Republican presidents, Harding and Coolidge. As a young man in Iowa, Wallace became fascinated by plant genetics, and later he founded hybrid seed companies that earned him a fortune. His restless intellect led him beyond agriculture to then-exotic interests including yoga, organic diets, and mystic religious philosophy. In 1933 President Franklin Roosevelt named him to the post his father formerly held, secretary of agriculture, and seven years later the president chose him as his running mate. The Roosevelt-Wallace ticket was victorious in 1940, and immediately after the election Wallace set off on a road trip through Mexico. Slowly he drifted away from the political consensus. In 1942 he delivered a speech that led Aaron Copland to compose his classic "Fanfare for the Common Man."

Some have spoken of the "American Century." I say that the century on which we are entering—the century which will come out of this war—can be and must be the century of the common man. . . . No nation will have the God-given right to exploit other nations. Older nations will have the privilege to help younger nations get started on the path to industrialization, but there must be neither military nor economic imperialism. . . . There can be no privileged peoples. We ourselves in the United States are no more a master race than the Nazis. And we cannot perpetuate economic warfare without planting the seeds of military warfare.

Views like these, along with Wallace's sympathy for the Soviet Union, displeased Roosevelt and his political advisers. In 1944, Wallace was dumped from the Democratic ticket and replaced by Senator Harry Truman. It was a fateful choice, since it allowed Truman rather than Wallace to succeed to the presidency after Roosevelt's death. When Truman ran for a full term in 1948, Wallace ran against him as a third-party candidate, denouncing his "imperialist policy," his "blind hatred of Russia," and his efforts "to intimidate the rest of mankind." Most Americans, however, had joined the Cold War consensus. Truman was elected, and Wallace finished with 2.4 percent of the vote.

Debate over foreign policy split the Republican Party as well. Its mainstream was solidly internationalist, confident in America's power and eager to project it around the world. Right-wing Republicans rose to challenge that mainstream, just as left-wing Democrats had.

In 1898 the richest tycoon in the United States, Andrew Carnegie, became an outspoken opponent of American intervention abroad. Half a century later, Representative Howard Buffett of Nebraska, not the country's richest tycoon but father of the man who would eventually claim that title, Warren Buffett, took up the same cause. "Our Christian ideals cannot be exported to other lands by dollars and guns," Buffett told the House of Representatives in 1947. "We cannot practice might and force abroad and retain freedom at home. We cannot talk world cooperation and practice power politics."

On the same day that Buffett spoke, Representative George Bender of Ohio rose to denounce President Truman's "new policy of interventionism" and "the whole Truman doctrine of drawing off the resources of the United States in support of every reactionary government in the world." Bender had become a key figure in Washington because of his close ties to Senator Robert Taft, the son of President William Howard Taft and one of the last old-style Republican anti-imperialists. In one of his most famous speeches, Taft opposed founding America's first peacetime military alliance, the North Atlantic Treaty Organization, because "the building up of a great army surrounding Russia" would set off "an inevitable arms race."

> An undertaking by the most powerful nation in the world to arm half the world against the other half goes far beyond any "right to collective defense if an armed attack occurs." It violates the whole spirit of the United Nations charter. . . . The Atlantic Pact moves in exactly the opposite direction from the purposes of the charter and makes a farce of further efforts to secure international justice through law and justice. It necessarily divides the world into two armed camps.

Taft ran for the Republican presidential nomination in 1948 but lost to Governor Thomas Dewey of New York, a mainstream Republican whose principal foreign policy adviser was the consummate international lawyer John Foster Dulles. Four years later he ran again, against Dwight Eisenhower—for whom Dulles also wrote speeches. Again he was defeated.

This was a pivotal moment in American political history. Both major political parties rejected challenges to the interventionist ethos. So did voters. That allowed American power to become truly global for the first time.

American intervention in foreign nations during the Cold War was different from all that had come before. It was shaped by two new realities. First, the United States now sought to influence events in every part of the world. John Foster Dulles, who became Eisenhower's secretary of state, liked to tell recalcitrant foreign leaders, "America's policy is global. You must be on one side or the other. Neutralism is immoral." This approach to world politics alienated leaders of "neutralist" countries such as Guatemala, Costa Rica, Egypt, Iran, India, Burma, Cambodia, and Indonesia.

The second reality of the Cold War era was Soviet military power. Marine invasions, which had been the ultimate instrument of American foreign policy for half a century, were no longer possible because they risked provoking counter-invasions by Soviet troops. American leaders needed a substitute. They found it in covert action.

Acting through the Central Intelligence Agency, which was created in 1947, President Eisenhower helped depose "neutralist" governments in Iran, Guatemala, and the Congo. He tried but failed in Albania, Egypt, Indonesia, and Cuba. In dozens of other countries, the CIA launched operations aimed at strengthening or weakening governments, according to their degree of fealty to the United States.

Eisenhower's successor, John F. Kennedy, devoured James Bond novels and developed a romantic attachment to covert action. In 1961, carrying out a plan bequeathed to him by Eisenhower, he allowed the CIA to direct a disastrous exile invasion of Cuba. Afterward he sought to destabilize the Cuban government and kill its leaders. Kennedy also escalated Eisenhower's military commitment in Vietnam. He said this was necessary to stop the advance of global Communism.

President Lyndon Johnson raised the Vietnam stakes even higher, ultimately destroying his presidency and forcing him to abandon his campaign for re-election in 1968. His successors in the White House also embraced the interventionist ethic. It dominated foreign policy thinking in both the Republican and Democratic Parties.

Richard Nixon ordered carpet bombing of both North Vietnam and neighboring Cambodia. He supported the government of Pakistan in its war against the secessionist province that became Bangladesh, during which hundreds of thousands of civilians were killed. Two years later, in 1973, he ordered the CIA to help overthrow the elected president of Chile, Salvador Allende.

The brief presidency of Gerald Ford was marked by covert American intervention in two civil wars. Ford gave ruling generals in Indonesia approval to invade and annex the former Portuguese colony of East Timor, then sent them large amounts of weaponry. Half a world away, in Angola, Ford armed warlords in a civil conflict that ballooned into a proxy war between the United States and the Soviet Union. East Timor gained its independence after a twenty-four-year rebellion against the American-backed Indonesian government. The civil war in Angola lasted for twenty-seven years and cost half a million lives.

During his successful campaign to defeat Ford in 1976, Jimmy Carter lamented "the deep hurt that's come to this country in the aftermath of Vietnam and Cambodia and Chile and Pakistan and Angola." As president, however, Carter launched an interventionist project that would itself cause the United States much hurt. In 1979 the Soviet Union sent troops to Afghanistan, and rather than allow them to sink slowly into the Afghan quagmire, as other imperial adventurers had before, Carter rushed to confront them. The forces he armed and financed became the Taliban, welcomed al-Qaeda, and brought the world waves of terror.

Ronald Reagan was every bit as interventionist as Carter but could at least claim that he never promised anything different. He intensified commitments to warlords in Africa and Afghanistan, sent aid to the Iraqi dictator Saddam Hussein during Saddam's eight-year war with Iran, fueled the "contra" rebellion against Sandinista rule in Nicaragua, and supported the governments of Guatemala and El Salvador in fierce campaigns against leftist rebels. In 1983 he sent troops to invade the Caribbean island of Grenada and depose its pro-Cuban government. That same year, however, after terrorists killed 241 U.S. Marines in Beirut, Reagan decided to withdraw American troops from Lebanon rather than start a new war by fighting back. He was another interventionist who sometimes recognized the limits of intervention.

In 1991, with the Cold War over, Reagan's successor, George H. W. Bush, proclaimed "a new world order" that the United States would dominate because "we have a unique responsibility to do the hard work of freedom." In pursuit of this new order, Bush ordered an invasion to depose the government of Panama. Later he organized an American-led coalition that pushed Iraqi troops out of Kuwait. After that victory, he decided to base thousands of U.S. troops on Saudi soil, outraging devout Saudis including Osama bin Laden. Then, toward the end of his term, he sent soldiers to intervene in a civil war raging in Somalia. The next president, Bill Clinton, ended the Somalia mission after Somali fighters shot down an American helicopter and dragged dead airmen through the streets of Mogadishu.

Clinton was attracted to the Wilsonian doctrine that came to be called "humanitarian intervention." By framing foreign wars as missions of mercy, he gave them an appealing patina. His invasion of Haiti in 1994 left the country no better off, and his success in wresting the province of Kosovo away from Serbia in 1999 was later used by Russian leaders to justify ripping apart other once-sovereign nations. In 1994, though, Clinton refused to support a modest multinational intervention with a truly humanitarian purpose. The commander of United Nations troops in Rwanda begged the UN to send him a few thousand peace-keepers to prevent the coming genocide, but Clinton used his influence to ensure that the UN refused.

George W. Bush promised during his campaign for the presidency that he would make the United States "a humble nation." In office, he ordered two of the most disastrous interventions in American history. He responded to the September 11, 2001, attacks on the Pentagon and World Trade Center not by targeted attacks on the bombers and their enablers, but with a full-scale assault on Afghanistan, followed by an open-ended occupation. Soon afterward he sent American troops into Iraq to depose Saddam Hussein. Never has the United States launched foreign wars that so decisively weakened its own security.

Like Reagan, Clinton, and George W. Bush, Barack Obama came to the presidency without experience in statecraft. Two of his "humanitarian intervention" projects backfired disastrously. In Sudan he intervened to promote secession and helped create a new nation, South Sudan, but instead of alleviating suffering that intervention intensified it. Then Obama ordered military operations to destroy the regime of Muammar Qaddafi in Libya. That threw Libya into chaos and opened Qaddafi's rich arsenals to terrorists across North Africa and beyond.

Obama, like presidents before him, seemed to learn lessons from his failed interventions. He resisted pressure to re-invade Afghanistan and Iraq when insurgencies in those countries showed strength. As civil war spread through Syria, he intervened without deploying large numbers of ground troops. "We should generally aim before we shoot," he reasoned.

Obama became the first president since Herbert Hoover to acknowledge limits to American power and adjust his foreign policy accordingly. On the surface they make an odd pair: Hoover a conservative Republican, Obama a liberal Democrat. Their agreement reflects a central truth that runs through the history of American anti-imperialism: while the broad center, built on alliances among political parties, the press, and multinational corporations, promotes overseas intervention, dissenters question its value.

During the Vietnam era, the most prominent of these dissenters was Senator George McGovern of South Dakota, who won the Democratic presidential nomination in 1972 on an anti-war platform. His speeches sounded much like those of senators who opposed the Philippine War seventy years before. "I will halt the senseless bombing of Indochina," McGovern promised after being nominated. "There will be no more Asian children running ablaze from bombed-out schools. There will be no more talk of bombing the dikes or the cities of the North. . . . And then let us resolve that never again will we send the precious young blood of this country to die trying to prop up a corrupt military dictatorship abroad."

McGovern went down to overwhelming defeat. The debacle of Vietnam, however, sobered many Americans. A conservative Republican, Patrick Buchanan, who sought his party's presidential nomination in 1992 and 1996, insisted that the United States betrayed its principles and undermined its own interests when it intervened in foreign countries.

"The steady increase of global commitments, as relative national power declines, is a prescription for endless wars and eventual disaster," Buchanan told Republicans. "We are not the party of empire. We are the party of liberty."

After Buchanan's defeats, a libertarian Republican, Representative Ron Paul of Texas, emerged as America's most insistent anti-imperialist. "We're still running a foreign policy of Woodrow Wilson, trying to make the world safe for democracy," Paul said during his 2012 campaign for the Republican presidential nomination. "We can't stay in 130 countries, get involved in nation building. We cannot have 900 bases overseas. We have to change policy." In another speech he described anti-imperialism as the essence of conservatism.

"Truly conservative, in the sense of the words 'to conserve our true values,' means being serious about taking our oath of office to the Constitution," Paul said. "If the U.S. is as great as I believe it should be and can be and has been, we will have influence around the world. We cannot spread our greatness and our goodness through the barrel of a gun. It fails because it destroys our goodness by doing it that way."

The first American imperialists failed to imagine the sorrows of empire. Part of the reason was their inability to recognize the cultural complexity of the peoples they set out to rule. They believed that most Asians,

Africans, and Latin Americans lived primitively and were barely capable of reasoning. Today such stereotypes have weakened, but the premise on which they were based remains strong. Many Americans truly believe that the United States has much to teach others and that the world will become better if nations near and far submit to its leadership. To suggest the opposite—that the United States might benefit from being a learning nation instead of a teaching nation—contradicts our deepest assumptions and seems vaguely un-American.

Early promoters of American intervention were zealous patriots. They loudly proclaimed their love for the United States, fidelity to its flag, and willingness to defend its sovereignty to the death. Yet they could not imagine that people in non-white countries might feel just as patriotic. To them, love of country was a mark of civilization, meaning that lesser peoples could not grasp it.

Anti-imperialists felt a different kind of patriotism. They believed that all power, even American power, is inherently limited—and that this is a good thing, because limits keep countries from launching self-defeating wars. Expansionists of 1898 were visionary radicals who wanted to pull the United States into a new age. Anti-imperialists were conservatives who looked back to old virtues, not ahead to global power.

Both sides in this debate saw their country as being in grave danger and wanted to rescue it. The threats they perceived, however, were quite different.

Imperialists wanted the United States to seize opportunities for economic and strategic power. They saw military force and covert action not as aggression but forward defense. Many of their interventions, however, produced the very security threats they were intended to prevent. They call to mind Bismarck's maxim "Preventive war is like committing suicide for fear of death."

Anti-imperialists believed the United States was threatened from within, not by enemy powers. The suffering that foreign wars brought pained them, but their deepest anguish came from what they saw as the corrosive effect these wars had on the American political system and the American soul. Empire and the wars that come with it, they warned, are inherently incompatible with republican government. They wanted the United States to be the champion of freedom, forever and unequivocally dedicated to its founding principle that people may be ruled only with their consent.

Americans are often described as ignorant about the world. We are, but so are most people everywhere. The difference is that most other countries' ignorance has no real effect. America's does, because the United States acts on its ignorance. Filled with a sense of mission and destiny, some American leaders see little reason to bother learning about the nations into whose affairs they intrude. In 1895 the sardonic editor of *The Nation*, E. L. Godkin, described this impulse in a passage that still rings true: "The situation seems to me this," Godkin wrote. "An immense democracy, mostly ignorant and completely secluded from foreign influence, finds itself in possession of enormous power and is eager to use it in brutal fashion against anyone who comes along, without knowing how to do it, and is therefore constantly on the brink of some frightful catastrophe."

Many of those catastrophes have unfolded years or even decades after seemingly successful interventions. Their effects resonate through history. Violent intervention in other countries always produces unintended consequences.

Turning Cuba into a protectorate seemed like a fine idea in 1901, but it led to a half-century of repression and ultimately the emergence of a bitterly anti-American regime. Intervention in the Philippines set off waves of nationalism across East Asia that contributed to the Communist takeover of China in 1949, and can also be seen as a progenitor of disasters from Pearl Harbor to Vietnam. Later American interventions also had terrible results that their planners never anticipated. From Iran and Guatemala to Iraq and Afghanistan, intervention has devastated societies and produced violent anti-American passion.

Deeply embedded assumptions guide American foreign policy. They make the United States different from other countries. No one who questions them is welcome in the corridors of power in Washington.

For generations, makers of American foreign policy have made decisions based on three assumptions: the United States is the indispensable nation that must lead the world; this leadership requires toughness; and toughness is best demonstrated by the threat or use of force. A host of subsidiary assumptions undergirds this catechism: the United States is inherently virtuous; its influence on the world is always benign; it must often intervene overseas because the risks of inaction are too high; its ideals are universal and can be exported; it welcomes support from other states but may act unilaterally when it chooses. Rather than see in the world a wide spectrum of forces, beliefs, cultures, and interests, Americans often see only good and evil. We rush to take the side of good. This usually brings trouble.

"It has generally been acknowledged to be madness to go to war for an idea," the British statesman Lord Salisbury observed before the United States set off on its imperial adventure, "but if anything, it is yet more unsatisfactory to go to war against a nightmare."

The United States will continue to project global power—but how? Americans have not reconciled the conflicting desires that shape our approach to the world. At times we are seized by martial impulses that lead us to launch pre-emptive wars and seek the absolute global power called "full-spectrum dominance." Periods of prudence follow, but they are temporary. Humility and arrogance coexist uncomfortably in the American psyche. Sometimes they war with each other.

Americans want to protect our country, promote freedom, and help others. Too often, however, we fail to realize that our power cannot wipe away deeply rooted patterns of culture and life. We intervene because we see bad situations, not because we have a clear plan to improve them. At moments of crisis or decision, emotion overcomes sober reasoning—and emotion is always the enemy of wise statesmanship.

Most Americans agree that the United States should act in its own interest. We cannot agree, however, what foreign policies truly *are* in our interest. Eager for quick results, we take rash steps to solve immediate problems. That often creates larger ones. History's great counsel to the United States is that it should more carefully weigh the long-term effects of its foreign interventions.

The United States has not discovered a magic formula that can produce happiness and prosperity everywhere. It cannot implant its ideals or values in vastly different social and political environments. Pre-emptive war and "regime change" operations reflect the quintessentially American view that the world is not a situation to be understood, but a problem to be solved.

Most American interventions are planned to achieve short-term objectives. They are not soberly conceived, with realistic goals and clear exit strategies. Many ultimately harm the target country while weakening the security of the United States.

Violent intervention always leaves a trail of "collateral damage" in the form of families killed, towns destroyed, and lives ruined. Usually these consequences are called mistaken or unavoidable. That does nothing to reduce the damage—or the anger that survivors pass down through generations.

The argument that the United States intervenes to defend freedom rarely matches facts on the ground. Many interventions have been designed to prop up predatory regimes. Their goal is to increase American power—often economic power—rather than to liberate the suffering.

Interventions aimed at "peacekeeping" often degenerate as well, because intervening forces naturally lean toward one side or another. Fighters on non-favored sides consider the peacekeepers their enemies and attack them. This is why the United States Marine barracks in Lebanon was blown up in 1983, and why American soldiers were killed in Somalia during the "Black Hawk Down" debacle a decade later. Americans may still cling to the fantasy that our soldiers are neutrals, fighting only for the good of humanity. Few others see them that way.

Interventions multiply our enemies. They lead people who once bore no ill will toward the United States to begin cursing its name. Every village raid, every drone strike, every shot fired in anger on foreign soil produces anti-American passion. Americans are shocked and incensed when that passion leads to violent counterattacks. They should not be. The instinct to protect one's own and to strike back against attackers is older than humanity itself.

American intervention overseas is hugely expensive. The United States spends more on its military than the next seven countries combined, including trillions of dollars to fight foreign wars. Meanwhile, American communities decay, infrastructure ages and withers, schoolchildren fall behind their counterparts in other countries, and millions go without housing, jobs, or health care. Even worse, at least symbolically, are the lifelong plagues that haunt many combat veterans. War brings "collateral damage" to Americans as well as foreigners.

Interventions are often imagined as discrete in-and-out operations. Once we impose a servile regime in a foreign country, however, we must remain indefinitely or return regularly to defend it against popular uprisings. Interventions rarely end quickly. Many never end at all. The "surgical" intervention that resolves an immediate problem without long-term effects is like a unicorn: an alluring fantasy that never becomes real.

Foreign intervention has weakened the moral authority that was once the foundation of America's political identity. The United States was once admired for its refusal to fight imperial wars or impose its will on distant nations. Today, many people around the world see it as a bully, recklessly invading foreign lands, blowing up entire societies, and leaving trails of destruction and conflict. They associate the name "United States" with bombing, invasion, occupation, night raids, covert action, torture, kidnapping, and secret prisons. History gives them the right to fear that their country may be "saved" the way the United States saved Iran, Guatemala, Vietnam, Chile, Nicaragua, Afghanistan, Iraq, Sudan, and Libya.

Some American leaders realized that these foreign interventions might set off upheaval in target countries. All presumed, however, that there would be no serious effects within the United States. For years this seemed reasonable. In the modern age, though, people with roots in countries whose history has been twisted by foreign intervention find ways to take revenge. It comes in forms from mass migration to terror attacks. These are bad results of assaults that we believed would have no bad results. We were foolish to presume that no matter how awful American or European interventions were, their effects would not reach the United States or Europe. The developed world—the invading world—is not an island or an impregnable fortress. Intervention takes a toll at home as well as abroad.

The distance between what the United States was and what it has become is nowhere more painfully clear than in the words of our noble patriarch. The advice George Washington left to posterity in his Farewell Address is now considered antique, quaint, a relic from bygone times. In fact, it is even more apt today than when he offered it in 1796. Future generations of Americans, Washington warned, would live in peace only if they avoided the traps that bring proud nations down:

—permanent alliances with any portion of the foreign world;

—frequent collisions, obstinate, envenomed, and bloody contests;

—overgrown military establishments which, under any form of government, are inauspicious to liberty, and which are to be regarded as particularly hostile to republican liberty;

—the mischiefs of foreign intrigue;

—love of power and proneness to abuse it;

—excessive partiality for one foreign nation and excessive dislike of another;

—the illusion of an imaginary common interest in cases where no real common interest exists;

—projects of hostility instigated by pride, ambition, and other sinister and pernicious motives.

Washington sensed that his warnings would one day be forgotten. "I dare not hope they will make the strong and lasting impression I could wish," he wrote. Yet he insisted on declaring the principle that he believed would "prevent our nation from running the course which has hitherto marked the destiny of nations."

"Give to mankind the magnanimous and too novel example of a people always guided by an exalted justice and benevolence," Washington advised. "Can it be that Providence has not connected the permanent felicity of a nation with its virtue?"

Nations lose their virtue when they repeatedly attack other nations. That loss, as Washington predicted, has cost the United States its felicity. We can regain it only by understanding our own national interests more clearly. It is late for the United States to change its course in the world—but not too late.

NOTES

1. WHITE AND PEACEFUL WINGS

5 Faneuil Hall meeting: *Boston Evening Transcript, Boston Globe, Boston Journal, New York Times*, June 16, 1898.

7 "annex the moon": James Grant, *Mr. Speaker!: The Life and Times of Thomas B. Reed, The Man Who Broke the Filibuster* (New York: Simon and Schuster, 2011), p. 360.

8 "Why quit our own": Carl Cavanaugh Hodges and Cathal J. Nolan, *U.S. Presidents and Foreign Policy: From 1789 to the Present* (ABC-CLIO, 2006), p. 388.

8 "If there be one principle": Thomas J. Randolph, ed., *Memoirs, Correspondence and Private Papers of Thomas Jefferson*, vol. 3 (London: Henry Colburn and Richard Bentley, 1829), p. 119.

8 "No man is good enough": Mario M. Cuomo and Harold Holzer, eds., *Lincoln on Democracy* (New York: Fordham University Press, 2004), p. 71.

8 "dogmas of the quiet past": Todd Brewster, *Lincoln's Gamble: The Tumultuous Six Months That Gave America the Emancipation Proclamation and Changed the Course of the Civil War* (New York: Scribner, 2014), p. 215.

8 "Since that fateful shot": *Congressional Record*, House of Representatives, Wednesday, June 15, 1898, pp. 5967–6019.

11 "the great God absolute!": Herman Melville, *Moby-Dick* (New York: Bantam, 2003), p. 131.

12 "jack-fools": Elting E. Morison, ed., *The Letters of Theodore Roosevelt*, vol. 4 (Cambridge, MA: Harvard University Press, 1951–54), p. 107.

12 "the man who loves other countries": Theodore Roosevelt, "The Monroe Doctrine," *Bachelor of Arts* (New York), vol. 2, no. 4 (March 1896).

13   "a majestic matron": William E. Phipps, *Mark Twain's Religion* (Macon, GA: Mercer University Press, 2003), p. 206.

13   *Connecticut Yankee*: Philip McFarland, *Mark Twain and the Colonel: Samuel L. Clemens, Theodore Roosevelt, and the Arrival of a New Century* (Lanham, MD: Rowman and Littlefield, 2007), p. 13.

13   "skin Mark Twain alive": Ibid., p. xiii.

14   "Jehovah deals with nations": *Boston Transcript*, June 15, 1898.

15   "History will vindicate the position": William Jennings Bryan and Mary Baird Bryan, *The Life and Speeches of Hon. Wm. Jennings Bryan* (Baltimore: R. H. Woodward, 1900), p. 59.

16   "Resolved, that a war begun": *Boston Journal*, June 20, 1898.

2. THERE MAY BE AN EXPLOSION

18   "Who's the dude?": Edmund Morris, *The Rise of Theodore Roosevelt* (New York: Coward, McCann and Geoghegan, 1979), pp. 161–62.

18   "given to sucking the knob": *Evening Observer* (Dunkirk, NY), March 10, 1883.

19   "a brilliant madman": *New York Times*, December 27, 1883.

19   "national figure of real importance": Morris, *Rise of Theodore Roosevelt*, p. 256.

20   His family had accumulated great wealth: *New York Times*, June 6, 1995; "Cabot Family" in Encyclopaedia Britannica: http://www.britannica.com /topic/Cabot-family.

20   his favorite outing: Karl Schriftgiesser, *The Gentleman from Massachusetts: Henry Cabot Lodge* (Boston: Atlantic–Little, Brown, 1944), p. 10.

20   Democrats ridiculed him: Ibid., p. 28.

21   When Roosevelt killed his first buffalo: Morris, *Rise of Theodore Roosevelt*, p. 212.

21   "He has no sympathy": Harriet E. Smith et al., eds., *The Autobiography of Mark Twain*, vol. 3 (Berkeley: University of California Press, 2015), p. 66.

22   Together they wrote a book: Warren Zimmerman, *First Great Triumph: How Five Americans Made Their Country a World Power* (New York: Farrar, Straus and Giroux, 2002), p. 63.

22   "We fear no encroachments": David Healey, *US Expansionism: The Imperialist Urge in the 1890s* (Madison: University of Wisconsin Press, 1970), p. 44.

22   "he would like above all": H. W. Brands, *The Reckless Decade: America in the 1890s* (New York: St. Martin's, 1995), p. 292.

22   "gushes over war": Wendy Graham, *Henry James's Thwarted Love* (Stanford, CA: Stanford University Press, 1999), p. 91.

22   "I should welcome almost any war": Kristen L. Hoganson, *Fighting for*

American Manhood: How Gender Politics Provoked the Spanish-American and Philippine-American Wars (New Haven: Yale University Press, 2000), p. 183.

23   "a bit of a spar": H. W. Brands, *T.R.: The Last Romantic* (New York: Basic, 1997), p. 222.

23   "I do not say": Zimmerman, *First Great Triumph*, p. 174.

23   Sometimes depression overwhelmed him: Ibid., p. 109.

23   "I am frankly an imperialist": Ibid., pp. 120–21, 418.

24   "Captain Mahan has written": Ibid., p. 100.

25   "The great nations": https://www.coursehero.com/file/11418079/Lodge-Our-Blundering-Foreign-Policy-Speech/.

25   "We are actually": Kathleen Dalton *Theodore Roosevelt: A Strenuous Life* (New York: Vintage, 2004), p. 163.

25   "We want a foreign market": Murat Halsted, *Life and Distinguished Services of Our Martyred President William McKinley* (Salem, MA: H. L. Barker, 1901), p. 143.

26   "cross of gold": Bryan, *Life and Speeches*, pp. 247–52.

27   "Bedlam broke loose": *Washington Post*, July 10, 1896.

27   Rockefeller, Vanderbilt, and Morgan: William T. Horner, *Ohio's Kingmaker: Mark Hanna, Man and Myth* (Athens; Ohio University Press, 2010), p. 199.

27   In his inaugural address: http://www.bartleby.com/124/pres40.html.

27   "one personal favor": Zimmerman, *First Great Triumph*, p. 175.

27   "Lodge did a brilliant selling job": Ibid., pp. 174–76.

27   She was the daughter of an admiral: John A. Garraty, *Henry Cabot Lodge: A Biography* (New York: Alfred A. Knopf, 1953), p. 102.

28   "she knew the names": Schriftgiesser, *Gentleman from Massachusetts*, p. 111.

28   "that ignorance which is born": Garraty, *Henry Cabot Lodge*, p. 101.

28   Nannie conducted an affair: Zimmerman, *First Great Triumph*, p. 78.

28   "It is unmitigated Boston": William C. Widenor, *Henry Cabot Lodge and the Search for an American Foreign Policy* (Berkeley: University of California Press, 1980), p. 3.

28   "a good deal disheartened": William Adam Russ, Jr., *The Hawaiian Republic (1894–98) and Its Struggle to Win Annexation* (Selinsgrove, PA: Susquehanna, 1961), p. 218.

28   NEXT TO WAR WITH SPAIN: *New York Journal*, January 13, 1898.

28   "Foreign correspondents at Havana": Charles H. Brown, *The Correspondents' War: Journalists in the Spanish-American War* (New York: Charles Scribner's Sons, 1967), pp. 140–41.

29   "The impetuosity and fierceness": Evan Thomas, *The War Lovers: Roosevelt, Lodge, Hearst, and the Rush to Empire, 1898* (New York: Back Bay, 2010), p. 198.

29 "There may be an explosion": Leon Wolff, *Little Brown Brother: America's Forgotten Bid for Empire Which Cost 250,000 Lives* (London: Longmans, 1961), p. 38.

30 settlement of a gambling debt: *New York Times*, June 26, 2012.

30 "an achievement not only unparalleled": *New York Journal*, November 5, 1896.

30 "deliberate and shameful lies": Upton Sinclair, *The Brass Check: A Study of American Journalism* (Champaign: University of Illinois Press, 2002), p. 94.

31 "long, deliberate, infallible destruction": Shelley Fisher Fishkin, ed., *A Historical Guide to Mark Twain* (Oxford: Oxford University Press, 2002), p. 231.

31 "a land of piracy and pillage": Frederick Anderson, ed., *Mark Twain: The Critical Heritage* (London: Routledge, 1997), p. 242.

31 "insult, humiliation, and forced labor": Larzer Ziff, *Mark Twain* (Oxford: Oxford University Press, 2004), p. 51.

31 Friends of Russian Freedom: Fishkin, *Historical Guide*, p. 235.

31 "In some cases the Germans": Dan Vogel, *Mark Twain's Jews* (Jersey City: KTAV, 2006), p. 65.

32 "impossible to exaggerate": *New York Journal*, February 10, 1898.

32 JOURNAL'S LETTER FREES COUNTRY: *New York Journal*, February 11, 1898.

32 "I laid down my pen": G.J.A. O'Toole, *The Spanish War: An American Epic, 1898* (New York: W. W. Norton, 1984), p. 21.

33 "no torpedo such as is known": Thomas, *War Lovers*, pp. 210–11.

34 the navy's false conclusion: *Official Report of the Naval Court of Inquiry into the loss of the Battleship Maine*, http://www.spanamwar.com/mainerpt.htm.

34 "*Maine* is a great thing": David Nasaw, *The Chief: The Life of William Randolph Hearst* (Boston: Houghton Mifflin, 2013), p. 171.

34 "Being a jingo": Joseph Bucklin Bishop, *Theodore Roosevelt and His Time as Shown in His Letters*, vol. 1 (New York: Charles Scribner's Sons, 1920), p. 105.

34 "Uncle Sam, tell us": https://archive.org/details/uncsamwait1898.

34 "I have been through one war": Jack McCallum, *Leonard Wood: Rough Rider, Surgeon, Architect of American Imperialism* (New York: New York University Press, 2006), p. 55.

35 "much nervous trouble": Thomas, *War Lovers*, p. 217.

35 "oppressed and care-worn": Ibid.

35 "mechanical massage" machine: Ivan Musicant, *Empire by Default: The Spanish-American War and the Dawn of the American Century* (New York: Henry Holt, 1998), p. 153.

35 As soon as Roosevelt realized: Stacy A. Cordery, *Theodore Roosevelt in the Vanguard of the Modern* (Belmont, CA: Thomson Wadsworth, 2003), p. 52; Garraty, *Henry Cabot Lodge*, p. 186.

35   "During my short absence": Thomas, *War Lovers*, p. 218.

35   "I have had letters": *Indianapolis News*, March 9, 1898.

36   "with as little apparent feeling": David A. Copeland, *The Greenwood Library of American War Reporting: The Indian Wars and the Spanish-American War* (Westport, CT: Greenwood, 2005), p. 326.

36   Proctor said he had set out for Cuba: Henry Benejah Russell, *The Story of Two Wars: An Illustrated History of Our War with Spain and Our War with the Filipinos* (Hartford: Hartford Publishing, 1899), pp. 33–46.

36   cleared his speech with McKinley: Ernest R. May, *Imperial Democracy: The Emergence of America as a Great Power* (New York: Harper and Row, 1961), p. 144.

36   to increase the market for gravestones: David Traxel, *1898: The Tumultuous Year of Victory, Invention, Internal Strife, and Industrial Strife that Saw the Birth of the American Century* (New York: Alfred A. Knopf, 1998), p. 117.

37   "Forcible intervention": John W. Tyler, *The Life of William McKinley* (Philadelphia: P. W. Ziegler, 1901), pp. 150–59.

37   "We are not in this crisis by accident": *Chicago Tribune*, April 14, 1898.

37   blocked bills to finance a bigger navy: Grant, *Mr, Speaker!*, p. 353.

38   Pandemonium broke out: Thomas, *War Lovers*, pp. 236–37.

38   Teller Amendment: *Chicago Tribune*, November 15, 1898.

39   "Dissuade them!": *New York Times*, April 7, 1898.

39   "It would very grievously hurt this Republic": *New York Journal*, April 8, 1898.

40   "During the stormy period": Claude M. Fuess, *Carl Schurz: Reformer* (New York: Dodd, Mead, 1932), p. 1.

40   "My country, right or wrong": Hans Louis Trefousse, *Carl Schurz: A Biography* (New York: Fordham University Press, 1998), p. 180.

40   "no jingo nonsense": H. Wayne Morgan, *William McKinley and His America* (Syracuse: Syracuse University Press, 1963), p. 223.

40   "would be criminal aggression": Ibid., p. 264.

40   "The man who in times of popular excitement": *Harper's Weekly*, April 16, 1898.

41   By 5:20 Dewey's maneuver was complete: Musicant, *Empire by Default*, p. 221.

41   Spain suffered 381 casualties: Gregg Jones, *Honor in the Dust: Theodore Roosevelt, War in the Philippines, and the Rise and Fall of America's Imperial Dream* (New York: New American Library, 2012), p. 49.

41   VICTORY! COMPLETE! GLORIOUS!: *New York Journal*, May 2, 1898.

41   An astonishing 1.6 million papers: Joseph E. Wisan, *The Cuban Crisis as Reflected in the New York Press, 1895–1898* (New York: Columbia University Press, 1934), p. 26.

41   "If old Dewey had just sailed away": John Taliaferro, *All the Great Prizes:*

The Life of John Hay, from Lincoln to Roosevelt (New York: Simon and Schuster, 2013), p. 331.

41   "The victory at Manila was at first": May, *Imperial Democracy*, p. 245.

41   "With our protective tariff wall": David Silbey, *A War of Frontier and Empire: The Philippine-American War 1899–1902* (New York: Hill and Wang, 2007), p. 54.

42   "somewhere away around": *The Dial*, vol. 60 (Chicago: Dial, 1916), p. 501.

42   "I could not have told you": Meredith Mason Brown, *Touching America's History: From the Pequot War Through World War II* (Bloomington: Indiana University Press, 2013), p. 152.

42   "whether it is your desire": David F. Trask, *The War with Spain in 1898* (Lincoln: University of Nebraska Press, 1996), p. 383.

42   "completing the reduction": Charles S. Olcott, *American Statesmen: William McKinley*, vol. 2 (Boston: Houghton Mifflin, 1916), pp. 166–67.

42   "He has lost his head": O'Toole, *Spanish War*, p. 195.

43   Roosevelt asked the governors: McCallum, *Leonard Wood*, p. 58.

43   "Colonel Wood is lost sight of": Dale E. Walker, *Boys of '98: Theodore Roosevelt and the Rough Riders* (New York: Forge, 1999), p. 101.

43   "I would have turned from my wife's deathbed": Ibid., p. 87.

43   "from Harvard, Yale, Princeton": Cordery, *Theodore Roosevelt in the Vanguard*, p. 55.

43   "millionaires, paupers, shyster lawyers": McCallum, *Leonard Wood*, p. 66.

43   Finally a correspondent: Traxel, *1898*, p. 147.

44   "The eyes of the civilized world": Walker, *Boys of '98*, p. 119.

44   Dewey meets Aguinaldo: Silbey, *War of Frontier and Empire*, p. 41; Brian McAllister Linn, *The Philippine War 1899–1902* (Lawrence: University of Kansas Press, 2000), p. 21; Wolff, *Little Brown Brother*, pp. 69–70.

44   "It is the word of a Malay adventurer": Stuart Creighton Miller, *"Benevolent Assimilation": The American Conquest of the Philippines, 1899–1903* (New Haven: Yale University Press, 1982), p. 37.

45   Schurz . . . was shocked: Frederic Bancroft, ed., *Speeches, Correspondence and Political Papers of Carl Schurz*, vol. 5 (New York: Negro Universities Press, 1913), p. 466.

46   "We need Hawaii": May, *Imperial Democracy*, p. 244.

46   to debate on annexation of Hawaii: U.S. Senate, *Senate Secret Debate on Seizure of the Hawaiian Islands, Tuesday, May 31, 1898*, http://www.hawaiiankingdom.org/pdf/Annex%2021.pdf.

47   "A sort of bellicose fever": May, *Imperial Democracy*, p. 143.

46   Reports from European newspapers: Giovanna Dell'Orto, *The Hidden Power of the American Dream: Why Europe's Shaken Confidence in the United States Threatens the Future of U.S. Influence* (Westport, CT: Praeger, 2008), pp. 37, 40, 41, 47.

47   "We desire to call attention": Murray Polner and Thomas E. Woods Jr.,

We Who Dared to Say No to War: American Antiwar Writing from 1812 to Now (New York: Basic, 2008), pp. 89–91.

48   "A generation has grown up": Robert Mann, *Wartime Dissent in America: A History and Anthology* (New York: Palgrave Macmillan, 2010), pp. 65–67.

3. THE GREAT DAY OF MY LIFE

49   "It is a great historical expedition": O'Toole, *Spanish War*, p. 246.

50   "The majority is always in the wrong": Jim Zwick, *Confronting Imperialism: Essays on Mark Twain and the Anti-Imperialist Movement* (West Conshohocken, PA: Infinity, 2007), p. 170.

50   "I have never enjoyed a war": Fishkin, *Historical Guide*, pp. 236–37.

50   "On your way": Leslie W. Walker, "Guam's Seizure by the United States in 1898," *Pacific Historical Review*, vol. 14, no. 1 (March 1945), pp. 1–12.

52   "The flag which had risen first": *Harper's*, July 1899.

52   HOW DO YOU LIKE THE JOURNAL'S WAR?: *New York Journal*, May 1, 1898.

52   an insolent letter: *New York Journal*, June 1, 1898.

53   His shipmates included a small army: Nasaw, *The Chief*, p. 137.

53   "the *Journal* had been the most potent influence": Thomas, *War Lovers*, p. 311.

53   "Roosevelt . . . jumped up and down": Walker, *Boys of '98*, p. 197.

54   "to my intense delight": Theodore Roosevelt, *The Autobiography of Theodore Roosevelt* (CreateSpace, 2009), p. 127.

54   in command of the Rough Riders: Cordery, *Theodore Roosevelt*, p. 436.

54   "The attack on Santiago is to begin": Brown, *Correspondents' War*, pp. 338–39.

54   "The instant I received the order": O'Toole, *The Spanish War*, pp. 315–16.

54   205 Americans and 215 Spaniards: Jones, *Honor in the Dust*, p. 77.

54   "the great day of my life": Morris, *Rise of Theodore Roosevelt*, p. 650.

54   "I wanted it for the *Journal*": Brown, *Correspondents' War*, p. 347.

55   blue polka-dot kerchief: Walker, *Boys of '98*, p. 214.

55   "Holy Godfrey": Edward Marshall and Richard F. Outcault, *The Story of the Rough Riders* (New York: G. W. Dillingham, 1899), p. 104.

55   "I closed in and fired twice": Thomas, *War Lovers*, p. 327.

56   Twenty-nine of them obediently came aboard: Nasaw, *The Chief*, pp. 139–40.

56   "You have won yourself a high place": Brands, *Last Romantic*, p. 361.

56   "On the day of the big fight": Ibid., p. 357.

57   "a group of correspondents would congregate": Garraty, *Henry Cabot Lodge*, p. 83.

57   "although the event was a crucial element": Angus Konstam, *San Juan Hill 1898: America's Emergence as a World Power* (Oxford: Osprey, 1998), pp. 70–71.

58   "I hear talk all the time": Thomas, *War Lovers*, p. 349.

58   "Ordinary rules do not apply to you": Zimmerman, *First Great Triumph*, p. 311.

58   "get that Medal of Honor for me": Thomas, *War Lovers*, p. 353.

58   "I don't ask this as a favor": Brands, *Last Romantic*, p. 372.

58   "extraordinary heroism": Glenda Richardson, *Medal of Honor Recipients 1979–2003* (New York: Novinka, 2003), p. 4.

58   "a splendid little war": Joseph Smith, *The Spanish-American War 1895–1902: Conflict in the Caribbean and the Pacific* (New York: Routledge, 1994), p. 212.

59   July 6 Senate debate on the annexation of Hawaii: *Congressional Record, Senate*, July 6, 1898, pp. 6693–6708.

60   "Hurrah for Hawaii!": Zimmerman, *First Great Triumph*, p. 292.

61   "Hawaii is ours": Ryan S., Waters, *The Last Jeffersonian: Grover Cleveland and the Path to Restoring the Republic* (Bloomington, IN: WestBow, 2012), p. 114.

61   "the Hawaiian monstrosity": E. Berkeley Tompkins, *Anti-Imperialism in the United States: The Great Debate 1890–1920* (Philadelphia: University of Pennsylvania Press, 1970), p. 101.

61   "dangerous perversions": *New York Times*, June 22, 1898.

61   "Our government was formed": *New York Journal*, June 23, 1898.

61   "Burdened with ponderous platitudinosities": *New York Journal*, June 23, 1898.

62   "The president I think feels very strongly about Cuba": Thomas, *War Lovers*, p. 353.

62   "I am feeling disgracefully well!": Walker, *Boys of '98*, p. 265.

62   "When I took it to Cuba": Morris, *Rise of Theodore Roosevelt*, p. 665.

62   "Will you be our next governor?": Ibid., pp. 664–65.

62   The War Department . . . refused to allow it: Walter Mills, *The Martial Spirit* (Cambridge: Literary Guild, 1931), p. 368.

63   "It is cheering to find a newspaper": *New York Journal*, March 19, 1898.

63   "ways of sultanic languor": Nasaw, *The Chief*, p. 135.

64   "I feel like hell": Thomas, *War Lovers*, p. 362.

64   "I guess I'm a failure": Ibid.

64   "That Roosevelt . . . was already so far ahead of him": Nasaw, *The Chief*, p. 147.

64   "The athlete does not win his race": Garraty, *Henry Cabot Lodge*, p. 206.

65   "The march of events": Scott Miller, *The President and the Assassin: McKinley, Terror, and Empire at the Dawn of the American Century* (New York: Random House, 2013), p. 235.

65   "The governor-general arranged with me": United States Senate, *Hearings Before the Committee on the Philippines of the United States Senate* (Washington, D.C.: Government Printing Office, 1902), p. 2929.

65   American commanders did not invite Aguinaldo: Linn, *Philippine War*, p. 25.

65   "Do not make peace": Arturo Morales Carrión, *Puerto Rico: A Political and Cultural History* (New York: W. W. Norton, 1983), p. 134.

66   "the annexation of . . . the entire world": Gore Vidal, *Empire* (New York: Vintage, 2000), p. 103.

66   By a wonderful quirk of history: Zimmerman, *First Great Triumph*, p. 295.

66   Lodge decorated one room: Garraty, *Henry Cabot Lodge*, pp. 195–96.

67   "Lodge is the Mephistopheles": Brands, *Last Romantic*, p. 333.

67   photo of Lodge in full drag: Garraty, *Henry Cabot Lodge*, facing p. 17.

67   "What a wonderful war": Zimmerman, *First Great Triumph*, p. 312.

67   "The government must not be held": Mills, *Martial Spirit*, p. 364.

68   "was not undertaken for territorial aggrandizement": Joseph Frazier Wall, *Andrew Carnegie* (Pittsburgh: University of Pittsburgh Press, 1989), p. 693.

68   "Cuba must be freed": Ibid., p. 691.

68   "Distant Possessions": Ibid., p. 698.

69   Schurz presented the anti-imperial case: Bancroft, *Speeches*, pp. 472–94.

70   "Mr. Schurz, you are too late!": *National Civic Federation Review* (New York), March 25, 1919.

70   The Saratoga conference convened for its final session: *Clinton Tribune*, August 22, 1898.

4. ISLANDS OR CANNED GOODS

72   In public, Roosevelt was still denying: Morris, *Rise of Theodore Roosevelt*, p. 668.

72   "If he becomes governor": Ibid., p. 666; United States Senate History, *Theodore Roosevelt, 25th Vice President,* http://www.senate.gov/artandhistory /history/common/generic/VP_Theodore_Roosevelt.htm.

73   "I always look at a public question": Cordery, *Theodore Roosevelt*, p. 59.

73   "would adopt no line of policy": Ferdinand Schevill, *The Rise and Progress of Democracy* (Chicago: Zalaz, 1915), p. 28.

73   Reformers . . . denounced him: Morris, *Rise of Theodore Roosevelt*, p. 676.

74   "There is no humiliation": Nasaw, *The Chief*, p. 148.

74   "We are told": Bancroft, *Speeches*, pp. 494–513.

75   "Would it not be perfectly feasible": Ibid., pp. 517–19.

75   the United States "cannot let go": Morgan, *William McKinley*, p. 410.

76   "Jammed from top to bottom": *Los Angeles Herald*, October 6, 1898.

76   "soaring, chauvinist oration": Stephen Glain, *State vs. Defense: The Battle to Define America's Empire* (New York: Broadway, 2012), p. 7.

76   "It sounded more like the oratory": Morris, *Rise of Theodore Roosevelt*, p. 680.

76   "There comes a time": *Chicago Tribune*, October 7, 1898.

76   He refused to feign: Morris, *Rise of Theodore Roosevelt*, p. 681.

77   "Expansion and our imperial destiny": *New York Times*, October 17, 1898.

77   whirlwind campaign tour: Morris, *Rise of Theodore Roosevelt*, pp. 684–85.

78   "When it came to the great day": Ibid., p. 683.

78   "wild imperialistic ideas": Bancroft, *Speeches*, p. 520.

78   "We have long been friends": Ibid., p. 521.

78   "He virtually asks us to endorse": Ibid., pp. 521–25.

79   "If we ever come to nothing": Widenor, *Henry Cabot Lodge*, p. 80.

79   "The chief of the reasons": *New York Times*, October 23, 1898.

80   "Unable to assail Roosevelt": Nasaw, *The Chief*, p. 148.

81   "map out and advocate": Paul C. Nagel, *This Sacred Trust: American Nationality 1778–1898* (New York: Oxford University Press, 1991), p. 295.

81   Beveridge launched his campaign: Claude G. Bowers, *Beveridge and the Progressive Era* (Boston: Houghton Mifflin, 1932), p. 73.

81   "March of the Flag": http://voicesofdemocracy.umd.edu/beveridge-march -of-the-flag-speech-text/.

82   Hoar made that clear: *Boston Globe*, November 2, 1898.

82   "Wobbly Willie": Laura B. Edge, *William McKinley* (Minneapolis: Twenty-First Century, 2006), p. 66.

83   McKinley gave fifty-seven speeches: Jones, *Honor in the Dust*, p. 105.

83   He found much enthusiasm: *New York World*, October 17, 1898.

83   "Shall we deny to ourselves": Zimmerman, *First Great Triumph*, p. 319.

83   According to the official transcript: William McKinley, *Speeches and Addresses of William McKinley from March 1, 1897, to May 30, 1900* (New York: Doubleday and McClure, 1900), pp. 122–23; Zimmerman, *First Great Triumph*, p. 319.

83   "Democracy has seriously begun to rule humanity": Fabian Hilfrich, *Debating American Exceptionalism: Empire and Democracy in the Wake of the Spanish-American War* (New York: Palgrave Macmillan, 2102), p. 80.

84   "This country has been most fortunate": *Sacramento Daily Union*, October 17, 1898.

84   "When Mr. Washington had given expression": Ibid.

85   "It is worse than folly": John Nichols, ed., *Against the Beast: A Documentary History of American Opposition to Empire* (New York: Nation, 2004), p. 114.

86   "We cannot avoid the serious questions": McKinley, *Speeches and Addresses*, pp. 133–36.

86   Mr. Dooley "probably did as much": Tompkins, *Anti-Imperialists*, p. 181.

86   "Mack r-rose up": Finley Peter Dunne, *Mr. Dooley in Peace and in War* (Boston: Small, Maynard, 1899), pp. 84–86.

87   "None of us have been able to move him": Mills, *Martial Spirit*, p. 383.

87   Various forces united to push McKinley: Richard E. Welch Jr., *Response to Imperialism: The United States and the Philippine-American War, 1899–1902* (Chapel Hill: University of North Carolina Press), p. 10.

87   "I went down on my knees": Daniel B. Schirmer and Stephen Rosskamm

Shalom, eds., *The Philippines Reader: A History of Colonialism, Neocolonialism, Dictatorship, and Resistance* (Boston: South End, 1987), p. 20.

88   "There is no denying": *Troy Times*, November 5, 1898.

88   "I have played it with bull luck": Morris, *Rise of Theodore Roosevelt*, p. 686.

88   "Willing or not": Mills, *Martial Spirit*, p. 387.

89   "Give to Hawaii a territorial government": George C. Boutwell, *The Crisis of the Republic* (Boston: Dana Estates, 1900), p. 85.

90   a check for $10,000: *Los Angeles Times*, November 20, 1898.

90   "address to the public": *St. Louis Post-Dispatch*, May 7, 1899.

91   "Should we undertake to hold the Philippines": Tompkins, *Anti-Imperialism*, p. 178.

91   "The true friend": Peter Krass, *Carnegie* (New York: Wiley, 2002), p. 370.

91   "When a jellyfish wishes": Wall, *Andrew Carnegie*, p. 696.

91   "If you should call upon the United States": *The Independent* (New York), May 18, 1899.

92   Harrison . . . opposed further expansion: Robert L. Beisner, *Twelve Against Empire: The Anti-Imperialists 1898–1900* (New York: McGraw-Hill, 1968), p. 189.

92   "a wild and frantic attack": Krass, *Andrew Carnegie*, p. 370.

92   "Few years in our history": Edward T. Roe, *The Life Work of William McKinley* (Chicago: Laird and Lee, 1901), p. 114.

92   "Treaty signed at 8:50": Halstead, *Illustrious Life*, p. 350.

93   "The President is naturally compelled to add": *London Chronicle*, December 7, 1898.

94   "We are going to have trouble": Garraty, *Henry Cabot Lodge*, p. 200.

94   "It seems impossible": Mills, *Martial Spirit*, p. 392.

94   "under the constitution": Tompkins, *Anti-Imperialism*, pp. 178–79.

94   "If we take the Philippines": Theodore L. Flood, ed., *The Chautauquan* (Meadeville, PA: T. L. Flood, 1899), p. 477.

94   Schurz called for a national plebiscite: Tompkins, *Anti-Imperialism*, p. 177.

94   Bryan gave a speech: *Los Angeles Herald*, December 23, 1898.

95   "What a singular collection": Morgan, *William McKinley*, p. 318.

95   "I know what I'd do": Dunne, *Mr. Dooley*, pp. 43–44.

97   "I would gladly pay twenty millions": Wall, *Andrew Carnegie*, p. 695.

97   He offered to strike a partnership: Nasaw, *The Chief*, p. 556; Wall, *Andrew Carnegie*, pp. 699–702.

5. IF THEY RESIST, WHAT SHALL WE DO?

99   Roosevelt sworn in as governor: Morris, *Rise of Theodore Roosevelt*, p. 691.

100   "one of those world powers": Edward P. Kohn, *Heir to the Empire City: New York and the Making of Theodore Roosevelt* (New York: Basic, 2013), p. 187.

100   McKinley's proclamation: http://www.msc.edu.ph/centennial/benevolent
       .html.

101   "the kicking Bostonese": *Los Angeles Times*, December 13, 1898.

101   a guide "for speakers or writers": Frederic Bancroft, ed., *Speeches, Corre-
       spondence and Political Papers of Carl Schurz*, vol. 6 (New York: Negro
       Universities Press, 1913), p. 1.

101   "You have brains": Nasaw, *Andrew Carnegie*, p. 556.

101   Schurz on American imperialism: Bancroft, *Speeches*, vol. 6, pp. 1–35.

102   "My nation cannot remain indifferent": Wolff, *Little Brown Brother*, p. 201.

103   McKinley tried to ease Hoar out: Richard E. Welch, *George Frisbie Hoar
       and the Half-Breed Republicans* (Cambridge, MA: Harvard University
       Press, 1971), p. 218.

103   "There is always a certain inherent drama": Ibid., p. 232.

104   "It is the greatest question ever discussed": *New York Times*, January 10,
       1899.

104   Congratulatory letters and telegrams poured: *Boston Transcript*, January 9,
       1899.

104   HOAR ATTACKS IMPERIALISM AND TREATY: *New York World*, January 9,
       1899.

105   "The literal application of the Senator's doctrine": *Congressional Record,
       Senate*, January 9, 1899, p. 501.

105   Trumbull's iconic painting: Daniel B. Schirmer, *Republic or Empire:
       American Resistance to the Philippine War* (Cambridge, MA: Schenkman,
       1972), p. 116.

105   "For over 100 years": *Boston Transcript*, January 10, 1899.

106   "I do not understand": *Boston Evening Transcript*, January 13, 1899; *Los
       Angeles Herald*, January 12, 1899; *Springfield Daily Republican*, January 14,
       1899.

107   "The Philippines are too far away": *Herald Democrat* (Leadville, CO),
       December 14, 1898.

107   Bryan's first and most radical gambit: Krass, *Carnegie*, pp. 371–72.

107   Pressed by reporters: *Los Angeles Herald*, December 23, 1898.

107   "When silver and iron fuse": *Boston Globe*, December 22, 1898.

107   "Just now I am talking against imperialism": Coletta, "Bryan," p. 134.

107   "You need not delude yourself": Morgan, *William McKinley*, p. 418.

108   "The Bible teaches us": Bryan, *Life and Speeches*, p. 68.

108   "I was so incensed": Mills, *Martial Spirit*, p. 401.

108   "Friends here who know tell me": W. Stull Holt, *Treaties Defeated by the Sen-
       ate: A Study of the Struggle Between President and Senate over the Conduct of
       Foreign Relations* (Baltimore: Johns Hopkins University Press, 1933), p. 175.

109   "Our friends assure me": Tompkins, *Anti-Imperialism*, p. 190.

109   "Your plan is dangerous": Coletta, "Bryan," p. 135.

109   "It is impossible now to make": Tompkins, *Anti-Imperialism*, pp. 190–91.

109   "Who can estimate": *New York Journal*, January 15, 1899.

109   "Naboth's Vineyard": Bryan, *Life and Speeches*, pp. 71–75.

110   "No one would venture an independent prediction": *Boston Transcript*, January 18, 1899.

110   "The fight that is being made": Theodore Roosevelt and Henry Cabot Lodge, *Selections of the Correspondence of Theodore Roosevelt and Henry Cabot Lodge, 1884–1918*, vol. 1 (New York: Charles Scribner's Sons, 1925), p. 385.

110   along with colloquies: *Sacramento Daily Union*, January 24, 1899.

111   "We have beaten Spain": William Graham Sumner, *The Conquest of the United States by Spain*, http://praxeology.net/WGS-CUS.htm.

112   "The two speeches go before the country": *Boston Transcript*, January 24, 1899.

112   A group of educated Filipinos: Onofre D. Corpuz, *Saga and Triumph: The Filipino Revolution Against Spain* (Manila: University of the Philippines Press, 2002), p. 191.

113   "give to those people more freedom": Hilfrich, *Debating American Exceptionalism*, p. 213.

113   "the highest cruelty": Ibid., p. 44.

113   "Providence has given the United States": *Congressional Record, Senate*, January 20, 1899, p. 838.

113   "The President is puzzled": *Boston Transcript*, January 19, 1899.

113   "Final polling today": *Boston Transcript*, January 25, 1899.

113   "On the surface": Coletta, "Bryan," p. 136.

113   "To refuse to ratify the treaty": Brands, *Last Romantic*, p. 386.

114   "It is difficult for me to speak": Morgan, *William McKinley*, pp. 416–17.

114   "I told the President": Holt, *Treaties Defeated*, p. 167.

114   "The President . . . cannot be sent back": Morgan, *William McKinley*, p. 419.

114   "really is against the Philippines": Paolo E. Coletta, "Bryan, McKinley, and the Treaty of Paris," *Pacific Historical Review*, vol. 26, no. 2 (May 1957), p. 136.

114   "we have been for a whole century": *Chicago Tribune*, January 28, 1899.

115   "ought not to be ratified until provision is inserted": *Sacramento Daily Union*, February 6, 1899.

115   "The week of tedious maneuverings": *Boston Transcript*, February 4, 1899.

116   a poem called "Imperialism": *Liberty Poems Inspired by the Crisis of 1898–1900* (Boston: James H. West, 1900), p. 18.

6. STINKPOT

117   "Where these sassy niggers": Silbey, *War of Frontier*, pp. 61–62.

117   "a striking point": *Boston Transcript*, January 25, 1899.

118   orders to patrol aggressively: Schirmer, *Republic or Empire*, p. 128.

118   One of Hoar's informants cabled: Ibid.

118   General Otis . . . cabled his superiors: Ibid., p. 126.

118   "unoccupied territory the insurgents regarded": Ibid., p. 129.

118 "Something rose up slowly": Charles Edward Russell, *The Outlook for the Philippines* (New York: Century, 1922), p. 93.

118 sixty Americans and three thousand Filipinos lay dead: Miller, *"Benevolent Assimilation,"* p. 68.

118 "We had a pre-arranged plan": Schirmer, *Republic or Empire*, p. 129.

119 "How foolish these people are": Morgan, *William McKinley*, p. 421.

119 "the insane attack": *New York Times*, February 7, 1899.

119 "crush the power of Aguinaldo": Schirmer, *Republic or Empire*, p. 130.

119 "Time alone will tell": Ibid.

119 Senators on both sides: *New York Times*, February 6, 1899.

119 "I have tried to avoid": Schirmer and Shalom, *Philippines Reader*, p. 20.

121 the White House was "moving heaven and earth": Welch, *George Frisbie Hoar*, p. 237.

121 "McKinley himself remained unobtrusive": Morgan, *William McKinley*, p. 420.

121 Pettigrew . . . stormed furiously into the office: Richard F. Pettigrew, *Imperial Washington* (Chicago: Charles H. Kerr, 1922), pp. 204–5.

121 Bryan was unmoved: Wall, *Andrew Carnegie*, pp. 702–3.

122 Carnegie was . . . "beside himself with rage": Morgan, *William McKinley*, p. 418.

122 "President McKinley, our 'War Lord'": *New York World*, January 30, 1899.

122 they talked ceaselessly: Garraty, *Henry Cabot Lodge*, p. 85.

122 "The excitement in Washington": *Boston Transcript*, February 6, 1899.

122 "the greatest Arctic outbreak in history": Paul J. Kocin et al., "The Great Arctic Outbreak and East Coast Blizzard of February 1899," in *Weather and Forecasting*, December 1998.

122 "no conflict with the insurgents": Mills, *Martial Spirit*, p. 395.

123 Lodge later wrote that he was uncertain: Holt, *Treaties Defeated*, p. 168.

123 "Anxiety was due not only": *San Francisco Call*, February 7, 1899.

123 "At the time the Senate went into executive session": *Boston Transcript*, February 7, 1899.

124 NO TRIFLING WITH FILIPINOS NOW: *San Francisco Call*, February 7, 1899.

124 Few in Washington were surprised: Coletta, "Bryan," pp. 138–40; Holt, *Treaties Defeated*, p. 173; Schirmer, *Republic or Empire*, pp. 122–23; Tompkins, *Anti-Imperialism*, p. 195; Welch, *George Frisbie Hoar*, pp. 244–45.

124 They had reason to be bitter: Carnegie, *Autobiography*, p. 352; Coletta, "Bryan," p. 138; Garraty, *Henry Cabot Lodge*, p. 201; Hoar, *Autobiography of Seventy Years*, vol. 2 (1903), p. 322; Pratt, *Expansionists of 1898*, p. 357.

124 "more responsible than any other": Coletta, "Bryan," p. 140.

124 "but for Mr. Bryan's personal interposition": Tompkins, *Anti-Imperialism*, p. 194.

124 "One word from Mr. Bryan": Carnegie, *Autobiography*, p. 364.

125 "But for Bryan and his influence": Holt, *Treaties Defeated*, p. 174.

125   "When the Spanish Treaty was pending": Pettigrew, *Imperial Washington*, pp. 270–71.

125   Bryan "let his friendliness for McKinley": John Cuthbert Long, *Bryan, the Great Commoner* (New York: D. Appleton, 1928), p. 131.

125   "How could he avoid expansion": Paulo Coletta, "McKinley, the Peace Negotiations, and the Acquisition of the Philippines," *Pacific Historical Review*, vol. 30, no. 4 (November 1961), p. 134.

126   "To the Honorable Eugene Hale": Welch, *George Frisbie Hoar*, p. 249.

126   "It had been a narrow thing": Mills, *Martial Spirit*, p. 403.

126   PEACE TREATY RATIFIED: *New York Journal*, February 6, 1899.

127   "Last Tuesday morning": Beisner, *Twelve Against Empire*, p. 158.

127   "There has never been an act of oppression": H. W. Brands, *The Reckless Decade: America in the 1890s* (New York: St. Martin's, 1995), p. 334.

127   "The country is now fairly embarked": David Milne, *Worldmaking: The Art and Science of American Diplomacy* (New York: Farrar, Straus and Giroux, 2015), p. 61.

128   "Until the fight was over": Garraty, *Henry Cabot Lodge*, pp. 201–2.

128   "As in the Roman Senate": *Liberty Poems*, p. 66.

128   a large cartoon: *New York Journal*, February 8, 1899.

129   "Iloilo City was a blackened ruin": Linn, *Philippine War*, p. 68.

129   "A message of tyranny": *Sacramento Daily Union*, February 15, 1899.

130   Twenty inches of snow: http://www.washingtonpost.com/blogs/capital-weather-gang/post/what-is-washington-dcs-weather-like-in-february-breaking-down-norms-and-extremes/2012/02/12/gIQAXDkUDR_blog.html.

130   Home Market Club: *Sacred Heart Review* (Cambridge), February 4, 1899; *Boston Herald, Boston Advertiser, Boston Globe, Boston Transcript*, February 17, 1899; *Christian Science Sentinel* (Boston), February 23, 1899.

133   James poured out his anguished soul: William James, *Essays, Comments, and Reviews* (Cambridge, MA: Harvard University Press, 1987), pp. 154–58.

134   "the President's own Pandora's box": Wall, *Andrew Carnegie*, p. 707.

134   "If the nation would declare": Bryan, *Life and Speeches*, p. 76.

135   "They labored under the decided disadvantage": Brands, *Last Romantic*, p. 333.

135   "On ship and on shore": McKinley, *Speeches and Addresses*, p. 305.

136   "We went to the Sandwich Islands": Jennifer C. James, *A Freedom Bought with Blood: African American War Literature from the Civil War to World War II* (Chapel Hill: University of North Carolina Press, 2007), p. 126.

136   Colored National Anti-Imperial League: Richard Seymour, *American Insurgents: A Brief History of American Anti-Imperialism* (Chicago: Haymarket, 2012), p. 50.

136   "to satisfy the robbers": E. Nathaniel Gates, *Race and U.S. Foreign Policy*

in the Ages of Territorial and Market Expansion, 1840–1900 (New York: Routledge, 1998), p. 8.

136   "one of the most unrighteous acts": *The Defender* (Philadelphia), January 27, 1900.

136   "the white man's burden is never so heavy": Jackson Lears, *Rebirth of a Nation: The Making of Modern America, 1877–1920* (New York: Harper-Collins, 2009), p. 216.

136   The mathematician and sociologist: Kelly Miller, "The Effect of Imperialism on the Negro Race," in *Anti-Imperialist Broadside*, no. 11 (Boston: Anti-Imperialist League, 1899).

136   "We are eternally opposed": Linda O. McMurry, *To Keep the Waters Troubled : The Life of Ida B. Wells* (New York: Oxford University Press, 1998), p. 253.

136   "The colored people of Boston": Schirmer and Shalom, *Philippines Reader*, p. 32.

137   "the lowering of a great race": Henry Cabot Lodge, *Speeches and Addresses 1884–1909* (Boston: Houghton Mifflin, 1909), p. 264.

137   Roosevelt attributed humanity's rise: Theodore Roosevelt, *Presidential Addresses and State Papers and European Addresses* (New York: Review of Reviews, 1910), p. 2073.

137   "a warped, perverse and silly morality": Jean M. Yarborough, *Theodore Roosevelt and the American Political Tradition* (Lawrence: University of Kansas Press, 2012), p. 77.

137   "made up very considerably of black people": Gerald Linderman, *The Mirror of War: American Society and the Spanish-American War* (Ann Arbor: University of Michigan Press, 1974), p. 138.

137   "You are undertaking to annex": *Farmer and Mechanic* (Raleigh, NC), January 24, 1899.

138   "a mess of Asian pottage": Thomas G. Paterson, *American Imperialism and Anti-Imperialism* (New York: Crowell, 1973), p. 114.

138   "They are not all one": *Los Angeles Herald*, February 4, 1899.

138   Gompers . . . frankly admitted: Stuart B. Kaufman, *The Samuel Gompers Papers*, vol. 5: *An Expanding Movement at the Turn of the Century, 1898–1902* (Urbana: University of Illinois Press, 1995), p. 28.

138   "We have hoisted our flag": Brands, *Reckless Decade*, p. 343.

138   "There must be control": Lears, *Rebirth of a Nation*, p. 203.

139   "For the first time in history": *Manchester Guardian*, January 3, 1899.

7. I TURN GREEN IN BED AT MIDNIGHT

140   "America had made so vast a stride": Mills, *Martial Spirit*, p. 405.

140   a series of long essays: *Harper's*, February, March, May, June, and July 1899.

141   "For thirty years": *Harper's*, June 1899.

141   patriotic dispatches: *Saturday Evening Post*, March 17 and 23, 1899.

142   "conspiracy against the government": Stanley Karnow, *In Our Image: America's Empire in the Philippines* (New York: Ballantine, 1990), p. 148.

142   "There are towns": Wolff, *Little Brown Brother*, p. 241.

142   "the American outlook": Karnow, *In Our Image*, p. 155.

142   "be good Indians": Morgan, *William McKinley*, p. 438.

142   "bold and defiant": Elwell S. Otis, *Report of Maj. Gen. E. S. Otis, United States Army, Commanding Division of the Philippines, Military Governor: September 1, 1899 to May 5, 1900* (Washington, D.C.: Government Printing Office, 1900), p. 10.

142   "An air of gloom": Linn, *Philippine War*, p. 117.

142   "I turn green": David R. Contosta and Robert Muccigrosso, eds., *Henry Adams and His World* (Philadelphia: American Philosophical Association, 1993), p. 42.

142   its membership numbered in the hundreds of thousands: Michael Patrick Cullinane, *Liberty and American Anti-Imperialism, 1898–1900* (New York: Palgrave Macmillan, 2012), p. 25.

143   Eager to seize the moment: Jones, *Honor in the Dust*, p. 160.

143   a meeting at Boston's historic Tremont Temple: *Protest Against the Philippine Policy: Anti-Imperialist Meeting, Tremont Temple, April 4, 1899* (Boston: Anti-Imperialist League, 1899).

143   "Chicago Liberty Meeting": *Chicago Liberty Meeting Held at Central Music Hall, April 30, 1899* (Chicago: Central Anti-Imperialist League, 1899).

144   "the essential manliness of the American character": Hoganson, *American Manhood*, p. 188.

144   "supple, feminine, and illogical": Lodge, *Studies in History*, p. 148.

144   "women's auxiliary": *Springfield Daily Republican*, May 30, 1899.

144   "We, women of the United States": Janette Thomas Greenwood, *The Gilded Age: A History in Documents* (New York: Oxford University Press, 2003), p. 151.

144   "allowed these disenfranchised citizens": Erin L. Murphy, "Women's Anti-Imperialism, 'The White Man's Burden,' and the Philippine-American War," *Asia-Pacific Journal*, vol. 77, issue 27, no. 1 (July 2009), p. 5.

145   "free those Filipino people": *The Freeman* (Indianapolis), March 4, 1899.

145   "So strong thou art": *Liberty Poems*, p. 35.

145   Atkinson drew up an ambitious list: Beisner, *Twelve Against Empire*, pp. 98–99.

145   The postmaster general promptly declared them "seditious": *Literary Digest*, no. 18 (1899), pp. 541–42; Tompkins, *Anti-Imperialism*, p. 208.

145   "I really think members of the Cabinet": Murray M. Rothbard, ed., *Left and Right: A Journal of Libertarian Thought* (Auburn, AL: Ludwig von Mises, 2007), p. 267.

146   ("Filipinos everywhere are alike hostile"): *The Anti-Imperialist*, 1899, no. 4., p. 24.

146   ("You are a foreign people"): Ibid., p. 21.

146   COLOSSAL BOTCH AND BUNGLE: *Pittsburgh Post*, September 1, 1899; *The Anti-Imperialist*, 1899, no. 5, p. 13.

146   ("From Vladivostok"): *The Anti-Imperialist*, 1899, no. 6, p. 37.

146   On July 4: *The Anti-Imperialist*, 1899, no. 3, p. 1.

146   "We've taken up the white man's burden": *New York World*, July 15, 1899.

146   Hearst had become an anti-imperialist: Nasaw, *The Chief*, p. 148.

147   "which I would not miss": Morris, *Rise of Theodore Roosevelt*, p. 703.

147   "It would really be difficult": Brands, *Last Romantic*, p. 389.

147   This tour's high point: Theodore Roosevelt, *The Strenuous Life: Essays and Addresses* (New York: Century, 1902), pp. 1–24.

148   "He is more than a presidential possibility": Morris, *Rise of Theodore Roosevelt*, p. 704.

148   "No, no, none of that": Ibid., p. 708.

148   "I have never known a hurrah": Morris, *Rise of Theodore Roosevelt*, p. 705.

148   Lodge . . . had "but two great desires": Widenor, *Henry Cabot Lodge*, p. 121.

149   "Thank the President for me": David F. Healy, *The United States in Cuba, 1898–1902: Generals, Politicians, and the Search for Policy* (Madison: University of Wisconsin Press, 1963), p. 109.

149   Roosevelt . . . scorned the choice: Morgan, *William McKinley*, p. 433.

149   "If I were a candidate": Schriftgiesser, *Gentleman from Massachusetts*, p. 185.

149   "a position with more work in it": Morris, *Rise of Theodore Roosevelt*, p. 705.

150   In six months: Wolff, *Little Brown Brother*, p. 249.

150   "his body becomes an object frightful to contemplate": *New York Evening Post*, April 8, 1902.

150   "To make them confess—what?": Charles Nieder, ed., *Life as I Find It: A Treasury of Mark Twain Rarities* (New York: Cooper Square, 1961), p. 251.

150   "it is the duty of the landlord": Travis L. Crosby, *Joseph Chamberlain: A Most Radical Imperialist* (London: I. B. Tauris, 2011), p. 115.

150   "I wish to God": Philip S. Foner, *Mark Twain: Social Critic* (New York: International, 1958), p. 265.

151   "Last night one of our boys": *Soldiers' Letters: Being Materials for the History of a War of Criminal Aggression* (Boston: Anti-Imperialist League, 1899), p. 15.

151   "They assailed our sovereignty": Morgan, *William McKinley*, p. 436.

151   the triumphal Dewey Arch: "The Dewey Arch," *Architects and Builders' Magazine*, December 30, 1900; David Brody, *Visualizing American Empire: Orientalism and Imperialism in the Philippines* (Chicago: University of Chicago Press, 2010), p. 133.

152   "Build up your arch": *Liberty Poems*, p. 22.

152   SELF-GOVERNMENT: Charles Sumner Olcott, *The Life of William McKinley*, vol. 2 (Boston: Houghton Mifflin, 1916), p. 97.

153   "concede to them the independence": Schirmer and Shalom, *Philippines Reader*, pp. 30–31.

153   "These meetings recalled vividly": *New York Post*, October 18, 1900.

153   a biting speech by Carl Schurz: Bancroft, *Speeches*, vol. 6, pp. 77–120.

154   "I didn't read": Jesse Stellato, *Not in Our Name: American Antiwar Speeches, 1846 to the Present* (University Park: Pennsylvania State University Press, 2013), p. 69.

154   He gave occasional interviews: Jones, *Honor in the Dust*, p. 158.

154   "peace-at-any-price men": Roosevelt, *Strenuous Life*, p. 100.

154   "We have got to put down": *Chicago Tribune*, November 11, 1899.

154   "I cannot understand": Ibid.

155   "A country at war is very intolerant": *North American Review* (February 1901).

155   "The so-called Filipino Republic is destroyed": Wolff, *Little Brown Brother*, p. 279.

155   "In the vice presidency": Morris, *Rise of Theodore Roosevelt*, p. 718.

156   "It is a matter of congratulation": Morgan, *William McKinley*, p. 435.

156   Beveridge stood to report: *Congressional Record, Senate*, January 9, 1900, pp. 705–11.

157   pulled a rock from his pocket: Miller, *"Benevolent Assimilation,"* p. 131.

158   "I have heard much": Karnow, *In Our Image*, p. 164.

158   "the psychological moment": *Chicago Times Herald*, January 10, 1900.

158   "If his Americanism": *Springfield Daily Republican*, January 10, 1900.

8. WHAT A CHOICE FOR A PATRIOTIC AMERICAN!

159   "I would like to see you in Washington": James R. Arnold, *Jungle of Snakes: A Century of Counterinsurgency Warfare from the Philippines to Iraq* (New York: Bloomsbury, 2009), p. 34; Bradley, *Imperial Cruise*, p. 144; Jonathan Lurie, *William Howard Taft: The Travails of a Progressive Conservative* (Cambridge: Cambridge University Press, 2014), pp. 39–40.

160   "When the United States sent word": Albert Bigelow Paine, *Mark Twain: A Biography* (New York: Harper and Brothers, 1912), p. 1064.

162   "I have thought it over a great deal": Morris, *Rise of Theodore Roosevelt*, p. 711.

162   Platt began telling friends: Ibid., p. 715.

163   "It is quite on the cards": Brands, *Last Romantic*, p. 396.

163   "Under no circumstances": Morris, *Rise of Theodore Roosevelt*, pp. 720–21.

163   rejecting "the divine right": *New York Journal*, February 11, 1900.

164   a bitingly ingenious cover: Wolff, *Little Brown Brother*, p. 272.

164   "Twice you have failed us": Edward McNall Burns, *David Starr Jordan: Prophet of Freedom* (Stanford, CA: Stanford University Press, 1953), pp. 23–24.

164   His hopes were raised: Joseph Frazier Wall, *Andrew Carnegie* (Pittsburgh: University of Pittsburgh Press, 1989), p. 708.

165   "It has been stated over and over again": Julia Ward Howe, ed., *Master-pieces of American Eloquence* (Whitefish, MT: Kessinger, 2011), pp. 355–61.

166   "You are the only man": Schriftgiesser, *Gentleman from Massachusetts*, p. 88.

166   FOR VICE PRESIDENT: Ibid., p. 213.

166   "the most famous": Morris, *Rise of Theodore Roosevelt*, p. 726.

166   "We will have this war": Brands, *Last Romantic*, p. 395.

167   "You're crazy, Roosevelt!": Ibid., p. 395.

167   "Do whatever you damn please!": Ibid., p. 397.

167   "at torrential speed": Morris, *Rise of Theodore Roosevelt*, p. 728.

167   "We stand at the threshold": Ibid., p. 729.

168   "The Wily One has won": Schriftgiesser, *Gentleman from Massachusetts*, p. 193.

168   "My purpose in this": Ibid., p. 194.

170   "Bryan threatened to withdraw": Library of Congress, "Democratic National Political Conventions 1832–2008," http://www.loc.gov/rr/main/democratic_conventions.pdf.

170   dictated by Bryan himself: Fred R. Harrington, "The Anti-Imperialist Movement in the United States, 1898–1900," *Mississippi Valley Historical Review*, vol. 22, no. 2 (September 1935), p. 226.

170   Platform: L. White Busbey et al., eds., *The Battle of 1900: An Official Handbook for Every American Citizen* (Chicago: Thompson and Hood, 1900), pp. 481–89.

171   "the paramount issue of the campaign": *Salina* (Kansas) *Daily Union*, July 6, 1900.

171   "a deluge of shouting": *Springfield Daily Republican*, April 6, 1900.

172   "rather be wrong than president": Morgan, *William McKinley*, p. 319.

172   "He is his own best opponent": Ibid., p. 502.

172   "We cannot set": Bryan, *Life and Speeches*, p. 299.

172   "Can it be our duty to kill": Ibid., p. 402.

172   "This appears to have been a colossal blunder": Thomas A. Bailey, "Was the Presidential Election of 1900 a Mandate on Imperialism?," *Mississippi Valley Historical Review*, vol. 24, no. 1 (June 1937).

173   "eyesore and disgrace": cited in *New York Times*, May 10, 1992.

173   "One morning the work lay on the ground": *New York Times*, December 30, 1900.

173   to form a third party: Miller, *"Benevolent Assimilation,"* p. 138.

173   "I am for Bryan": George Boutwell, *Bryan on Imperialism* (Boston: New England Anti-Imperialist League, 1900), pp. 15–16.

174   "the most effective means": *Herald Democrat* (Leadville, CO), August 17, 1900.

174   "The 1900 election might have marked its triumph": Zwick, *Confronting Imperialism*, pp. 6–7.

174   In every speech: Michael Kazin, *A Godly Hero: The Life of William Jennings Bryan* (New York: Alfred A. Knopf, 2006), p. 105.

174   compared Bryan's supporters to the Paris Commune: James L. Sundquist, *Dynamics of the Party System: Alignment and Realignment of Political Parties in the United States* (Washington, D.C.: Brookings, 1983), p. 156.

174   "All the lunatics": Kazin, *Godly Hero*, p. 105.

174   "a small man": Brands, *Last Romantic*, p. 403.

175   "I wish to see the United States": David McCullough, *The Path Between the Seas: The Creation of the Panama Canal, 1870–1914* (New York: Simon and Schuster, 1977), p. 255.

175   "We are for expansion": Wolff, *Little Brown Brother*, p. 332.

175   "only imperialistic in the sense": Ibid., pp. 401–2.

175   He called them "Chinese half-breeds": Ibid., p. 331.

175   Roosevelt made 567 campaign stops: Morris, *Rise of Theodore Roosevelt*, pp. 730–31.

175   "he needs no whiskey": Morgan, *William McKinley*, p. 507.

175   "If thayse annywan r-runnin'": Morris, *Rise of Theodore Roosevelt*, p. 770.

176   Their true intent: Hilfrich, *Debating American Exceptionalism*, p. 65.

176   "The leading argument": Ibid.

176   cost him anti-imperialist votes: Schirmer, *Republic or Empire*, pp. 209–11.

176   THE NATION'S CHOICE—OF EVILS: *The Nation*, October 18, 1900.

176   "masterly inactivity": Beisner, *Twelve Against Empire*, p. 191.

176   "Bryanism and McKinleyism!": Miller, *"Benevolent Assimilation,"* p. 140.

176   Carl Schurz lamented: Bailey, "Was the Presidential Election," p. 45; Carl Schurz et al., *The Reminiscences of Carl Schurz*, vol. 3 (Garden City, NY: Doubleday, Page, 1908), p. 445.

176   "the most distasteful thing": Tompkins, *Anti-Imperialism*, p. 235.

176   "McKinley stands for war": Nasaw, *Andrew Carnegie*, p. 609.

177   expose them to charges of collaboration: Schirmer, *Republic or Empire*, pp. 219–20.

177   "On this day": Wolff, *Little Brown Brother*, p. 329.

177   "a clear mandate to govern": Ibid., p. 332.

177   "After McKinley and Hanna": Brands, *Last Romantic*, p. 404.

177   Roosevelt told friends: Morgan, *William McKinley*, p. 508.

177   "We're off to Washington": Morris, *Rise of Theodore Roosevelt*, p. 734.

9. THE CONSTITUTION DOES NOT APPLY

178   Before leaving London: *New York World*, October 6, 1900

178   "Well, I am": *Chicago Tribune*, October 15, 1900.

179   "I left these shores": *New York Herald*, October 15, 1900.

179   "Bryan was all wrong": McFarland, *Mark Twain and the Colonel*, p. 62.

179   "Candidly and absolutely": Mark Zwonitzer, *The Statesman and the Story-teller: John Hay, Mark Twain, and the Rise of American Imperialism* (Chapel Hill, NC: Algonquin, 2016), p. 415.

180   "The standard of honor": Ibid., p. 417.

180   "political channel-finder": Zwick, *Confronting Imperialism*, pp. 113, 117, 120.

180   "I dropped into his wake": Mark Twain, "Carl Schurz: Pilot," in *Harper's*, May 26, 1906.

180   "I bring you the stately matron": *New York Herald*, December 30, 1900.

180   "most perfect single piece": William M. Gibson, "Mark Twain and Howells: Anti-Imperialists," *New England Quarterly*, vol. 20 (1947), p. 451.

180   compared it to the Gettysburg Address: Morton N. Cohen, "Mark Twain and the Philippines: Containing an Unpublished Letter," *Journal of the Central Mississippi Valley American Studies Association*, vol. 1, no. 2 (Fall 1960), p. 29.

180   "Give her the glass": *New York Herald*, October 15, 1900.

181   "Yes, I shall be glad": Jim Zwick, ed., *Mark Twain's Weapons of Satire: Anti-Imperialist Writings on the Philippine-American War* (Syracuse: Syracuse University Press, 1992), p. xxii.

181   "To the Person Sitting in Darkness: Tom Quirk, ed., *The Portable Mark Twain* (New York: Penguin, 2004), pp. 489–510.

182   The American Anti-Imperialist League published it as a pamphlet: Zwick, *Confronting Imperialism*, p. 162.

182   "Mark Twain . . . has suddenly become": Ibid., pp. 114–15.

182   "There's a new Gospel of Saint Mark": Paine, *Mark Twain*, vol. 3, p. 1133.

183   "He did not write the Declaration": Zwick, *Weapons of Satire*, p. 85.

183   "The Boxer is a patriot": Hoganson, *American Manhood*, pp. 61–62.

184   "We find a whole heap of fault": Gary Scharnhorst, *Mark Twain: The Complete Interviews* (Tuscaloosa: University of Alabama Press, 2006), p. 390.

184   "Will you allow me to say": Zwick, *Weapons of Satire*, p. 61.

184   Twain even rewrote "The Battle Hymn": William A. Link and Susannah J. Link, eds., *The Gilded Age and Progressive Era: A Documentary Reader* (Malden, MA: Blackwell, 2012), p. 301.

185   "I think that England sinned": Paul Fatout, ed., *Mark Twain Speaking* (Iowa City: University of Iowa Press, 1976), p. 369.

185   "He hadn't anything personal against me": Ibid., p. 394.

186   "Does it help the world": Fred Kaplan, *The Singular Mark Twain: A Biography* (New York: Anchor, 2005), p. 602.

186   "as caustic, fiendish and devilish as possible": Van Wyck Brooks, *The Ordeal of Mark Twain* (New York: E. P. Dutton, 1920), p. 13.

186   "as savage as Fuller's poetry": Fred Harvey Harrington, "Literary Aspects of American Anti-Imperialism," *New England Quarterly*, vol. 10, no. 4 (December 1937), p. 661.

186   raised enough money: Henry Blake Fuller, *The New Flag: Satires* (Chicago: Henry Blake Fuller, 1899).

186   Among the lesser literary products: Ernest Crosby, *Captain Jinks, Hero* (Rochester, NY: Scholar's Choice, 2015).

187   The humorist George Ade: George Ade, *George Ade's Stories of Benevolent Assimilation* (Quezon City, Philippines: New Day, 1985).

187   Nearly one hundred of the better efforts: *Liberty Poems*.

187   Bates . . . wrote a vividly anti-war companion piece: Katharine Lee Bates, *America the Beautiful and Other Poems* (New York: Thomas Y. Crowell, 1911), p. 80.

188   "We say to thim": Finley Peter Dunne, *Mr. Dooley in the Hearts of His Countrymen* (Boston: Small, Maynard, 1899), pp. 4–5.

188   "a self-denying ordinance": Louis A. Perez Jr., *The War of 1898: United States and Cuba in History and Historiography* (Chapel Hill: University of North Carolina Press, 1998), p. 28.

188   "impulsive but mistaken generosity": Ibid.

188   "no more fit for self-government": Ibid., p. 29.

188   "Given a solemn and unmistakable promise": *New York Evening Post*, February 1, 1901.

189   "If this democracy": David Healy, *U.S. Expansionism: The Imperialist Urge in the 1890s* (Madison: University of Wisconsin Press, 1970), pp. 217–18.

190   Some suggested formally repealing: Lars Schoult, *Beneath the United States: A History of U.S. Policy Toward Latin America* (Cambridge, MA: Harvard University Press, 1998), p. 142.

190   "while saying as little as possible": Healy, *U.S. Expansionism*, p. 84.

190   came up with a more elegant solution: Healy, *United States in Cuba*, pp. 113–14.

190   "The new Cuba": Olcott, *Life of William McKinley*, vol. 2, p. 206.

190   "political jumping-jacks": Healy, *United States in Cuba*, p. 148.

191   "independence and self-government were assured": Ibid., p. 149.

191   the constitution would have to guarantee: Ibid., p. 154.

191   the Platt Amendment: Ibid., pp. 163–64.

192   "soothed into acquiescence": Ibid., p. 166.

192   "little or no independence left Cuba": McCallum, *Leonard Wood*, p. 187.

192   "a very silly letter": Healy, *United States in Cuba*, p. 136.

192   he offered Gómez a sinecure: Ibid., p. 127.

192   "None of us thought": Perez, *War of 1898*, p. 23.

193   "a desperate undertaking": Silbey, *War of Frontier and Empire*, p. 176.

193   With that, Funston saluted: Karnow, *In Our Image*, pp. 182–84; Wolff, *Little Brown Brother*, p. 342.

193   "We have failed to waken": Michael Golay, *Spanish-American War* (New York: Chelsea House, 2010), p. 131.

194   "almost complete unity of action": *New Outlook*, February 23, 1901.

194   "Start a vigorous campaign": *Boston Herald*, November 19, 1900.

194   "European methods": Schirmer, *Republic or Empire*, p. 225.

194   "Forbearance has ceased to be a military virtue": *San Francisco Call*, November 19, 1900.

195   "The Spaniard used the torture of water": Louis Freeland Post et al., eds., *The Public: Issues 158–209* (Charleston, SC: Nabu, 2012), p. 814.

195   None of this bothered General MacArthur: Schirmer, *Republic or Empire*, p. 226.

195   "Whenever action is necessary": Brian McAllister Linn, *The Philippine War 1899–1902* (Lawrence: University Press of Kansas, 2000), p. 213.

196   "McKinley, our mortal enemy": Silbey, *War of Frontier and Empire*, p. 161.

196   He considered Filipinos "a semi-savage people": H. W. Brands, *Bound to Empire: The United States and the Philippines* (New York: Oxford University Press, 1992), p. 58.

197   "The poor little 'Macs'": Frederick Funston, *Memories of Two Wars: Cuban and Philippine Experiences* (London: Constable, 1912), p. 420.

197   "Is this not some joke?": O'Toole, *Spanish War*, p. 392.

198   Edison made a film: Karnow, *In Our Image*, p. 184.

198   There was talk of his running for governor: Wolff, *Little Brown Brother*, p. 346.

198   "Th' consul at Ding Dong": Dunne, *Hearts of His Countrymen*, p. 9.

198   casually mentioned to a newspaper reporter: Richard Slotkin, *Gunfighter Nation: The Myth of the Frontier in Twentieth-Century America* (Norman: University of Oklahoma Press, 1998), pp. 118–19.

198   "The loss of life by killing alone": Schirmer, *Republic or Empire*, p. 231.

198   "Our men have been relentless": *Philadelphia Ledger*, November 11, 1901.

199   he issued a manifesto: *Chicago Tribune*, April 20, 1901.

199   "The pacification of the Philippines": McFarland, *Mark Twain and the Colonel*, p. 141.

200   "The Constitution does not apply": FindLaw, *Downes v. Bidwell*, http://caselaw.findlaw.com/us-supreme-court/182/244.html.

202   Even Mr. Dooley noticed the political tint: Tompkins, *Anti-Imperialists*, p. 245.

202   "I'm only a common soldier": Richard E. Welch, *Response to Imperialism: The United States and the Philippine-American War, 1899–1902* (Chapel Hill: University of North Carolina Press, 1979), p. 313.

203   issued its first major statement: Post, *The Public*, pp. 221–23.

204   several prominent activists quit: Zwick, *Confronting Imperialism*, pp. 8–9.

204   "very drastic" tactics: Schirmer, *Republic or Empire*, p. 227.

205   Roosevelt approached Justice White: Edmund Lester Pearson, *Theodore Roosevelt* (New York: Macmillan, 1920), pp. 78–79.

205   Pan-American Exposition: Walter Hines Page and Arthur Wilson Page, *The World's Work: A History of Our Time*, vol. 2 (New York: Doubleday, Page, 1901), pp. 1013–1101; *Official Catalogue and Guide Book to the Pan-American Exposition* (Buffalo: Charles Ahrhart, 1901), pp. 11–61; *Africans, Darkies and Negroes: Black Faces at the Pan American Exposition of 1901, Buffalo, New York*, http://www.buffalonian.com/history/articles/1901-50/ucqueens/old_plantation.htm.

206   "that kind of idealism": Alfred Henry Lewis, ed., *A Compilation of the Messages and Speeches of Theodore Roosevelt, 1901–1905* (Washington, D.C.: Bureau of National Literature and Art, 1906), p. 633.

206   "It is our duty": Robert C. V. Myers, *Theodore Roosevelt: Patriot and States-man* (Philadelphia: P. W. Ziegler, 1902), p. 356.

206   "giving to the Philippines a degree of freedom": *Burlington Free Press*, September 6, 1901.

206   "I am interested in all furred": *Burlington Free Press*, September 7, 1901.

206   "Friends, a cloud has fallen: Ibid.; C. S. Forbes, "Theodore Roosevelt," *The Vermonter*, vol. 7, no. 4 (November 1901), pp. 363–72.

10. YOU WILL GET USED TO IT

208   "Our capacity to produce": Samuel Fallows, ed., *Life of William McKinley, Our Martyred President* (Chicago: Regan, 1901), p. 290.

209   "No one would wish to hurt me": Morgan, *William McKinley*, pp. 520–21.

209   "My wife—be careful": Ibid., p. 521.

209   X-ray machine: McFarland, *Mark Twain and the Colonel*, p. 143.

209   "Condition at the conclusion": *New York Times*, September 7, 1901.

210   "Lose no time coming": Carlton Putnam, *Theodore Roosevelt: The Formative Years* (New York: Charles Scribner's Sons, 1958), p. 474.

210   "I killed the President": *New York Times*, October 30, 1901.

210   HIGH PRIESTESS OF ANARCHY: *Chicago Daily News*, September 8, 1901.

211   A ditty by Ambrose Bierce: *New York Journal*, April 10, 1901.

211   "If bad institutions": Nasaw, *The Chief*, p. 156.

211   "variously garbled": Ibid., p. 157.

211   "His reclamation": *New Yorker*, September 26, 1901.

211   "Every scoundrel like Hearst": Brands, *Last Romantic*, p. 413.

212   "All that distresses me": Nasaw, *The Chief*, p. 158.

213   "continue absolutely unbroken": Edmund Morris, *Theodore Rex* (New York: Random House, 2001), p. 14.

213   "I told William McKinley": Richard F. Hamilton, *President McKinley, War and Empire*, vol. 2: *President McKinley and America's "New Empire"* (New Brunswick, NJ: Transaction, 2007), p. 173.

214   "I hope it is so": Schriftgiesser, *Gentleman from Massachusetts*, p. 196.

214   "Hardly a day passed": Ibid., p. 200.

214   that "the Anti-Imperialist League should for the time being": Zwick, *Confronting Imperialism*, pp. 116–17.

215   The scandal broke from Samar: Silbey, *War of Frontier*, p. 190; Linn, *Philippine War*, pp. 310–12.

215   Mark Twain spat back into the public eye: Zwick, *Weapons of Satire*, p. 132.

215   Chaffee . . . blamed the Balangiga attack: Karnow, *In Our Image*, p. 191.

216   Senate Committee on the Philippines: United States Senate, *Hearings Before the Committee on the Philippines* (Washington, D.C.: Government Printing Office, 1902).

216   "the committee room was totally inadequate": *New York Journal*, February 13, 1902.

216   "all the power of a judge": Schriftgiesser, *Gentleman from Massachusetts*, p. 203.

217   "all sorts of trouble for us": John Braeman, *Albert J. Beveridge: American Nationalist* (Chicago: University of Chicago Press, 1971), p. 60.

217   "never had a war been conducted": *New York Journal*, February 5, 1902.

217   "some retaliation": *New York Times*, February 6, 1902.

217   "in substantially every case": *Los Angeles Herald*, February 20, 1902; *New York Journal*, February 20, 1902.

218   Senator Hoar demanded to know: *New York Journal*, February 6, 1902.

218   "a thrilling and sensational scene": *New York Journal*, February 23, 1902.

219   "Scarcely had [Tillman] resumed his seat": *New York Times*, February 23, 1902.

219   "During my absence": United States Senate, *The Senators from South Carolina: 57th Congress, 1st Session, Document 228* (Washington, D.C.: Government Printing Office, 1902), pp. 1–12.

220   "The Senate never in its history": *New York Times*, Feb. 23, 1902.

220   Washington remained tense: Silbey, *War of Frontier and Empire*, p. 200; *New York Journal*, April 15, 17, 18, and 22 and May 4, 1901.

220   Rawlins of Utah drew him out: United States Senate, *Hearings Before the Committee on the Philippines*, p. 559.

221   "It is most provoking": *New York Evening Post*, May 3, 1902.

221   "I want no prisoners": Miller, *"Benevolent Assimilation,"* p. 220.

222   "If we are to 'benevolently assimilate'": Silbey, *War of Frontier and Empire*, p. 203.

222   Public outrage: *New York Journal*, April 16, 1902.

222   Smith turned out to be an ideal villain: Karnow, *In Our Image*, pp. 193–94.

222   "Having the devil to fight": *Harper's*, May 2, 1902.

223   "I personally strung up": *New York Sun*, May 10, 1902.

223   "Defense of General Funston": *North American Review* (May 1, 1902).

223   "It was impossible": John Sutton Tuckey, *The Devil's Race-Track: Mark Twain's Dark Writings* (Berkeley: University of California Press, 1966), p. 376.

224   "She has lost her unique position": Beisner, *Twelve Against Empire*, p. 81.

224   Its last large campaign: Karnow, *In Our Image*, p. 188; Wolff, *Little Brown Brother*, pp. 359–96.

224   "If I were in the Philippines": Foner, *Mark Twain*, p. 377.

225   "The American public . . . sips its coffee": *New York World*, March 16, 1902.

225   Roosevelt issued a proclamation: *Proclamation 483, July 4, 1902: Granting Pardon and Amnesty to Participants in Insurrection in the Philippines*, http://www.presidency.ucsb.edu/ws/?pid=69569.

225   A total of 120,000 American soldiers: Karnow, *In Our Image*, p. 194.

225 During those forty-one months: Thomas Schoonover, *Uncle Sam's War of 1898 and the Origins of Globalization* (Lexington: University of Kentucky Press, 2005), p. 95.

225 Twain was in a foul mood: Wolff, *Little Brown Brother*, p. 363.

226 "equitable distribution of wealth": Nasaw, *The Chief*, p. 172.

226 "we are defeated for the time": Beisner, *Twelve Against Empire*, p. 83.

11. THE DEEP HURT

227 Days after the election: *Report of the Sixth Annual Meeting of the Anti-Imperialist League, November 26, 1904* (Boston: Anti-Imperialist League, 1904), https://archive.org/stream/reportofannualme0607anti /reportofannualme0607anti_djvu.txt.

228 "far and away the worst": Bernard DeVoto, ed., *Mark Twain in Eruption* (New York: Harper and Brothers, 1940), p. 34.

228 "Our forefathers faced certain perils": Frederick E. Drinker and Jay Henry Mobray, *Theodore Roosevelt: His Life and Work* (Washington, D.C.: National Publishing, 1919), p. 138.

229 "heel of Achilles": Stephen Wertheim, "Reluctant Liberator: Theodore Roosevelt's Philosophy of Self-Government and Preparation for Philippine Independence," *Presidential Studies Quarterly*, vol. 39, no. 3 (September 2009).

232 "to choose the sovereignty": George Maclean Harper, ed., *President Wilson's Addresses* (New York: Henry Holt, 1918), p. 176.

232 "to elect good men": Harley A. Notter, *The Origins of the Foreign Policy of Woodrow Wilson* (New York: Russell and Russell, 1965), p. 274.

232 "America is the only idealistic nation": Herbert Hoover, *The Ordeal of Woodrow Wilson* (Washington, D.C.: Woodrow Wilson Center, 1992), p. ix.

234 "resolving international differences": *Indianapolis Star*, January 17, 1928.

234 In one speech he asserted: William Appleton Williams, *The Tragedy of American Diplomacy* (New York: W. W. Norton, 1959), pp. 156–57.

236 "a high-class muscle man": Mark Strecker, *Smedley D. Butler, USMC: A Biography* (Jefferson, NC: McFarland, 2011), p. 153.

237 "The 20th century": Henry R. Luce, "The American Century," http://www -personal.umich.edu/~mlassite/discussions261/luce.pdf.

238 "Some have spoken of the 'American Century' ": John C. Culver and John Hyde, *American Dreamer: A Life of Henry A. Wallace* (New York: W. W. Norton, 2000), p. 277.

239 "to intimidate the rest of mankind": Ibid., p. 417.

239 "Our Christian ideals": *Congressional Record, House of Representatives*, March 18, 1947, p. 2217.

239 "new policy of interventionism": Ronald Radosh, *Prophets on the Right: Profiles of Conservative Critics of American Globalism* (New York: Simon and Schuster, 1975), p. 158.

240 "An undertaking by the most powerful nation": Robert A. Taft, *A Foreign Policy for Americans* (Garden City, NY: Doubleday, 1951), p. 91.

240 "America's policy is global": Paul F. Gardner, *Shared Hopes, Separate Fears: Fifty Years of U.S.-Indonesian Relations* (Boulder, CO: Westview, 1997), p. 128.

241 Carter lamented "the deep hurt": *St. Louis Post-Dispatch*, October 7, 1976.

242 "a new world order": George Bush, *State of the Union Address*, http://www .thisnation.com/library/sotu/1991gb.html.

243 "We should generally aim before we shoot": "President Obama Speaks with Vice News," https://news.vice.com/video/president-barack-obama -speaks-with-vice-news.

244 "I will halt the senseless bombing": Richard Panchyk, *The Keys to American History: Understanding Our Most Important Historic Documents* (Chicago: Chicago Review, 2008), p. 210.

244 "The steady increase of global commitments": Patrick Buchanan, *A Republic, Not an Empire: Reclaiming America's Destiny* (Washington, D.C.: Regnery, 1999), pp. 34, 390.

244 "We're still running a foreign policy": *On the Issues*, "Ron Paul on Foreign Policy," http://www.ontheissues.org/2012/Ron_Paul_Foreign_Policy.htm.

244 "Truly conservative": Council on Foreign Relations, "Paul's Speech at CPAC," http://www.cfr.org/elections/pauls-speech-cpac/p15478.

245 "Preventive war is like committing suicide": Margaret MacMillan, *The War That Ended Peace: The Road to 1914* (New York: Random House, 2014), p. 558.

246 "The situation seems to me this": Healy, *U.S. Expansionism*, p. 218.

247 "It has generally been acknowledged to be madness": R. W. Seton-Watson, *Disraeli, Gladstone, and the Eastern Question: A Study in Diplomacy and Politics* (New York: Macmillan, 1935), p. 168.

249 Washington warned: Avalon Project, "Washington's Farewell Address," 1796, http://avalon.law.yale.edu/18th_century/washing.asp.

BIBLIOGRAPHY

Adams, Henry. *The Education of Henry Adams: An Autobiography.* Boston: Mariner, 2000.

Addams, Jane. *Democracy or Militarism: The Chicago Liberty Meeting.* Chicago: Central Anti-Imperialist League, 1899.

Ade, George. *George Ade's Stories of Benevolent Assimilation.* Quezon City, Philippines: New Day, 1985.

Anderson, Frederick, ed. *Mark Twain: The Critical Heritage.* London: Routledge, 1997.

Andrews, Wayne, ed. *The Autobiography of Theodore Roosevelt.* New York: Octagon, 1975.

Anti-Imperialist League. *Soldiers' Letters: Being Materials for the History of a War of Criminal Aggression.* Boston: Anti-Imperialist League, 1899.

Arnold, James R. *Jungle of Snakes: A Century of Counterinsurgency Warfare from the Philippines to Iraq.* New York: Bloomsbury, 2009.

Bailey, Thomas A. "Was the Presidential Election of 1900 a Mandate on Imperialism?" *Mississippi Valley Historical Review,* vol. 24, no. 1 (June 1937).

Bancroft, Frederic, ed. *Speeches, Correspondence and Political Papers of Carl Schurz.* 6 vols. New York: G. P. Putnam's Sons, 1913.

Bates, Katharine Lee. *America the Beautiful and Other Poems.* New York: Thomas Y. Crowell, 1911.

Beale, Howard. *Theodore Roosevelt and the Rise of America to World Power.* Baltimore: Johns Hopkins University Press, 1956.

Bederman, Gail. *Manliness and Civilization: A Cultural History of Gender and Race in the United States, 1880–1917.* Chicago: University of Chicago Press, 1995.

Beisner, Robert. *Twelve Against Empire: The Anti-Imperialists 1898–1900*. New York: McGraw-Hill, 1968.

Bishop, Joseph Bucklin. *Theodore Roosevelt and His Time as Shown in His Letters*, vol. 1. New York: Charles Scribner's Sons, 1920.

Boutwell, George C. *The Crisis of the Republic*. Boston: Dana Estates, 1900.

Bowers, Claude G. *Beveridge and the Progressive Era*. Boston: Houghton Mifflin, 1932.

Bradford, James C., ed. *Crucible of Empire: The Spanish-American War*. Ann Arbor: University of Michigan Press, 1974.

Bradley, James. *The Imperial Cruise: A Secret History of Empire and War*. New York: Back Bay, 2009.

Braeman, John. *Albert J. Beveridge: American Nationalist*. Chicago: University of Chicago Press, 1971.

Brands, H. W. *Bound to Empire: The United States and the Philippines*. New York: Oxford University Press, 1992.

———. *Reckless Decade: America in the 1890s*. New York: St. Martin's, 1995.

———. *T.R.: The Last Romantic*. New York: Basic, 1997.

Brooks, Van Wyck. *The Ordeal of Mark Twain*. New York: E. P. Dutton, 1920.

Brown, Charles H. *The Correspondents' War: Journalists in the Spanish-American War*. New York: Charles Scribner's Sons, 1967.

Brown, Meredith Mason. *Touching America's History: From the Pequot War Through World War II*. Bloomington: Indiana University Press, 2013.

Bryan, William Jennings. *Bryan on Imperialism: Speeches, Newspaper Articles and Interviews*. Chicago: Bentley, 1900.

———, and Ruth Baird Bryan. *Life and Speeches of Hon. Wm. Jennings Bryan*. Baltimore: R. H. Woodward, 1900.

Buchanan, Patrick. *A Republic, Not an Empire: Reclaiming America's Destiny*. Washington, D.C.: Regnery, 1999.

Budd, Louis J. *Our Mark Twain: The Making of His Public Personality*. Philadelphia: University of Pennsylvania Press, 1983.

Busbey, L. White, et al., eds. *The Battle of 1900: An Official Handbook for Every American Citizen*. Chicago: Thompson and Hood, 1900.

Carrión, Arturo Morales. *Puerto Rico: A Political and Cultural History*. New York: W. W. Norton, 1983.

Central Anti-Imperialist League. *The Chicago Liberty Meeting, Held at Central Music Hall, April 30, 1899*. Chicago: Central Anti-Imperialist League, 1899.

Challener, Richard D. *Admirals, Generals, and American Foreign Policy, 1898–1914*. Princeton: Princeton University Press, 1973.

Chatfield, Charles. *The American Peace Movement: Ideals and Activities*. New York: Twayne, 1992.

Cohen, Morton N. "Mark Twain and the Philippines: Containing an Unpublished Letter." *Journal of the Central Mississippi Valley American Studies Association*, vol. 1, no. 2 (Fall 1960).

Coletta, Paulo. "McKinley, the Peace Negotiations, and the Acquisition of the Philippines." *Pacific Historical Review*, vol. 30, no. 4 (November 1961), p. 134.

Contosta, David R., and Robert Muccigrosso, eds. *Henry Adams and His World.* Philadelphia: American Philosophical Association, 1993.

Copeland, David A. *The Greenwood Library of American War Reporting: The Indian Wars and the Spanish-American War.* Westport, CT: Greenwood, 2005.

Cordery, Stacy A. *Theodore Roosevelt in the Vanguard of the Modern.* Belmont, CA: Wadsworth, 2003.

Corpuz, Onofre D. *Saga and Triumph: The Filipino Revolution Against Spain.* Manila: University of the Philippines Press, 2002.

Cosmas, Graham A. *An Army for Empire: The United States Army in the Spanish-American War.* Columbia: University of Missouri Press, 1971.

Crapol, Edward P. *James G. Blaine: Architect of Empire.* Wilmington, DE: Scholarly Resources, 2000.

Creelman, James. *On the Great Highway: The Wanderings and Adventurings of a Special Correspondent.* Boston: Lothrop, 1901.

Crosby, Ernest. *Captain Jinks, Hero.* Rochester, NY: Scholar's Choice, 2015.

Crosby, Travis L. *Joseph Chamberlain: A Most Radical Imperialist.* London: I. B. Tauris, 2011.

Cullinane, Michael Patrick. *Liberty and American Anti-Imperialism, 1898–1909.* New York: Palgrave Macmillan, 2012.

Culver, John C., and John Hyde. *American Dreamer: A Life of Henry A. Wallace.* New York: W. W. Norton, 2000.

Curti, Merle Eugene. *Bryan and World Peace.* New York: Octagon, 1969.

Dalton, Kathleen. *Theodore Roosevelt: A Strenuous Life.* New York: Vintage, 2004.

Dell'Orto, Giovanna. *The Hidden Power of the American Dream: Why Europe's Shaken Confidence in the United States Threatens the Future of U.S. Influence.* Westport, CT: Praeger, 2008.

DeVoto, Bernard, ed. *Mark Twain in Eruption: Hitherto Unpublished Pages about Men and Events.* New York: Harper and Brothers, 1940.

Dobson, John. *America's Ascent: The United States Becomes a Great Power, 1880–1914.* DeKalb: Northern Illinois University Press, 1978.

———. *Reticent Expansionism: The Foreign Policy of William McKinley.* Pittsburgh: Duquesne University Press, 1988.

Drinker, Frederick E., and Jay Henry Mobray. *Theodore Roosevelt: His Life and Work.* Washington, D.C.: National Publishing, 1919.

Dunne, Finley Peter. *Mr. Dooley in Peace and War.* Boston: Small, Maynard, 1899.

———. *Mr. Dooley in the Hearts of His Countrymen.* Boston: Small, Maynard, 1899.

Dyer, Thomas. *Theodore Roosevelt and the Idea of Race.* Baton Rouge: Louisiana State University Press, 1980.

Edge, Laura B. *William McKinley.* Minneapolis: Twenty-First Century, 2006.

Esthus, Raymond A. *Theodore Roosevelt and International Rivalries.* Waltham, MA: Ginn-Blaisdell, 1970.

Fallows, Samuel, ed. *Life of William McKinley, Our Martyred President.* Chicago: Regan, 1901.

Fatout, Paul, ed. *Mark Twain Speaking.* Iowa City: University of Iowa Press, 1976.

Fishkin, Shelley Fisher, ed. *A Historical Guide to Mark Twain.* Oxford: Oxford University Press, 2002.

Flood, Theodore L., ed. *The Chautauquan.* Meadeville, PA: T. L. Flood, 1899.

Foner, Philip S. *Mark Twain: Social Critic.* New York: International, 1958.

———. *The Spanish-Cuban-American War and the Birth of American Imperialism.* Vol. 1, *1895–1898.* New York: Monthly Review, 1972.

———. *The Spanish-Cuban-American War and the Birth of American Imperialism.* Vol. 2, *1898–1902.* New York: Monthly Review, 1972.

———, and Richard C. Winchester, eds. *The Anti-Imperialist Reader: A Documentary History of Anti-Imperialism in the United States.* New York: Holmes and Meier, 1984.

Freidel, Frank. *The Splendid Little War: The Dramatic Story of the Spanish-American War.* Boston: Little, Brown, 1958.

Fuess, Claude M. *Carl Schurz: Reformer.* New York: Dodd, Mead, 1932.

Fuller, Henry Blake. *The New Flag: Satires.* Chicago: Henry Blake Fuller, 1899.

Gardner, Lloyd C., ed. *A Different Frontier: Selected Readings in the Foundations of American Economic Expansion.* Chicago: Quadrangle, 1966.

Gardner, Paul F. *Shared Hopes, Separate Fears: Fifty Years of U.S.-Indonesian Relations.* Boulder, CO: Westview, 1997.

Garraty, John A. *Henry Cabot Lodge: A Biography.* New York: Alfred A. Knopf, 1953.

Gibson, William M. "Mark Twain and Howells: Anti-Imperialists." *New England Quarterly,* no. 20 (1947).

Glad, Paul W. *McKinley, Bryan, and the People.* Philadelphia: Lippincott, 1964.

Glain, Stephen. *State vs. Defense: The Battle to Define America's Empire.* New York: Broadway, 2012.

Gould, Lewis I. *The Spanish-American War and President McKinley.* Lawrence: University of Kansas Press, 1982.

Grant, James. *Mr. Speaker!: The Life and Times of Thomas B. Reed—The Man Who Broke the Filibuster.* New York: Simon and Schuster, 2012.

Greenwood, Janette Thomas. *The Gilded Age: A History in Documents.* New York: Oxford University Press, 2003.

Halsted, Murat. *The Illustrious Life of William McKinley, Our Martyred President.* Salem, MA: H. L. Barker, 1901.

Hamilton, Richard F. *President McKinley, War and Empire.* Vol. 1, *President McKinley and the Coming of War, 1898.* New Brunswick, NJ: Transaction, 2006.

———. *President McKinley, War and Empire.* Vol. 2, *President McKinley and America's "New Empire."* New Brunswick, NJ: Transaction, 2007.

Harper, George Maclean, ed. *President Wilson's Addresses.* New York: Henry Holt, 1918.

Harrington, Fred Harvey. "Literary Aspects of American Anti-Imperialism." *New England Quarterly*, vol. 10, no. 4 (December 1937).

Harris, Susan K. *God's Arbiters: Americans and the Philippines, 1898–1902*. Oxford: Oxford University Press, 2011.

Hawley, Joshua David. *Theodore Roosevelt: Preacher of Righteousness*. New Haven: Yale University Press, 2008.

Healy, David F. *The United States in Cuba 1898–1902: Generals, Politicians, and the Search for Policy*. Madison: University of Wisconsin Press, 1963.

———. *US Expansionism: The Imperialist Urge in the 1890s*. Madison: University of Wisconsin Press, 1970.

Hilfrich, Fabian. *Debating American Exceptionalism: Empire and Democracy in the Wake of the Spanish-American War*. New York: Palgrave Macmillan, 2012.

Hill, Hamlin. *Mark Twain: God's Fool*. Chicago: University of Chicago Press, 2010.

Hoar, George Frisbie. *Autobiography of Seventy Years*, New York: Charles Scribner's Sons, 1903.

Hodge, Carl Cavanagh, and Cathal J. Nolan, eds. *U.S. Presidents and Foreign Policy: From 1789 to the Present*. Oxford: ABC-CLIO, 2006.

Hoffman, Andrew. *Inventing Mark Twain: The Lives of Samuel Langhorne Clemens*. New York: William Morrow, 1997.

Hofstadter, Richard. *The Paranoid Style in American Politics*. New York: Vintage, 1952.

Hoganson, Kristin L. *Fighting for American Manhood: How Gender Politics Provoked the Spanish-American and Philippine-American Wars*. New Haven: Yale University Press, 1988.

Holt, W. Stull. *Treaties Defeated by the Senate: A Study of the Struggle between President and Senate over the Conduct of Foreign Relations*. Baltimore: Johns Hopkins University Press, 1933.

Home Market Club. *Souvenir of the Visit of President McKinley and Members of the Cabinet to Boston, February 1899*. Boston: Home Market Club, 1899.

Hoover, Herbert. *The Ordeal of Woodrow Wilson*. Washington, D.C.: Woodrow Wilson Center, 1992.

Horner, William T. *Ohio's Kingmaker: Mark Hanna, Man and Myth*. Athens: Ohio University Press, 2010.

Immerman, Richard H. *Empire for Liberty: A History of American Imperialism from Benjamin Franklin to Paul Wolfowitz*. Princeton: Princeton University Press, 2010.

James, Jennifer C. *A Freedom Bought with Blood: African American War Literature from the Civil War to World War II*. Chapel Hill: University of North Carolina Press, 2007.

Jones, Gregg. *Honor in the Dust: Theodore Roosevelt, War in the Philippines, and the Rise and Fall of America's Imperial Dream*. New York: New American Library, 2012.

Judis, John B. *The Folly of Empire: What George W. Bush Could Learn from Theodore Roosevelt and Woodrow Wilson*. Oxford: Oxford University Press, 2004.

Kaplan, Fred. *The Singular Mark Twain: A Biography*. New York: Anchor, 2005.

Kaplan, Justin. *Mr. Clemens and Mark Twain*. New York: Simon and Schuster, 1991.

Karnow, Stanley. *In Our Image: America's Empire in the Philippines*. New York: Random House, 1989.

Kauffman, Bill. *Ain't My America: The Long, Noble History of Antiwar Conservatism and Middle-American Anti-Imperialism*. New York: Metropolitan, 2008.

Kaufman, Stuart B. *The Samuel Gompers Papers*. Vol. 5, *An Expanding Movement at the Turn of the Century, 1898–1902*. Urbana: University of Illinois Press, 1995.

Kazin, Michael. *A Godly Hero: The Life of William Jennings Bryan*. New York: Alfred A. Knopf, 2006.

Keenan, Jerry. *Encyclopedia of the Spanish-American and Philippine-American Wars*. Santa Barbara, CA: ABC-CLIO, 2001.

Kohn, Edward P. *Heir to the Empire City: New York and the Making of Theodore Roosevelt*. New York: Basic, 2014.

Konstam, Angus. *San Juan Hill 1898: America's Emergence as a World Power*. Oxford: Osprey, 1998.

LaFeber, Walter. *The New Empire: An Interpretation of American Expansion, 1860–1898*. Ithaca, NY: Cornell University Press, 1963.

Langellier, John P. *Uncle Sam's Little Wars: The Spanish-American War, Philippine Insurrection and Boxer Rebellion, 1898–1902*. London: Greenhill, 1999.

Lears, Jackson. *Rebirth of a Nation: The Making of Modern America, 1877–1920*. New York: HarperCollins, 2009.

Lewis, Alfred Henry, ed. *A Compilation of the Messages and Speeches of Theodore Roosevelt 1901–1905*. Washington, D.C.: Bureau of National Literature and Art, 1906.

Linderman, Gerald. *The Mirror of War: American Society and the Spanish-American War*. Ann Arbor: University of Michigan Press, 1974.

Link, William A., and Susannah J. Link, eds. *The Gilded Age and Progressive Era: A Documentary Reader*. Malden, MA: Blackwell, 2012.

Linn, Brian McAllister. *Guardians of Empire: The U.S. Army and the Pacific, 1902–1940*. Chapel Hill: University of North Carolina Press, 1997.

———. *The Philippine War 1899–1902*. Lawrence: University of Kansas Press, 2000.

Littlefield, Roy Everett III. *William Randolph Hearst: His Role in American Progressivism*. New York: University Press of America, 1980.

Lodge, Henry Cabot. *Speeches and Addresses, 1884–1909*. Boston: Houghton Mifflin, 1909.

———. *The War with Spain*. New York: Harper and Brothers, 1899.

Long, John Cuthbert. *Bryan, the Great Commoner*. New York: D. Appleton, 1928.

Lurie, Jonathan. *William Howard Taft: The Travails of a Progressive Conservative*. Cambridge: Cambridge University Press, 2014.

MacMillan, Margaret. *The War That Ended Peace: The Road to 1914*. New York: Random House, 2014.

Manela, Erez. *The Wilsonian Moment: Self-Determination and the International Origins of Anticolonial Nationalism.* Oxford: Oxford University Press, 2007.

Mann, Robert. *Wartime Dissent in America: A History and Anthology.* New York: Palgrave Macmillan, 2010.

Marshall, Edward, and Richard F. Outcault. *The Story of the Rough Riders.* New York: G. W. Dillingham, 1899.

May, Ernest R. *Imperial Democracy: The Emergence of America as a Great Power.* New York: Harper Torchbooks, 1961.

McCallum, Jack. *Leonard Wood: Rough Rider, Surgeon, Architect of American Imperialism.* New York: New York University Press, 2006.

McCullough, David. *Mornings on Horseback.* New York: Simon and Schuster, 1981.

——. *The Path Between the Seas: The Creation of the Panama Canal, 1870–1914.* New York: Simon and Schuster, 1977.

McFarland, Philip. *Mark Twain and the Colonel: Samuel Clemens, Theodore Roosevelt, and the Arrival of a New Century.* Lanham, MD: Rowman and Littlefield, 2012.

McKinley, William. *Speeches and Addresses of William McKinley from March 1, 1897, to May 30, 1900.* New York: Doubleday and McClure, 1900.

McMurry, Linda O. *To Keep the Waters Troubled : The Life of Ida B. Wells.* New York: Oxford University Press, 1998.

Miller, Nathan. *Theodore Roosevelt: A Life.* New York: William Morrow, 1992.

Miller, Scott. *The President and the Assassin: McKinley, Terror, and Empire at the Dawn of the American Century.* New York: Random House, 2011.

Miller, Stuart Creighton. *"Benevolent Assimilation": The American Conquest of the Philippines, 1899–1903.* New Haven: Yale University Press, 1982.

Mills, Walter. *The Martial Spirit.* Cambridge, MA: Riverside, 1931.

Milne, David. *Worldmaking: The Art and Science of American Diplomacy.* New York: Farrar, Straus and Giroux, 2015.

Morgan, H. Wayne. *America's Road to Empire: The War with Spain and Overseas Empire.* New York: John Wiley and Sons, 1966.

——. *William McKinley and His America.* Syracuse: Syracuse University Press, 1963.

Morison, Elting E., ed. *The Letters of Theodore Roosevelt.* Cambridge, MA: Harvard University Press, 1951–54.

Morris, Edmund. *The Rise of Theodore Roosevelt.* New York: Coward, McCann and Geoghegan, 1979.

——. *Theodore Rex.* New York: Random House, 2001.

Murphy, Erin L. "Women's Anti-Imperialism, 'The White Man's Burden,' and the Philippine-American War." *Asia-Pacific Journal,* vol. 77, issue 27, no. 1 (July 2009).

Musicant, Ivan. *Empire by Default: The Spanish-American War and the Dawn of the American Century.* New York: Henry Holt, 1998.

Nagel, Paul C. *This Sacred Trust: American Nationality 1778–1898.* New York: Oxford University Press, 1991.

Nasaw, David. *The Chief: The Life of William Randolph Hearst.* Boston: Houghton Mifflin, 2000.

———. *Andrew Carnegie.* New York: Penguin, 2007.

New England Anti-Imperialist League. *Liberty Poems Inspired by the Crisis of 1898–1900.* Boston: James H. West, 1900.

Nichols, John, ed. *Against the Beast: A Documentary History of American Opposition to Empire.* New York: Nation, 2004.

Nieder, Charles, ed. *Life as I Find It: A Treasury of Mark Twain Rarities.* New York: Cooper Square, 1961.

Notter, Harley A. *The Origins of the Foreign Policy of Woodrow Wilson.* New York: Russell and Russell, 1965.

Olcott, Charles S. *The Life of William McKinley.* Boston: Houghton Mifflin, 1916.

Otis, Elwell S. *Report of Maj. Gen. E. S. Otis, United States Army, Commanding Division of the Philippines, Military Governor: September 1, 1899 to May 5, 1900.* Washington, D.C.: Government Printing Office, 1900.

O'Toole, G. J. A. *The Spanish War: An American Epic, 1898.* New York: W. W. Norton, 1984.

Page, Walter Hines, and Arthur Wilson Page. *The World's Work: A History of Our Time.* New York: Doubleday, Page, 1901.

Paine, Albert Bigelow. *Mark Twain: A Biography.* New York: Harper and Brothers, 1912.

Panchyk, Richard. *The Keys to American History: Understanding Our Most Important Historic Documents.* Chicago: Chicago Review, 2008.

Patterson, Thomas G., ed. *American Imperialism and Anti-Imperialism.* New York: Thomas Y. Crowell, 1973.

Pérez, Louis A. *The War of 1898: The United States and Cuba in History and Historiography.* Chapel Hill: University of North Carolina Press, 1990.

Pettigrew, Richard F. *Imperial Washington.* Chicago: Charles H. Kerr, 1922.

Phipps, William E. *Mark Twain's Religion.* Macon, GA: Mercer University Press, 2003.

Polner, Murray, and Thomas E Woods Jr., eds. *We Who Dared to Say No to War: American Antiwar Writing from 1812 to Now.* New York: Basic, 2008.

Powers, Ron. *Mark Twain: A Life.* New York: Free Press, 2006.

Pratt, Julius, *Expansionists of 1898: The Acquisition of Hawaii and the Spanish Islands.* Baltimore: Johns Hopkins University Press, 1936.

Putnam, Carlton. *Theodore Roosevelt: The Formative Years.* New York: Charles Scribner's Sons, 1958.

Quirk, Tom, ed. *The Portable Mark Twain.* New York: Penguin, 2004.

Radosh, Ronald. *Prophets on the Right: Profiles of Conservative Critics of American Globalism.* New York: Simon and Schuster, 1975.

Richardson, Glenda. *Medal of Honor Recipients 1979–2003.* New York: Novinka, 2003.

Roe, Edward T. *The Life Work of William McKinley.* Chicago: Laird and Lee, 1901.

Roosevelt, Theodore. *The Autobiography of Theodore Roosevelt.* CreateSpace, 2009.

——. *Presidential Addresses and State Papers and European Addresses*. New York: Review of Reviews, 1910.

——. *The Strenuous Life: Essays and Addresses*. New York: Century, 1902.

——, and Henry Cabot Lodge. *Selections of the Correspondence of Theodore Roosevelt and Henry Cabot Lodge, 1884–1918*, vol. 1. New York: Charles Scribner's Sons, 1925.

Rothbard, Murray M., ed. *Left and Right: A Journal of Libertarian Thought*. Auburn, AL: Ludwig von Mises, 2007.

Russ, William Adam, Jr. *The Hawaiian Republic (1894–1898) and Its Struggle to Win Annexation*. Selinsgrove, PA: Susquehanna University Press, 1992.

Russell, Charles Edward. *The Outlook for the Philippines*. New York: Century, 1922.

Russell, Henry Benejah. *The Story of Two Wars: An Illustrated History of Our War with Spain and Our War with the Filipinos*. Hartford: Hartford Publishing, 1899.

Scannell, Ruth Hamilton. *The Senate and the Philippines: The Debate in the Senate of the Fifty-Fifth Congress on the Ratification of the Peace Treaty with Spain, December 6, 1898–February 6, 1899*. Stanford, CA: Stanford University Press, 1960.

Schevill, Ferdinand. *The Rise and Progress of Democracy*. Chicago: Zalaz, 1915.

Schirmer, Daniel B. *Republic or Empire: American Resistance to the Philippine War*. Cambridge, MA: Schenkman, 1972.

——, and Stephen Rosskamm Shalom. *The Philippines Reader: A History of Colonialism, Nationalism, Neocolonialism, Dictatorship, and Resistance*. Boston: South End, 1987.

Schoonover, Thomas. *Uncle Sam's War of 1898 and the Origins of Globalization*. Lexington: University of Kentucky Press, 2003.

Schoult, Lars. *Beneath the United States: A History of U.S. Policy Toward Latin America*. Cambridge, MA: Harvard University Press, 1998.

Schriftgiesser, Karl. *The Gentleman from Massachusetts: Henry Cabot Lodge*. Boston: Atlantic–Little, Brown, 1944.

Schurz, Carl. *The Reminiscences of Carl Schurz*. Boston: Adamant, 2001.

Seton-Watson, R. W. *Disraeli, Gladstone, and the Eastern Question: A Study in Diplomacy and Politics*. New York: Macmillan, 1935.

Seymour, Richard. *American Insurgents: A Brief History of American Anti-Imperialism*. Chicago: Haymarket, 2012.

Silbey, David J. *A War of Frontier and Empire: The Philippine-American War, 1899–1902*. New York: Hill and Wang, 2007.

Sinclair, Upton. *The Brass Check: A Study of American Journalism*. Champaign: University of Illinois Press, 2002.

Slotkin, Richard. *Gunfighter Nation: The Myth of the Frontier in Twentieth-Century America*. New York: Harper Perennial, 1992.

Smith, Harriet E., et al., eds. *The Autobiography of Mark Twain*, vol. 3. Berkeley: University of California Press, 2015.

Smith, Joseph. *The Spanish-American War, 1895–1902: Conflict in the Caribbean and the Pacific*. New York: Routledge, 1994.

Spector, Ronald. *Admiral of the New Empire: The Life and Career of George Dewey.*
     Baton Rouge: Louisiana State University Press, 1974.

Stellato, Jesse. *Not in Our Name: American Antiwar Speeches, 1846 to the Present.*
     Philadelphia: Pennsylvania State University Press, 2013.

Storey, Moorfield, and Marcial P. Lichauco. *The Conquest of the Philippines by the
     United States, 1898–1925.* New York: G. P. Putnam's Sons, 1926.

Strecker, Mark. *Smedley D. Butler, USMC: A Biography.* Jefferson, NC: McFarland,
     2011.

Sundquist, James L. *Dynamics of the Party System: Alignment and Realignment of
     Political Parties in the United States.* Washington, D.C.: Brookings, 1983.

Swanberg, W. A. *Citizen Hearst.* New York: Charles Scribner's Sons, 1961.

Taft, Robert A. *A Foreign Policy for Americans.* Garden City, NY: Doubleday, 1951.

Taliaferro, John. *All the Great Prizes: The Life of John Hay, from Lincoln to Roose-
     velt.* New York: Simon and Schuster, 2013.

Thomas, Evan. *The War Lovers: Roosevelt, Lodge, Hearst, and the Rush to Empire,
     1898.* New York: Little, Brown, 2010.

Tompkins, E. Berkeley. *Anti-Imperialism in the United States: The Great Debate,
     1890–1920.* Philadelphia: University of Pennsylvania Press, 1970.

Trask, David F. *The War with Spain in 1898.* Lincoln: University of Nebraska Press,
     1996.

Traxel, David. *1898: The Tumultuous Year of Victory, Invention, Internal Strife,
     and Industrial Strife That Saw the Birth of the American Century.* New York:
     Alfred A. Knopf, 1998.

Trefousse, Hans Louis. *Carl Schurz: A Biography.* New York: Fordham University
     Press, 1998.

Tuchman, Barbara. *The Proud Tower: A Portrait of the World Before the War,
     1890–1914.* New York: Macmillan, 1966.

Tuckey, John Sutton. *The Devil's Race-Track: Mark Twain's Dark Writings.* Berkeley:
     University of California Press, 1966.

Tyler, John W. *The Life of William McKinley.* Philadelphia: P. W. Ziegler, 1901.

Tyrrell, Ian, and Jay Sexton, eds. *Empire's Twin: U.S. Anti-Imperialism from the
     Founding Era to the Age of Terrorism.* Ithaca, NY: Cornell University Press, 2015.

United States Senate. *Hearings Before the Committee on the Philippines of the United
     States Senate,* vol. 3. Washington, D.C.: Government Printing Office, 1902.

———. *The Senators from South Carolina: 57th Congress, 1st Session, Document 228.*
     Washington, D.C.: Government Printing Office, 1902.

Vidal, Gore. *Empire.* New York: Vintage, 2000.

Vogel, Dan. *Mark Twain's Jews.* Jersey City: KTAV, 2006.

Walker, Dale L. *The Boys of '98: Theodore Roosevelt and the Rough Riders.* New
     York: Tom Doherty, 1998.

Walker, Leslie W. "Guam's Seizure by the United States in 1898." *Pacific Historical
     Review,* vol. 14, no. 1 (March 1945), pp. 1–12.

Wall, Joseph Frazier. *Andrew Carnegie.* Pittsburgh: University of Pittsburgh Press,
     1989.

Waters, Ryan S. *The Last Jeffersonian: Grover Cleveland and the Path to Restoring the Republic.* Bloomington, IN: WestBow, 2012.

Welch, Richard E., Jr. *George Frisbie Hoar and the Half-Breed Republicans.* Cambridge, MA: Harvard University Press, 1971.

———. *Imperialists vs. Anti-Imperialists: The Debate over Expansionism in the 1890s.* Itasca, IL: F. E. Peacock, 1972.

———. *Response to Imperialism: The United States and the Philippine-American War, 1899–1902.* Chapel Hill: University of North Carolina Press, 1979.

Wertheim, Stephen. "Reluctant Liberator: Theodore Roosevelt's Philosophy of Self-Government and Preparation for Philippine Independence." *Presidential Studies Quarterly,* vol. 39, no. 3 (September 2009).

Widenor, William C. *Henry Cabot Lodge and the Search for an American Foreign Policy.* Berkeley: University of California Press, 1980.

Williams, William Appleton. *The Tragedy of American Diplomacy.* New York: W. W. Norton, 1959.

Wisan, Joseph E. *The Cuban Crisis as Reflected in the New York Press, 1895–1898.* New York: Columbia University Press, 1934.

Yarbrough, Jean M. *Theodore Roosevelt and the American Political Tradition.* Lawrence: University of Kansas Press, 2012.

Ziff, Larzer. *Mark Twain.* Oxford: Oxford University Press, 2004.

Zimmerman, Warren. *First Great Triumph: How Five Americans Made Their Country a World Power.* New York: Farrar, Straus and Giroux, 2002.

Zwick, Jim. *Confronting Imperialism: Essays on Mark Twain and the Anti-Imperialist Movement.* West Conshohocken, PA: Infinity, 2007.

———, ed. *Mark Twain's Weapons of Satire: Anti-Imperialist Writings on the Philippine-American War.* Syracuse, NY: Syracuse University Press, 1992.

Zwonitzer, Mark. *The Statesman and the Storyteller: John Hay, Mark Twain, and the Rise of American Imperialism.* Chapel Hill, NC: Algonquin, 2016.

ACKNOWLEDGMENTS

Much of the material in this book comes from old newspapers and magazines, and from historical archives. I appreciate the cooperation and resources of the Boston Public Library, the New York Public Library, Widener Library at Harvard University, the John D. Rockefeller Jr. Library at Brown University, and the Massachusetts Historical Society.

My sister, Jane Kinzer, an acute editor, read an early version of the manuscript and provided a detailed critique that helped shape later drafts. Jonathan Sperber and James Stone contributed insightful observations. Two eminent American historians, Walter LaFeber and Walter Nugent, made valuable suggestions.

I am grateful to Richard Locke, who as director of what is now the Watson Institute for International and Public Affairs at Brown University gave me the encouragement necessary to complete this project. My colleagues at the Watson Institute have created a rich intellectual environment from which works like this, in addition to scholarly research, can emerge and contribute to public debate.

A talented Brown student, Samantha Creighton, spent many hours assembling the photos and images that illustrate this text. My editor, Paul Golob, provided steady guidance with his usual precision and wit.

ILLUSTRATION CREDITS

INDEX

ABOUT THE AUTHOR

Stephen Kinzer is the author of *The Brothers, Reset, Overthrow, All the Shah's Men*, and other books. An award-winning foreign correspondent, he served as Latin America correspondent for the *Boston Globe* and as the *New York Times* bureau chief in Nicaragua, Germany, and Turkey. He is a senior fellow at the Watson Institute for International and Public Affairs at Brown University and writes a column on world affairs for the *Boston Globe*. He lives in Boston.